POWELL ON PIANO   MEL POWELL   *Capitol*   C   8

BLUES   SUNG BY   *Teddy Grace*   DECCA ALBUM   59

OT JAZZ CLASSICS • Teddy Wilson – Billie Holiday   C61

INK SPOTS   ★   DECCA ALBUM   477

Chicago JAZZ ALBUM   DECCA ALBUM   121

in the groove *vintage record graphics 1940-1960*

EW AMERICAN JAZZ   *Capitol*   SET A-3

ACCORDIANA • Charles Magnante   G53

WALLER ON THE IVORIES   ~   ~   ~   P-109   VICTOR

SONGS BY THE DINNING SISTERS   *Capitol*   ALBUM B-D   7

RODGERS-HART: Musical Comedy Hits   C-11

RHUMBA DE CUBA   CHUY REYES   *Capitol*   BD   74

the voice of

FRANK SINATRA

orchestra under the direction of
Axel Stordahl

set c·112 ℗

you go to my head
i don't know why
these foolish things
a ghost of a chance
why shouldn't i?
try a little tenderness
someone to watch over me
paradise

COLUMBIA RECORDS

in the groove

vintage record graphics 1940-1960

by eric kohler

CHRONICLE BOOKS

SAN FRANCISCO

Rosemary Clooney holding a favorite
Billie Holiday album at the Commodore
Music Shop in New York, 1950.
Photograph by Charles Peterson.

Printed in Hong Kong.

Library of Congress Cataloging-in-Publication
Data: Kohler, Eric. In the groove :
vintage record graphics. 1940–1960 / Eric Koh
p. cm. ISBN 0-8118-2121-8 (pbk.)
1. Sound recordings—Album covers—
United States—Catalogs. I. Title. NC1883.U6K6
1999 741.6'6'097309044—dc21 98-40008 C

Cover and book design: Eric Kohler
Author photograph: Lisa Kohler
Cover and interior photography: Les Morsillo

Distributed in Canada by Raincoast Books,
8680 Cambie Street, Vancouver BC V6P 6M9

10 9 8 7 6 5 4 3 2 1

Chronicle Books,
85 Second Street, San Francisco, CA 94105
www.chroniclebooks.com

Album opposite title page:
Designer: UNKNOWN   Label: COLUMBIA
Released: 1946

Tony Bennett at Columbia Records studios in New York, 1950. Photograph by Herman Leonard.

foreword

BY TONY BENNETT

The book you hold in your hands offers a memorable pictorial history of some of the greatest cover art from the years 1940 to 1959. This was the golden era of American popular music, a time when the public was exposed to and gravitated to only the best.

During those early years I would take frequent trips to the record shop where I would scour the bins for new releases. Although the lure of great artists such as Frank Sinatra, Billie Holiday, Ella Fitzgerald, and Harry James was enough for me, it was often the striking cover art that first caught my eye. If you are, like myself, one of those people who long for the bygone days of the twelve-inch vinyl LPs, then you can easily recall the thrill of possessing these albums. They were large enough to make you feel like you were taking home your very own work of art. Seeing the cover art always gave me my first sense of what I was about to hear. On the train ride home, filled with anticipation, I would carefully study the album cover. Even the feel of the thick cardboard would give me the impression that my purchase would last forever. I would almost immediately turn over the record to reveal the printed liner notes on the back (printed large enough to actually read, I might add). There I would find invaluable background information about the artist and all the performers on the recording. This was an education in itself.

The power of illustration is evident in its ability to convey the mood and style of each individual artist and the music within. As a teenager I attended the High School of Industrial Arts in New York (later the High School of Art and Design) and have continued to study art my whole life. I have always been confused by the fact that art critics rarely consider illustrators to be qualified artists. History has proven them wrong. We can easily look back and recognize legitimate works of art, executed in an illustrative style as diverse as William Blake's illustrations of his poetry, Michelangelo's depiction of the Last Judgement in the Sistine Chapel, and Norman Rockwell's depictions of American life. In fact, I have become so fond of illustrators, that although I've never belonged to a society of anything, I became a member of the Society of Illustrators. I've learned a lot about painting by visiting with the instructors and listening to lectures on their works. Anyone who does not consider illustration an art form is doing themselves a tremendous disservice by missing out on a whole new way of experiencing art.

There is such a vast number of fabulous album covers created by so many illustrators and designers (David Stone Martin, under the watchful eye of producer Norman Granz, Alex Steinweiss, Ben Shahn, Andy Warhol, and Rudolph deHarak) that it is quite impossible to recall them all. The selection represented in this book serves to focus on the best. Reading this book conjures up memories of my own record collection and the endless joy of owning my own personal library of recordings.

I envy anyone who had the foresight not to throw out their old record albums in an age where the five-inch CD now dominates the record scene. This book is a testament to a time and an attitude when art and music were fully appreciated and hard to separate.

As we say to all young students, understanding our past is the key to unlocking our future. This book illustrates a glorious history of album art that is truly inspirational.

Tony Bennett

COLUMBIA

CBS

35254
(WCO 26133)

RCA VICTOR

LPM

"NEW ORTHOPHONIC" HIGH FIDELITY

Capitol RECORDS

PRESTIGE

★ 446 W. 50th ST., N. Y. C.

MILES DAVIS
ALL STARS

Hi Fi

SOLAR

PRLP 7076 B

THE HUT-SUT SONG
3810 A

DECCA

CLOUD 7
TONY BENNETT
MY REVERIE

NOTHING
BUT THE SO
(BLAKEY)
SPOTLIGHT ON DRUMS

(BN 536)

ART BLAKEY
A DRUM IMPROVISA
BLUE NOTE RECORDS, 767

BLUE NOTE

VERVE RECORDS

ALL OR NO

1. DO NOTHIN' TILL YOU
(Ellington-Russell) Robbins
2. CHEEK TO CHEEK
(Berlin) Irving Berlin Mus
3. ILL WIND
(Arlen-Koehler) Mills Mus
4. SPEAK LOW
(Weill-Nash) Chappell & C
5. I WISHED ON THE MO
(Rainger-Parker) Famous Mu
6. BUT NOT FOR ME
(George and Ira Gershwin) Ne
Corp. – ASCAP
(Under the personal supervision o

MG V-8329-
(50,790)

VERVE RECORDS, INC.   MADE IN

OKeh

PLATTERBRAINS
Fox Trot
-Basie-T. Smith-
COUNT BASIE and his ORCHESTRA

preface

My interest in music and album cover art began with the visual splendor of my parents' collection of turn-of-the-century phonographs. I spent my childhood in Washington, D.C., drawing the horned Edison, Victor, and Columbia phonographs that I loved. The music from these "talking machines" also intrigued me, and at an early age I listened to Sousa marches, Caruso, and Fritz Kreisler. The passion for collecting phonographs led to a passion for collecting jazz records of the 1930s and 1940s, beginning with a copy of Glenn Miller's "In the Mood" I found in the bottom cabinet of a Victrola. I spent most of my time scouring the bins at the Salvation Army and ringing neighbors' doorbells, all in a quest for 78s and early LPs. In my teens, my drawing gave way to aspirations to become a graphic designer, and record covers became the inspiration for my design work. As an art student at Cooper Union in New York, I studied graphic design with Rudolph deHarak, who designed covers for Columbia Records in the early 1950s that appear in this collection.

My idea for this book came about ten years ago out of a desire to design something I really loved and to document the first golden age of an era that had come to an end. This year, 1998, the LP celebrates its fiftieth anniversary, a poignant one at best, as the compact disc has replaced the LP almost overnight and the impact of the twelve-inch album cover has been reduced to an anti-climactical four and three-fourths. Indeed, the words *record* and *phonograph* have already become "quaint" terms to teens who grew up in the 1980s. To me, this seemed like a perfect time to do a book on covers that are in danger of being forgotten. I had always bought every book on record art I could find, but they always concentrated on airbrushed rock covers from the 1960s and 1970s that interested me little. It then occurred to me that there had never been a book on the 1940s, the first decade of album cover art, or a comprehensive one on the 1950s. I found this strange, as this period "invented" popular music as we know it today. It also addressed, for the first time, the market for popular music. The album cover, disc jockey, jukeboxes, and most important, the first music superstars like Frank Sinatra, all rose to a popularity unheard of before the 1940s. This popularity, incidentally, rivaled that bestowed on later icons such as Elvis Presley and the Beatles. It is a coincidence, of course, that the era most overlooked is the era I am most passionate about. I hope this book begins to fill that gap.

Most of the two hundred and fifty album covers that appear in this book were drawn from my own collection of over three thousand records. These covers were chosen by me for their design merit alone — work that I think is beautiful or, in some way, represents the era stylistically. Because I decided early on that aesthetics would rule my decisions, I did not include work that was only "kitschy" or "camp" unless it had, at least to me, some design value. My intention in my choices is to represent a wide variety of design styles. For this reason, the book contains covers that range from the minimalist Swiss design of Erik Nitsche to the more elaborate, surreal work of Alex Steinweiss, the humorous illustrations of Jim Flora, and the vivacious and exotic Yma Sumac covers for Capitol. For the designers I could identify as well as those who were the most prolific, I have included biographical information. In my search I found little previously written about most of these designers, so the bulk of my information was compiled through personal interviews with the designers and their recollections of the deceased. Many covers had names of designers I could not obtain any information about and even more had no name at all. Record company files for this type of material are so incomplete that actual release dates of some albums are only approximate. In any case, I have tried to include as much factual information as possible.

ERIC KOHLER August 20th, 1998

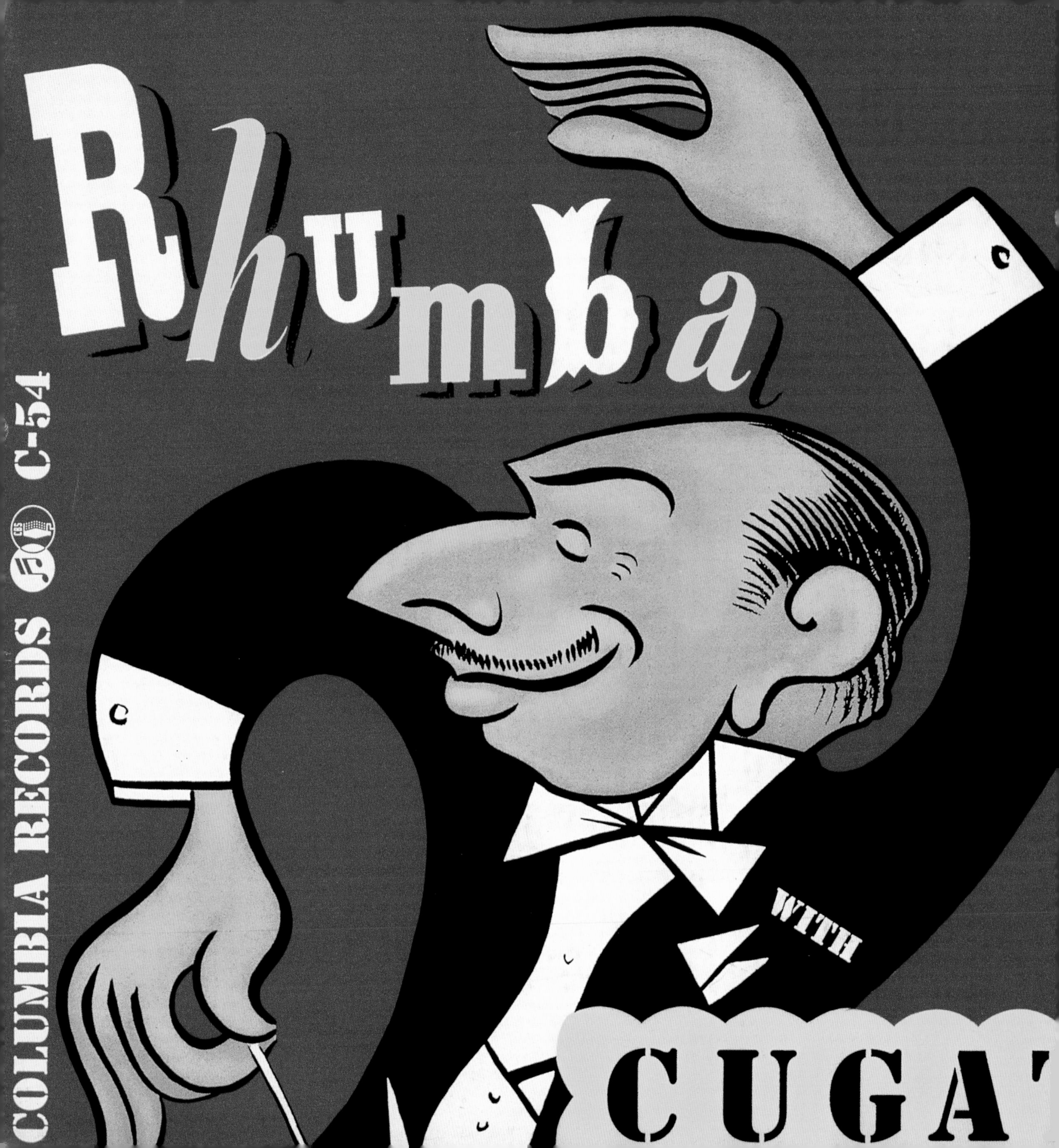
Rhumba
with
CUGA
COLUMBIA RECORDS
C-54

1 9 4 0

*I*t's hard to imagine today's recording industry without the driving force of marketing. But before 1940, that was exactly the case. The phonograph, invented in 1877 and widely popular and perfected between 1900 and 1920, was dominated by three companies: Edison, Victor, and Columbia. All three placed more emphasis on promoting the "talking machines" they produced than the records played on them. At the time, records were available only as singles in paper sleeves with graphics that promoted the record company rather than the artist. By the 1920s, classical records began to appear in album form (usually four to six twelve-inch 78 rpm discs bound in volumes with gold or silver spines emulating books) but still with no graphics relating to the music. A store that sold only records was a rarity, as they were typically sold in music or appliance stores along with phonographs and sheet music. Because of their lack of visual enticement, records were usually placed on shelves in the back of the store or behind a sales counter, forcing a customer to have to ask for a recording as they would a can on the top shelf. However, in these pre-radio days, the phonograph had no real competition. Intense marketing of recordings was not really necessary, and by 1920 the Victrola was commonplace in most American homes.

The growing popularity of radio during the 1920s brought a wide variety of free music (not to mention news, sports, and serial dramas) into homes without the expense and bother of buying records and phonograph needles. The steady decline in phonograph and record sales this brought about was so rapid that by 1928 the world's largest record company, the Victor Talking Machine Company, was forced to merge with the world's largest radio manufacturer, the Radio Corporation of America. If radio caused the recording industry to suffer, the stock market crash in the following year all but finished it. The Edison Company ceased producing records, as well as the phonograph it had invented, and Columbia Records was absorbed by the American Phonograph Company in 1934 and the name Columbia dropped. The era of the phonograph record seemed to have come to an end, yet the factors that would revive it were just around the corner.

Although the Great Depression nearly destroyed the record industry, it was, ironically, also responsible for creating certain social conditions that would soon allow it to rise out of the ashes. The repeal of prohibition in 1933 brought an end to the secretive world of the speakeasy, and in its place, thousands of bars and taverns appeared, filled with depression-weary patrons eager for cheap entertainment. Prohibition's end, combined with two major events in 1935, would change the fate of the record industry. That year, the first commercially successful jukeboxes were introduced by Wurlitzer, Seeburg, and Rock-Ola, and Benny Goodman's Orchestra had its first ground-breaking success at the Palomar

COLUMBIA RECORDS
IMPERIAL
ORCH UNDER
RICH. RODGERS
SMASH SONG HITS
BY RODGERS & HART
249

ballroom in Chicago, ushering in "The Swing Era" and the concept of popular music as it exists today. The popularity of the big bands was initially spread across the country by radio, which broadcast live "remotes" from the hundreds of ballrooms where the bands played nightly. Quite quickly, the most popular bandleaders became household names, as did the bands' sidemen and vocalists. This initial burst of popularity created a demand for big band records, which stocked thousands of new jukeboxes in bars and restaurants and the homes of teenagers and young adults who became fanatical record collectors. By 1938, more than half of all broadcast music would consist of recordings of popular music[1] and the disc jockey became a new phenomenon. In 1939, it was estimated that jukeboxes alone consumed thirty million records a year. In five short years, 1935 to 1940, the record industry went from near extinction with sales of 5.5 million, to an industry with great marketing potential and sales reaching 48.4 million.[2]

In 1940, the way that music was marketed and packaged took a dramatic turn with the appearance of an album on Columbia Records of four ten-inch 78s of the musical hits of Rodgers and Hart. What made this album stand apart from those before was that it had cover art created especially for it by a young designer named Alex Steinweiss. Steinweiss was hired by Columbia Records in 1939 as their first advertising and promotional designer. A year earlier, the company was bought by CBS, restructured, and the name Columbia revived for the new label. Steinweiss designed posters, catalogs, and other promotional material. But, like the other labels, Columbia had no intention of spending money on individual album covers, relying instead on the same generic all-type covers with gold-lettered spines that had been the norm during the 1920s and 1930s. It was Steinweiss who came up with the idea of specially designed cover art shortly after he was hired. Although his request was initially opposed because of a fear of rising production costs, Columbia finally capitulated and produced the first Steinweiss covers. These new covers were an instant success, and Columbia soon realized that the extra production cost required was well worth it when sales figures of albums with the Steinweiss covers rose dramatically in comparison to the same albums issued earlier with conventional plain covers. The popularity of Steinweiss's work prompted Columbia's marketing department to request cover art for all subsequent releases. At twenty-three, Steinweiss had single-handedly created a new medium in graphic design and changed forever the way recorded music was marketed and packaged.[3] He was hired first as a one-man design department, but the label soon allowed him to hire assistants. Later, they would hire staff or freelance designers to handle the increased volume of work. The other designers included Jim Flora, Robert Jones, Jim Amos, and Sydney Butchkes. Within a year after the first Steinweiss covers appeared, their success was such that it forced the other major labels, Victor and Decca, to follow suit. Yet despite all the other designers who quickly followed his lead, whether at Columbia or the other labels, it was the work of Alex Steinweiss that created the look of record packaging in the 1940s.

Perhaps because of World War II, the style of the 1940s has never been defined or given a name. Most often design from this decade is seen as a last gasp of Art Deco or, at best, a bridge between that style and 1950s Swiss Modernism. However, a look at the covers by Steinweiss or other early record cover designers shows distinct design innovations that belong to the 1940s. The heavy use of nineteenth-century type and engravings in a modern context (first used so effectively by Lester Beall and Herbert Bayer), vertical stripes, the ever present "shadow box," and the use of Surrealism, popularized by Dali's dream sequence in Hitchcock's 1944 film *Spellbound,* all became design images characteristic of the decade. Many design forms associated with the 1950s were actually extremely popular with designers in the 1940s. The

OPPOSITE: The first album cover designed by Alex Steinweiss for Columbia in 1940.

CONCERTO IN F

GERSHWIN

OSCAR

LEVANT

ANDRÉ

KOSTELANETZ

SET M-512

PHILHARMONIC-SYMPHONY ORCHESTRA OF NEW YO

COLUMBIA MASTERWORKS

CNY'S FRUITS HARDWARE BAR & GRILLE BAR GRILLE FISH BAKERY DRUGS-SODA

harlequin diamond, amoebic shapes, and all lower-case lettering can be found on hundreds of record covers from the forties. It is interesting to note that designers in the vanguard, like Paul Rand, Alvin Lustig and Saul Bass, had already abandoned these forms by the 1950s.

The 1940s also saw the record industry grow from its tentative rebirth in the 1930s into a major industry by the end of the decade. The popularity of the big bands that had done so much to boost record sales in the late 1930s gave way during the war years to an even bigger phenomenon in popular music: the vocalist. *The* vocalist was, of course, Frank Sinatra, responsible for more record sales during the decade than any other artist. By 1945, at the crest of Sinatra's first peak, industry-wide record sales would climb from 48.4 million in 1940 to 109 million. The late 1940s brought great technological changes that would revolutionize the industry with the introduction of the long-playing record, or LP. In 1944, CBS began researching a way to produce a slow-speed microgroove record that would play classical compositions without interruptions every four minutes as was the case with the current 78 disc. RCA Victor had begun similar experiments as far back as 1931, but had never produced a product ready for public consumption. Further developed by Peter Goldmark, a researcher at CBS, the LP was introduced by Columbia Records to the public in 1948. From the beginning, the advantages over the conventional 78 were clear. The long-playing discs held over thirty minutes of music per side, while the 78 held only four minutes. The LP was pressed on lightweight, unbreakable vinyl and offered a vast improvement in fidelity over the heavy, breakable, shellac-based 78. Even with these obvious improvements, Columbia had the formidable task of winning over an entire industry geared to, and quite content with, the 78.[4] Feeling that alliance with other major labels would help put their invention over, Columbia offered RCA Victor free rights to their LP. Probably because of earlier failed attempts to produce a similar product, Victor executives let their pride get the best of them and rejected the offer. A year after Columbia's introduction of the LP, RCA Victor counterattacked with the 45. This began what was referred to as "The War of Speeds." For a short time, recordings were issued in all three formats (33, 45, and 78) but by 1950 the LP was clearly the choice for extended works and albums, and the 45 the choice for popular singles. The only speed left out was the venerable old 78, which was left to suffer a slow demise. The last disc was issued in 1957.

The first popular LP issued by Columbia in 1948, CL 6001, was of their biggest seller, Frank Sinatra. The rather generic packaging was a result of their rush to get their new invention out on the market, and reflects their uncertainty of how the public would respond.

OPPOSITE: Designer: ALEX STEINWEISS   Label: COLUMBIA   Released: 1940

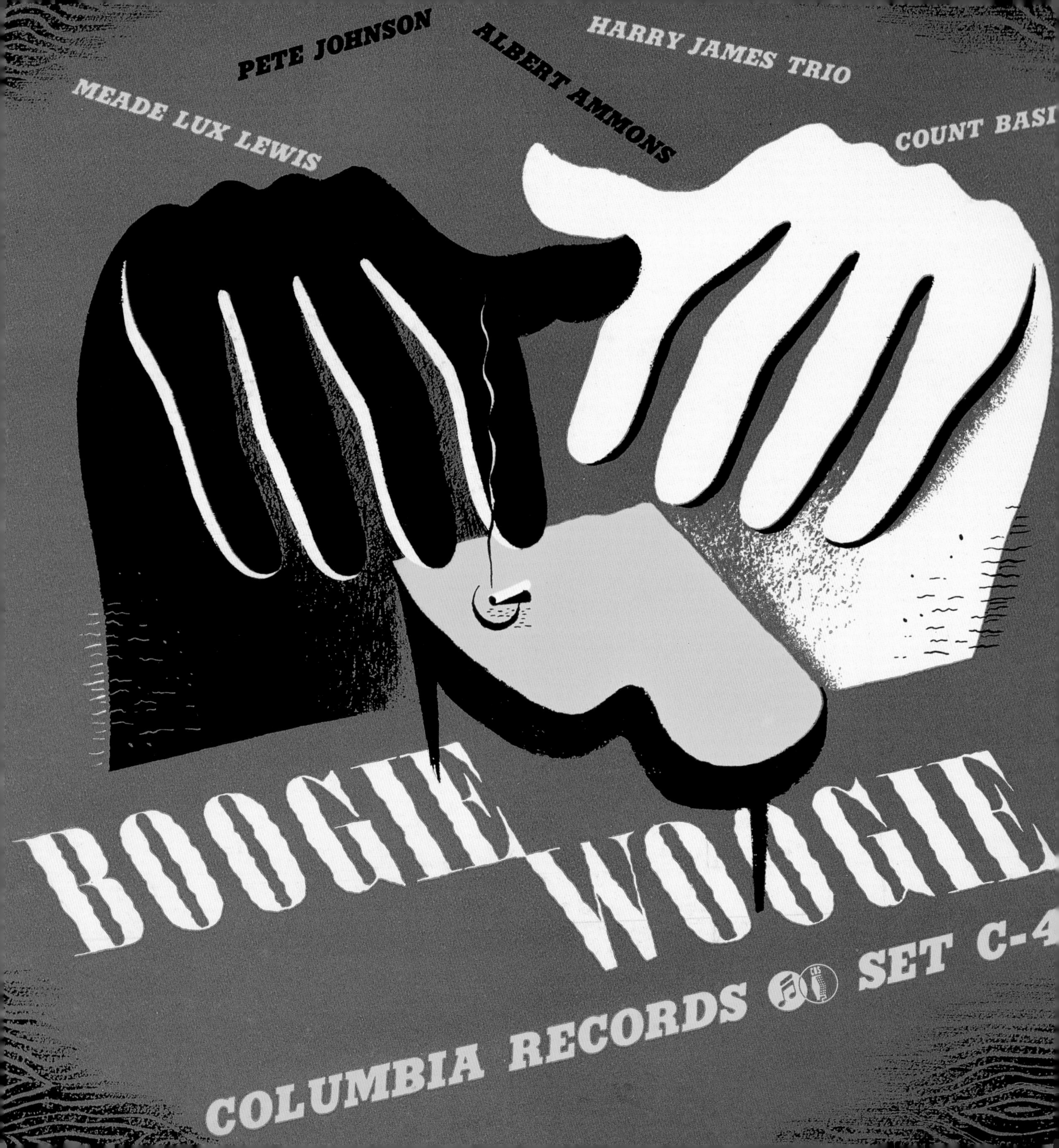

MEADE LUX LEWIS

PETE JOHNSON   ALBERT AMMONS   HARRY JAMES TRIO

COUNT BASI

BOOGIE WOOGIE

COLUMBIA RECORDS   SET C-4

COLUMNBIA

RECORDS

alex

Steinweiss

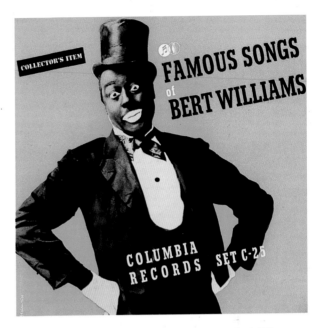

Designer: ALEX STEINWEISS Label: COLUMBIA Released: 1940

Alex Steinweiss was born in Brooklyn in 1917, graduated from Parson's School of Design in 1937, and worked as an assistant to Austrian poster designer Joseph Binder for three years before he was hired by Columbia Records. The look Steinweiss created for the label was inspired by the work of the great European poster artists of the '20s and '30s he had studied at school and, from an early age, a love of music that came from his father. Looking at the Steinweiss covers today, they have all the qualities of posters from the 1930s: bold use of type, flat colors, and a central theme with stylized images (seen in the abstract cocktail glass and tray of *Dinner Music* or an enormous flowing skirt for *Gypsy Music*). What sets the style apart, especially from covers done in more recent years, is the absence in almost all of

Designer: ALEX STEINWEISS Label: COLUMBIA Released: 1940

OPPOSITE: Designer: ALEX STEINWEISS Label: COLUMBIA Released: 1942

17

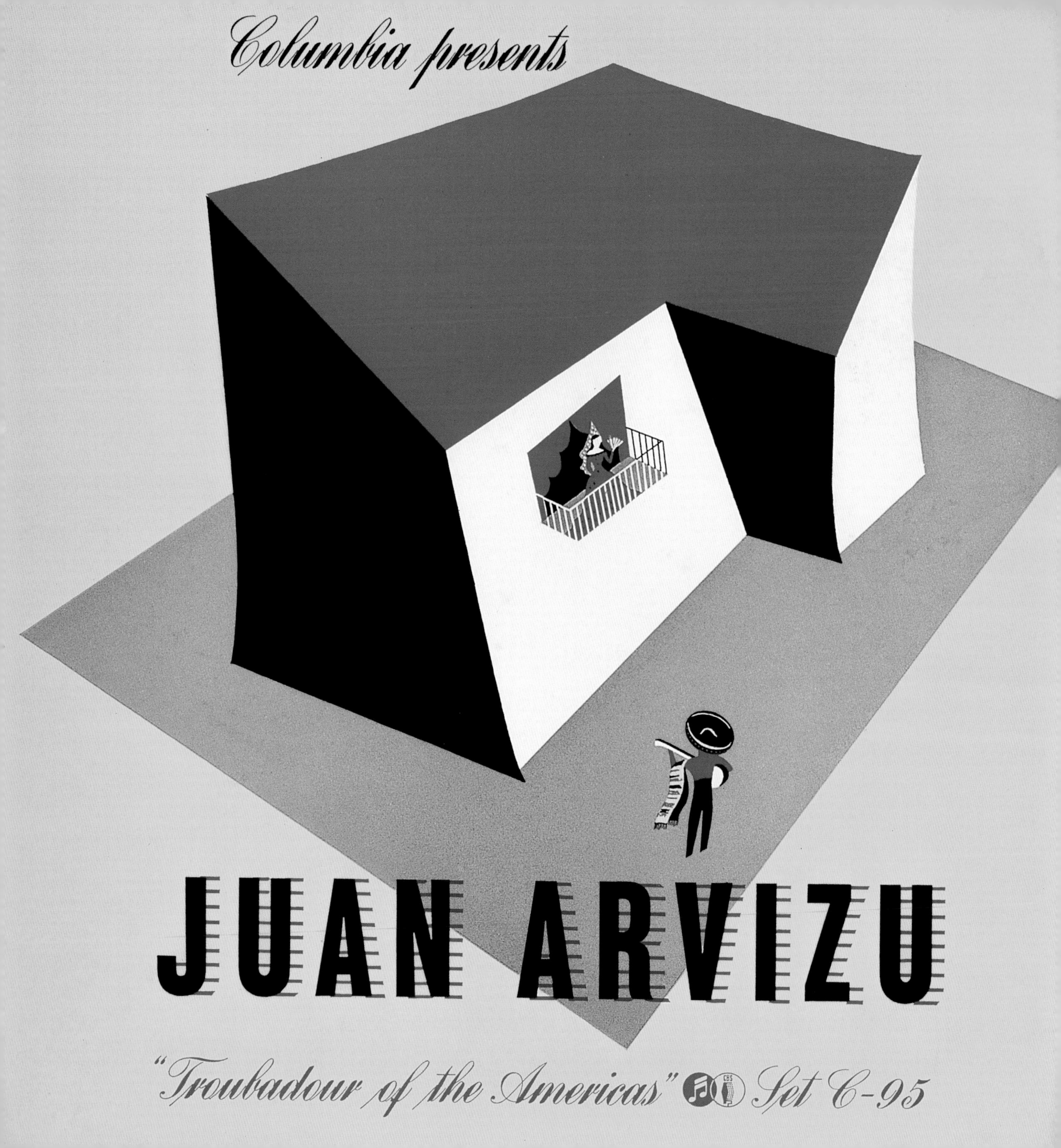

Columbia presents

JUAN ARVIZU

"Troubadour of the Americas" 🎵 *Set C-95*

them of a photo of the recording artist. Instead, Steinweiss employed a stylized Symbolist approach of musical and cultural elements to portray the music inside. For an album of music by Teddy Wilson and Billie Holiday, for example, a stylized entrance to a 52nd Street jazz club (where both artists were currently playing); a Broadway theater marquee for the hits of Rodgers and Hart; two large surreal hands, one black and one white, for an album of Boogie Woogie, symbolizing the black and white artists that appeared together on the album. On the cover of *Rhumba with Cugat*, it was Steinweiss's idea to use a large caricature of the bandleader drawn by Cugat himself (who had been a successful cartoonist before he embarked on a career in music). Steinweiss also created imagery from type, often treating the main title in a decorative fashion appropriate to the music, or creating type out of objects. In a cover for pianist Frankie Carle, the letters "Carle" are composed out of parts of a piano. The most instantly recognizable trademark of Steinweiss's style was a typeface he created called "Steinweiss Scrawl." This loose, hand-lettered script with quirky curls appears on hundreds of the covers he created for Columbia. Steinweiss developed this script out of necessity; it was often hard to obtain typesetting fast enough and the type styles available were often limiting, so he found it easier to hand-letter his loose script for each album when appropriate. Later, in the 1950s, after Steinweiss stopped producing covers for Columbia, Steinweiss Scrawl became a legitimate typeface available to others when it was bought by Photolettering, Inc.

In 1947, Ted Wallerstein, the president of Columbia records, approached Alex Steinweiss with a packaging problem for a newly developed recording that would revolutionize the

Designer: ALEX STEINWEISS Label: COLUMBIA Released: 1940

OPPOSITE: Designer: ALEX STEINWEISS Label: COLUMBIA Released: 1942

Designer: ALEX STEINWEISS Label: COLUMBIA Released: 1941

Dvořák

New World Symphony

Eugene Ormandy

conducting The Philadelphia Orchestra • Set MM-570

Columbia Masterworks

industry. Steinweiss was soon hard at work developing another first: the industry standard jacket for the long playing record, or LP. Ironically, these early discs were not sold with the same covers Steinweiss and other designers had created for the standard 78 rpm versions of the same recordings. Instead the first LPs were sold in generic paper envelopes, just as 78 discs had been before Steinweiss designed his first covers back in 1940. Not only did these packages not promote the music, they also did not protect the finer grooves and vinyl discs from damage in shipping. What Steinweiss developed to solve this problem (thin board folded in half and bound with a paper covering) became the standard LP jacket that would be used for forty years until the LP's demise in the 1980s. Although Steinweiss held the original patent on his invention, his Columbia contract required him to sign over his rights to them. Steinweiss ended the decade designing covers for Columbia on a freelance basis. His other projects included advertising and logo designs for Schenley liquors, and covers for *Fortune*. In his pioneering packaging and design work for Columbia, Steinweiss had single-handedly readied the record industry for the decade ahead.[5]

Designer: ALEX STEINWEISS   Label: COLUMBIA   Released: 1942

ALEX STEINWEISS, 1947

OPPOSITE: Designer: ALEX STEINWEISS   Label: COLUMBIA   Released: 1944

Designer: ALEX STEINWEISS   Label: COLUMBIA   Released: 1941

columbia presents
cante
FLAMENCO
la niña de los peines
set c-59

Designer: ALEX STEINWEISS   Label: COLUMBIA   Released: 1942

Designer: ALEX STEINWEISS   Label: COLUMBIA   Released: 1940

Designer: ALEX STEINWEISS   Label: COLUMBIA   Released: 1941

OPPOSITE: Designer: ALEX STEINWEISS   Label: COLUMBIA   Released: 1941

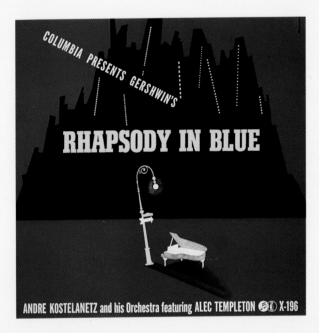

Designer: ALEX STEINWEISS   Label: COLUMBIA   Released: 1941

le **sacre**

du printemps

stravinsky
(the rite of spring)
the philharmonic-symphony
orchestra of new york with
stravinsky conducting ⊙⊙ set m-417

columbia masterworks

Designer: ALEX STEINWEISS   Label: COLUMBIA   Released: 1941

Designer: ALEX STEINWEISS   Label: COLUMBIA   Released: 1946

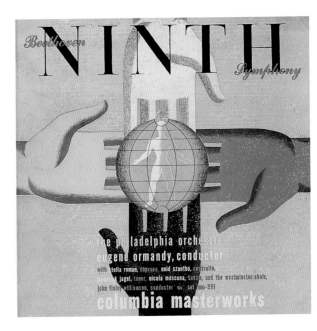

Designer: ALEX STEINWEISS   Label: COLUMBIA   Released: 1946

OPPOSITE: Designer: ALEX STEINWEISS   Label: COLUMBIA   Released: 1942

Designer: ALEX STEINWEISS   Label: COLUMBIA   Released: 1944

COLUMBIA presents

GYPSY music

V. Selinescu and his

Gypsy Ensemble ⒿⒸ C-64

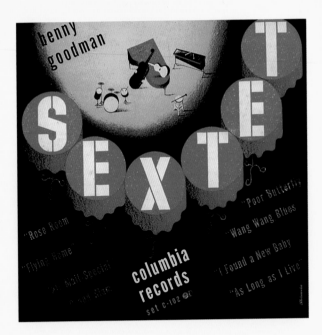

Designer: ALEX STEINWEISS   Label: COLUMBIA   Released: 1945

Designer: ALEX STEINWEISS   Label: COLUMBIA   Released: 1945

Designer: ALEX STEINWEISS   Label: COLUMBIA   Released: 1946

OPPOSITE: Designer: ALEX STEINWEISS   Label: COLUMBIA   Released: 1941

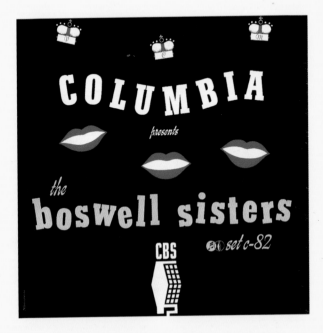

Designer: ALEX STEINWEISS   Label: COLUMBIA   Released: 1942

in the still of the night from "Anything Goes"

all through the night night from "Rosalie"

I concentrate on you

I've got you under my skin from "Born to Dance"
from "Broadway Melody of 1940"

ow, Gabriel, from "Mexican Hayride"

I love you from blow from "Anything Goes"

music of

Cole Porter

andre

Kostelanetz

and his orchestra

set mm-721

Columbia

masterworks

Designer: ALEX STEINWEISS   Label: COLUMBIA   Released: 1946

Designer: ALEX STEINWEISS   Label: COLUMBIA   Released: 1947

Designer: ALEX STEINWEISS   Label: COLUMBIA   Released: 1947

OPPOSITE: Designer: ALEX STEINWEISS   Label: COLUMBIA   Released: 1947

Designer: ALEX STEINWEISS   Label: COLUMBIA   Released: 1948

BIX and TRAM

BIX BEIDERBECKE . WITH FRANKIE TRUMBAUER'S ORCHESTRA

flora

SET C-144 . A HOT JAZZ CLASSIC . #20 IN A SERIES THAT MADE JAZZ HISTORY

COLUMBIA RECORDS

Born in Bellefontaine, Ohio, in 1914, Jim Flora originally had aspirations to be an architect and in 1933 won a scholarship to the Boston Architectural League. Since this was the height of the Great Depression, the only job he could find was as a busboy in a restaurant that paid him $7 a week for seven full days of work. This left him no time to devote to school, so he saw his scholarship ultimately go to someone else. A year later, when he had managed to save some money, he attended the Art Academy of Cincinnati. During his school years, Flora spent his summers working as an assistant to the muralist Carl Zimmerman who became his mentor. Graduating in 1939, he remained in Cincinnati and quickly found work as a freelance illustrator. It was Flora's passion for jazz that prompted him to send Pat Dolan (the advertising manager at Columbia Records and the man who originally hired Alex Steinweiss) a series of ideas for album covers for their jazz reissue series. Dolan liked Flora's work so much that he hired him in 1942 to handle the bulk of the label's jazz covers while Steinweiss concentrated more on the company's classical artists. Moving from Cincinnati to Connecticut, near Columbia's main office in Bridgeport, Flora found himself working alongside Steinweiss. The two became good friends and when Steinweiss went into the army in 1943, Flora took over his job as art director. During this period, Flora hired other designers including Robert Jones, Jim Amos, and Sydney Butchkes. Columbia promoted Flora from art director to advertising manager and then finally to sales promotion manager, both positions which gave him more money but no art work to do. Dissatisfied with the more corporate side of Columbia, he left the label in 1950 and set out on a fifteen-month trip with his family to Taxco, Mexico, to paint. Flora was an early admirer of the work of contemporary Mexican artists, including Rivera,

jim flora

Designer: JIM FLORA   Label: COLUMBIA   Released: 1947

OPPOSITE: Designer: JIM FLORA   Label: COLUMBIA   Released: 1947

LOUis ARMSTRONG'S hot 5

HOT FIVE VOL 2

Album #18 in a series
of reissues of the records
that made Jazz history

flora

COLUMBIA RECORDS · set C-139

Orozoco, Siquerios, and Taymayo. These influences, combined with Surrealism and the cartoon, became the inspiration for his cover designs. Upon his return to his home in Rowayton, Connecticut, he found freelance work with Leo Leonni doing covers and spot illustrations for *Fortune* magazine. In 1954, Robert Jones, now art director at RCA Victor, hired Flora as a freelancer to design covers. Jones gave Flora free rein at Victor and some of his best work was done for them. By 1956, however, the tide had turned against illustration at Victor, and the company specifically asked Jones for "no more Flora covers." His distinct and rather humorous style went against the slick set-up photography the company was starting to favor. However, the style proved perfectly suited for children's books. In 1954, Flora wrote and illustrated his first book, *The Fabulous Firework Family*. This began his long association with Harcourt Brace, for whom he would do seventeen children's books, the last published in 1982. From the late 1950s through the 1970s, Flora did editorial illustration work for numerous clients, including *Life*, *Look*, *Holiday*, *Newsweek*, and the *New York Times*. Flora spent the last fifteen years of his life devoting most of his time to painting until his death in 1998.

Designer: JIM FLORA   Label: COLUMBIA   Released: 1947

JIM FLORA, 1947

OPPOSITE: Designer: JIM FLORA   Label: COLUMBIA   Released: 1947

Designer: JIM FLORA   Label: COLUMBIA   Released: 1949

billie holiday

vol. 1

a
hot
jazz
classic

set
c-135

columbia

records

until the real thing comes al

i cover the water fr

i can't get star

when a woman loves a m

he's funny that w

a sailboat in the moonli

summerti

billie's bl

ROBERT JONES

Robert Jones was born in Goff, Kansas, in 1913. Growing up in Salt Lake City, he attended the California School of Fine Art. Jones's first job was in the art department at *Life* magazine, where he worked until he was drafted in 1942. After the war, Jones was hired by Jim Flora at Columbia Records, where he designed many of the company's popular and jazz covers until 1951. In 1953, RCA Victor hired him as their art director, a job he held through the late 1970s. Throughout most of his career, Jones ran a metaltype press at his home called the Glad Hand Press. Here he became well known for his exceptional limited editions and spent time lecturing on typography until his death in 1993.

Designer: ROBERT JONES   Label: COLUMBIA   Released: 1947

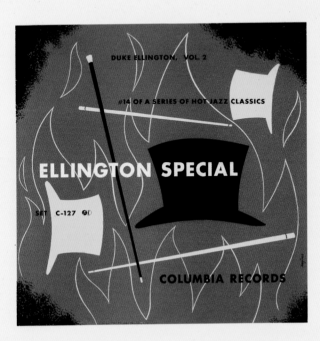

Designer: ROBERT JONES   Label: COLUMBIA   Released: 1948

OPPOSITE: Designer: ROBERT JONES   Label: COLUMBIA   Released: 1947

Designer: ROBERT JONES   Label: COLUMBIA   Released: 1947

a
SENTIMENTAL JOURNEY
with

LES BROWN
AND HIS ORCHESTRA

SENTIMENTAL JOURNEY

TWILIGHT TIME

BIZET HAS HIS DAY

A GOOD MAN IS HARD TO FIND

MEXICAN HAT DANCE

LEAP FROG

OUT OF NOWHERE

DAYBREAK SERENADE

SET C-131

COLUMBIA RECORDS

Designer: ROBERT JONES   Label: COLUMBIA   Released: 1947

Designer: ROBERT JONES   Label: COLUMBIA   Released: 1949

Designer: ROBERT JONES   Label: COLUMBIA   Released: 1946

OPPOSITE: Designer: ROBERT JONES   Label: COLUMBIA   Released: 1947

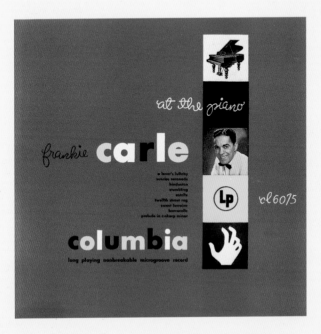

Designer: ROBERT JONES   Label: COLUMBIA   Released: 1949

I'm sorry I made you cry

I concentrate on you

how deep is the ocean

that old black magic

over the rainbow

all the things you are

she's funny that way

embraceable you

orchestra under the direction of **Axel Stordahl**

SONGS B

SINATRA

VOLUME I SET C-124

COLUMBIA

RECORDS

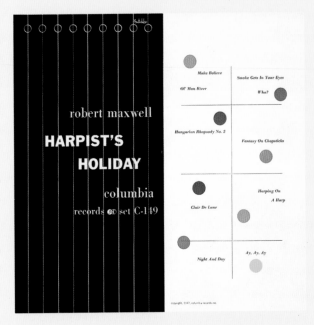

Designer: SYDNEY BUTCHKES Label: COLUMBIA Released: 1947

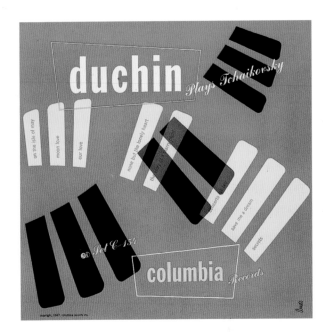

Designer: JIM AMOS Label: COLUMBIA Released: 1948

Designer: GEORGE MAAS Label: COLUMBIA Released: 1946

OPPOSITE: Designer: SYDNEY BUTCHKES Label: COLUMBIA Released: 1947

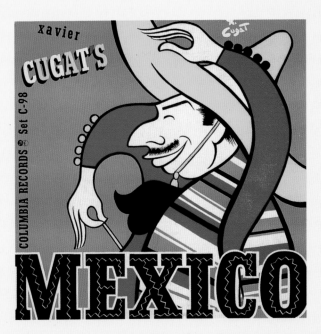

Designer: XAVIER CUGAT Label: COLUMBIA Released: 1945

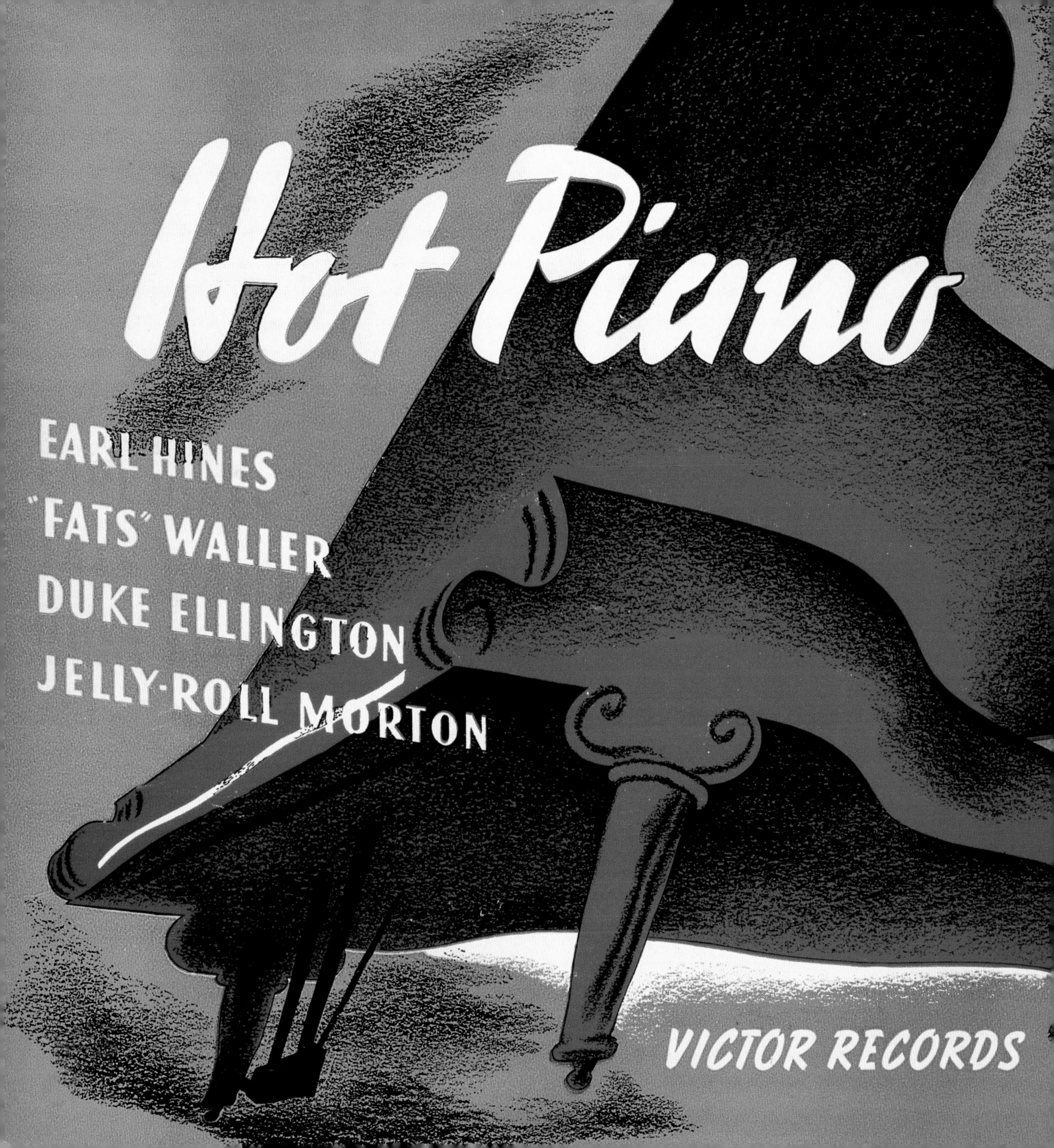

Hot Piano

EARL HINES
"FATS" WALLER
DUKE ELLINGTON
JELLY-ROLL MORTON

VICTOR RECORDS

"HIS MASTER'S VOICE"

VICTOR

Designer: UNKNOWN   Label: RCA VICTOR   Released: 1940

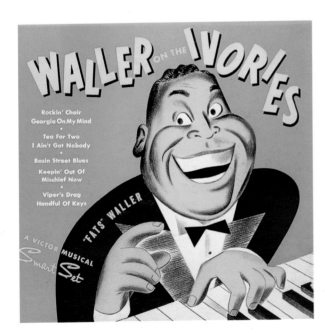

Designer: UNKNOWN   Label: RCA VICTOR   Released: 1942

OPPOSITE: Designer: UNKNOWN   Label: RCA VICTOR   Released: 1941

Designer: UNKNOWN   Label: RCA VICTOR   Released: 1947

EAST ST. LOUIS TOODLE-OO
THE MOOCHE
RING DEM BELLS
MOOD INDIGO
STOMPY JONES
DELTA SERENADE
DUSK
WARM VALLEY
A DUKE ELLINGTON
PANORAMA
A VICTOR MUSICAL Smart Set

Designer: UNKNOWN   Label: RCA VICTOR   Released: 1942

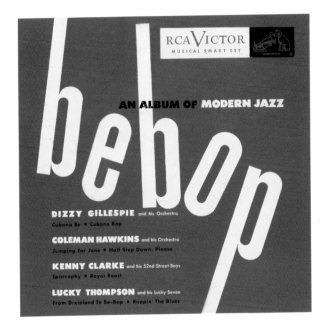

Designer: UNKNOWN   Label: RCA VICTOR   Released: 1948

Designer: UNKNOWN   Label: RCA VICTOR   Released: 1946

OPPOSITE: Designer: UNKNOWN   Label: RCA VICTOR   Released: 1942

Designer: UNKNOWN   Label: RCA VICTOR   Released: 1944

Designer: SCHURRER   Label: CAPITOL   Released: 1944

Designer: MEGGS   Label: CAPITOL   Released: 1945

OPPOSITE: Designer: UNKNOWN   Label: CAPITOL   Released: 1948

Designer: MEGGS   Label: CAPITOL   Released: 1944

Designer: MEGGS   Label: CAPITOL   Released: 1944

Designer: UNKNOWN   Label: CAPITOL   Released: 1946

Designer: UNKNOWN   Label: CAPITOL   Released: 1948

OPPOSITE: Designer: UNKNOWN   Label: CAPITOL   Released: 1948

Designer: BASS   Label: CAPITOL   Released: 1949

STAN KENTO

Encores

Designer: BOOTH   Label: CAPITOL   Released: 1945

Designer: UNKNOWN   Label: CAPITOL   Released: 1948

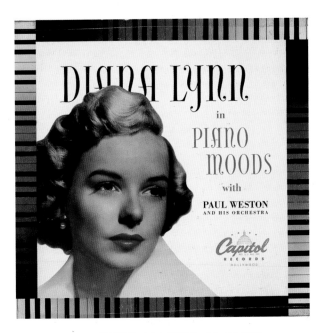

Designer: UNKNOWN   Label: CAPITOL   Released: 1949

OPPOSITE: Designer: UNKNOWN   Label: CAPITOL   Released: 1948

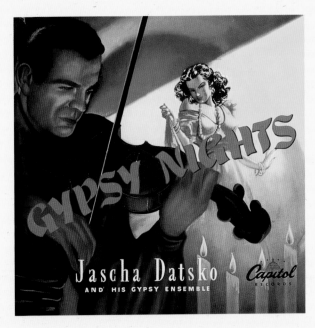

Designer: UNKNOWN   Label: CAPITOL   Released: 1947

Designer: UNKNOWN   Label: CAPITOL   Released: 1947

Designer: UNKNOWN   Label: CAPITOL   Released: 1947

Designer: UNKNOWN   Label: CAPITOL   Released: 1948

OPPOSITE: Designer: UNKNOWN   Label: CAPITOL   Released: 1947

Designer: UNKNOWN   Label: CAPITOL   Released: 1945

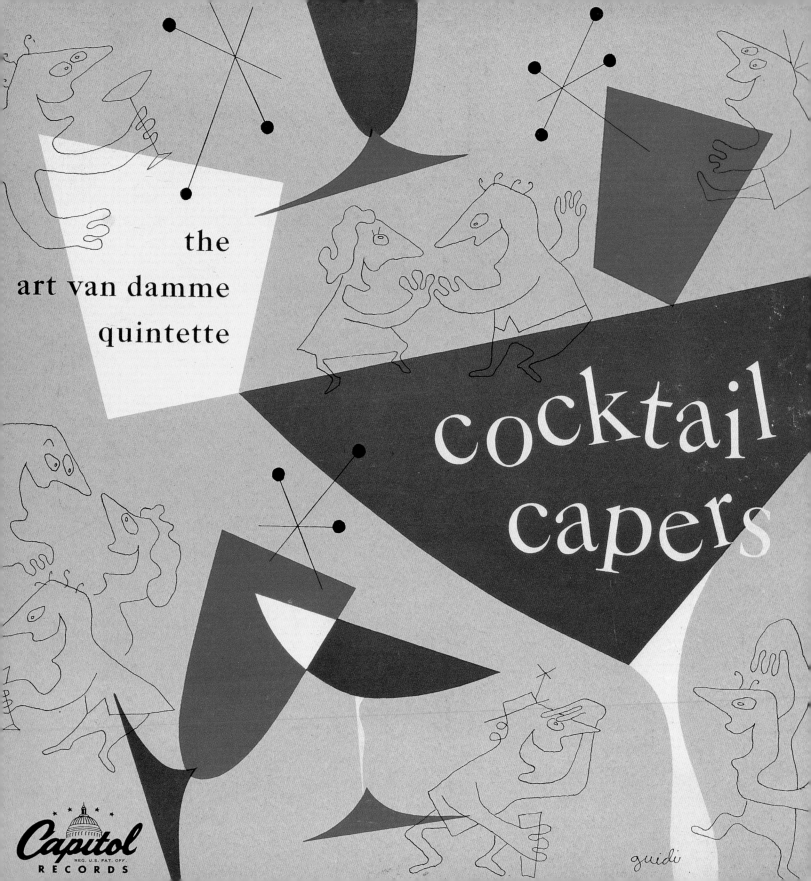

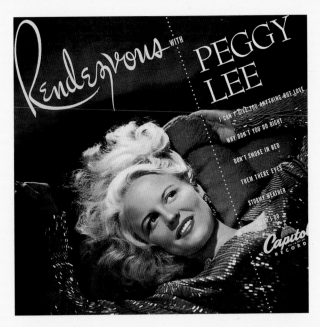

Designer: UNKNOWN   Photo: TED ALLAN   Label: CAPITOL   Released: 1948

Designer: McAVIN   Label: CAPITOL   Released: 1949

Designer: GUIDI   Label: CAPITOL   Released: 1949

OPPOSITE: Designer: GUIDI   Label: CAPITOL   Released: 1948

Designer: UNKNOWN   Label: CAPITOL   Released: 1948

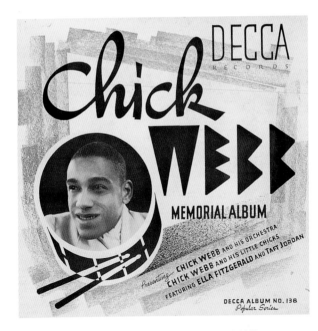

Designer: UNKNOWN   Label: DECCA   Released: 1940

Designer: UNKNOWN   Label: DECCA   Released: 1944

OPPOSITE: Designer: UNKNOWN   Label: DECCA   Released: 1941

Designer: UNKNOWN   Label: DECCA   Released: 1941

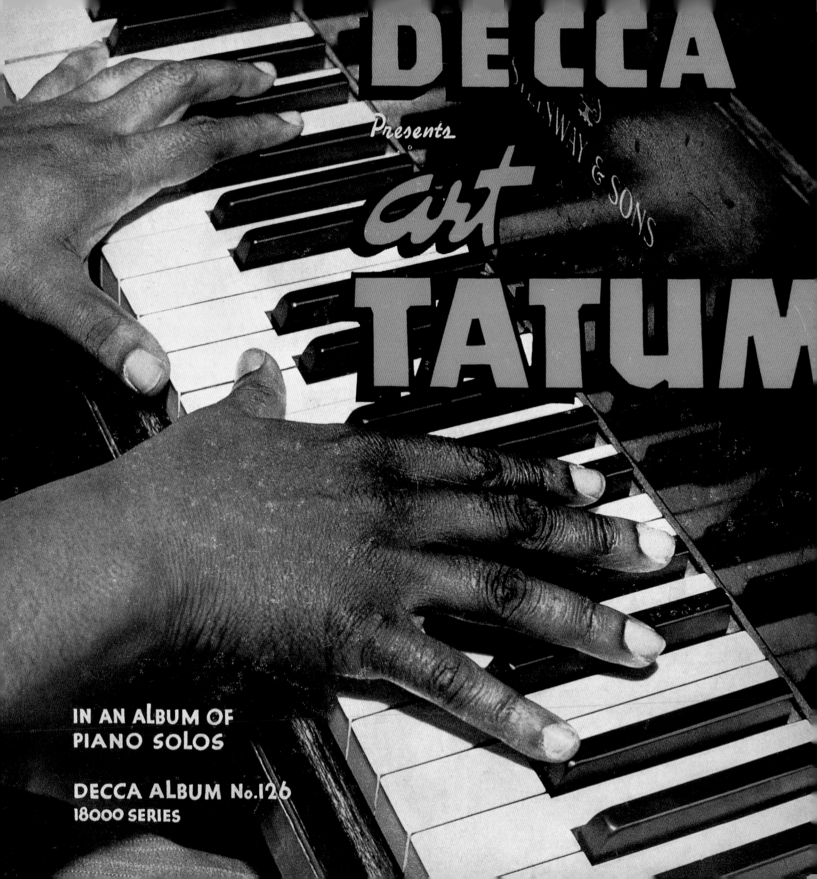

Designer: UNKNOWN   Label: DECCA   Released: 1941

Designer: UNKNOWN   Label: DECCA   Released: 1940

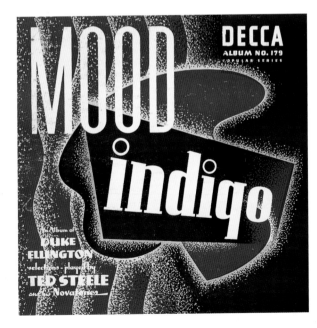

Designer: UNKNOWN   Label: DECCA   Released: 1941

OPPOSITE: Designer: UNKNOWN   Label: DECCA   Released: 1941

Designer: UNKNOWN   Label: DECCA   Released: 1941

DECCA
presents

MARLENE DIETRICH

NEW UNIVERSAL STAR · IN A COLLECTION OF SONGS FROM
HER NEW UNIVERSAL PICTURES, AND HER OTHER FAVORITES.

DECCA ALBUM No.115

Designer: BAIRD   Label: DECCA   Released: 1947

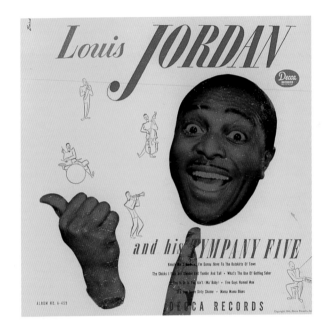

Designer: BAIRD   Label: DECCA   Released: 1947

Designer: UNKNOWN   Label: DECCA   Released: 1941

OPPOSITE: Designer: UNKNOWN   Label: DECCA   Released: 1941

Designer: UNKNOWN   Label: DECCA   Released: 1941

JOHN DE VRIES

Billie Holiday

COMMODORE RECORDS

david lambert
buddy stewart
red rodney
charlie ventura
neal hefti
chubby jackson

B E B O P

keynote album 140

Designer: GEORGE MAAS   Label: KEYNOTE   Released: 1947

KEYNOTE ALBUM 136

babe russin
corky corcoran
coleman hawkins
herbie haymer
don byas
ted nash

tenor jazz

Designer: GEORGE MAAS   Label: KEYNOTE   Released: 1947

Designer: GIKOW   Label: ASCH   Released: 1946

OPPOSITE: Designer: JOHN DE VRIES   Label: COMMODORE   Released: 1947

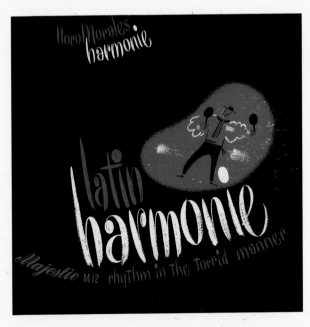

Designer: UNKNOWN   Label: MAJESTIC   Released: 1946

The 1950s were promising years for the phonograph record. With the LP firmly established as the preferred format in recording, new options in the industry opened up that were never before feasible. Because of the LP, more music was being issued in album form in the 1950s than ever before. Unlike with the 78, it was now possible to record extended works of music without interruptions every three or four minutes. This gave birth to the idea of the "concept" album (a collection of songs chosen with a common theme or mood) which was first introduced with Frank Sinatra's *Songs for Young Lovers* for Capitol in 1953. Another musical genre greatly influenced by this new extended format was "mood music," a name now synonymous with the 1950s. Artists such as Mantovanni, Jackie Gleason, André Kostelanetz, Paul Weston, and Percy Faith turned out hundreds of best-selling albums with titles like *Music for Lovers Only*, *Music to Remember Her By*, *Music for Memories*, *Music for the Fireside*, and even *Music to Change Her Mind*. Not only did the LP lead to an enormous amount of newly recorded music, but the desire to replace cumbersome libraries of 78s with LPs created another jump in record sales in reissues of 78 material. With the vast improvement in sound of the LP, "High Fidelity" became a household word and launched a whole generation of hi-fi fans who built large collections of LPs and played them on the best Marantz and Macintosh equipment. Record labels capitalized on this fad with hi-fi slogans on their covers, promising "New Orthophonic High Fidelity," "360 Sound," "Full Color Fidelity," or "Panoramic True High Fidelity." Most of these terms were bogus, dreamt up by the marketing or advertising department rather than the sound engineers. For his Clef label, Norman Granz's slogan "A Muenster-Dummel Hi-Fi Recording" implied some special European sound process when, in actuality, it was named after his favorite cheese and his sound engineer, Jack Dummel.[6]

With the unprecedented boost in record production, album cover art would play an increasingly important role. Early in the decade, design styles continued along the lines of the 1940s. Columbia Records produced covers by Alex Steinweiss and newcomers like Rudolph deHarak, while designers such as Jim Flora and Robert Jones switched to RCA Victor. By 1955, however, the technical advances in design, printing, and physical packaging pioneered by Steinweiss in the 1940s would, ironically, become the cause for the individual style he created to fall out of fashion with the larger record companies. With advanced printing techniques and growing budgets for cover art, slick photography came into vogue, and the big labels — Columbia, along with RCA Victor, Capitol, and Decca — opted for a more corporate, less individual look. Indeed, the beginning of the trend away from illustrative design to photography had begun to take over in all areas of advertising

OPPOSITE: Designer: DAVID STONE MARTIN   Label: NORGRAN   Released: 1955

RCA VICTOR
45EP   EPA-637

Pete Jolly Duo

Buddy Clark, bass

Flora

Pete Jolly, piano

and design around the middle of the decade. The influence of the post-war mentality (realism as opposed to the idealized), the growing influence of Swiss design with the introduction of new "unadorned" typefaces such as Helvetica, and the Americanization of the International Style in architecture erased all lingering elements of the pre-war Art Deco and streamlined Moderne styles. These lofty new design ideals, combined with the more commercial effects photography could produce, contributed to the demise of the illustrative, hand-lettered approach to design. When this changing of the guard hit Columbia Records in the mid-fifties, Alex Steinweiss, the man every cover designer followed in the 1940s, found himself out of a job. He began doing cover work for Decca and purposely altered his style to keep up with the times, even working under a pseudonym, Piedra Blancha (Spanish for Steinweiss), to differentiate between the two labels. But by the end of the decade, Steinweiss finally admitted that he was fighting a losing battle with photography.

Trends notwithstanding, the 1950s still produced some of the best cover designs in the illustrative and typographic genre. The commercial success of the LP was such that the major labels, or the "Big Four" as they were referred to, no longer completely dominated the market. By 1955, hundreds of smaller "specialty" labels had flooded the market, some quite sucessfully. Clef and Norgran (later Verve), Prestige, Blue Note, Pacific Jazz, Bethlehem, and Emarcy were devoted exclusively to jazz; Vox, Angel, and London to classical; Tico and Crescendo to Latin; Atlantic and Mercury to pop and rhythm and blues; and Folkways to folk. The more creative cover graphics were produced largely for these smaller companies, the jazz labels in particular. Ironically, rock and roll, the musical form most associated with the 1950s, had almost no impact on album cover art during the decade, as most of the releases first appeared as 45 rpm singles, a practice that lasted well into the 1960s. Instead, the 1950s was clearly the decade of the jazz record cover: the designs of Reid Miles, with illustrations by artists like Andy Warhol for Blue Note, Burt Goldblatt's illustrations and designs for Bethlehem, Rudolph deHarak's designs for Columbia, the work of Erik Nitsche for Decca, Jim Flora's humorous illustrations for RCA Victor, and especially the work of illustrator David Stone Martin for Verve. These artists defined the 1950s in cover graphics and carried on the concept initiated by Steinweiss of highly stylized, instantly recognizable cover art that became label trademarks.

An early 1950s Capitol album by an unknown designer likening abstract design and painting motifs to the abstract "bop" of such artists as Miles Davis, Stan Kenton, and Dizzy Gillespie.

OPPOSITE: Designer: JIM FLORA   Label: RCA VICTOR   Released: 1954

frank

Sinatra

dedicated
to
you

orchestra under the direction of axel stordahl

the music stopped
the moon was yellow
i love you
strange music
where or when
none but the lonely heart
always
why was i born

set c-197

Columbia

records

COLUMBIA

LP

RECORDS

Designer: VELDE   Label: COLUMBIA   Released: 1950

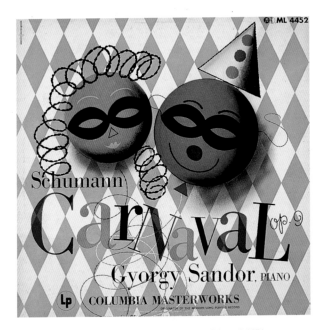

Designer: STANLEY   Label: COLUMBIA   Released: 1951

OPPOSITE: Designer: ROBERT JONES   Label: COLUMBIA   Released: 1950

Designer: UNKNOWN   Label: COLUMBIA   Released: 1953

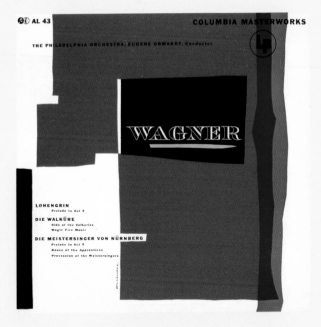

Designer: WILLAUMEZ   Label: COLUMBIA   Released: 1954

Designer: UNKNOWN   Label: EPIC   Released: 1954

Designer: WILLAUMEZ   Label: COLUMBIA   Released: 1953

OPPOSITE: Designer: JIM AMOS   Label: COLUMBIA   Released: 1950

Designer: NEIL FUJITA   Photo: HERMAN LEONARD   Label: COLUMBIA   Released: 1955

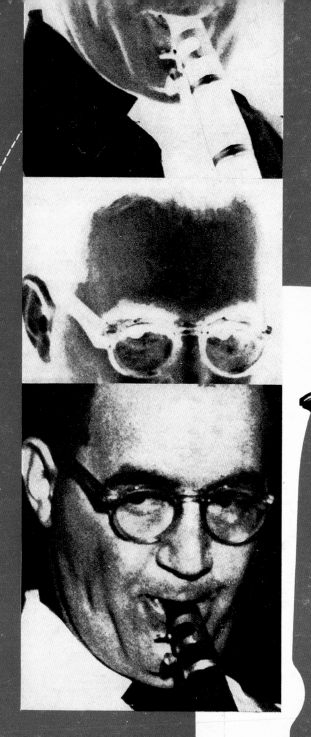

the golden era series

presents

benny goodman combos

columbia ʟᴘ

after you've gone
gilly
stardust
breakfast feud
benny's bugle
as long as i live
on the alamo
liza
shivers
ac-dc current
slipped disc
a smo-o-o-th one

Rudolph deHarak

Rudolph deHarak was born in Culver City, California, on April 10, 1924. When he was nine, his family moved to New York City where he would eventually attend the High School of Industrial Arts, studying drawing and commercial art. After service in World War II, the young deHarak returned to Los Angeles, where his first job was as an apprentice at a small advertising agency, doing mechanicals, layouts, and illustration. Winning an award for one of his early ads in a Los Angeles Art Director's Club design competition convinced him that he could be successful as a graphic designer. By the late 1940s, deHarak, along with six other designers, had formed the Los Angeles Society of Contemporary Designers, because they felt their impact might be greater on the design world as a group. Two of the designers in this group, Alvin Lustig and Saul Bass, were also early influences on deHarak's work. Lustig he admired for his interest in abstract forms and type, and Bass for his strong ideas. DeHarak, however, had little faith in Los Angeles as a progressive city and he moved to New York in 1950, taking a job as a promotion art director at *Seventeen* magazine. By 1951, deHarak was out on his own and designing covers for Columbia Records. His first cover for them, *Benny Goodman Combos,* brought to the label a new approach that was less elaborate than Steinweiss's work, but also relied heavily on type and symbolic shapes rather than working around a photograph of the recording artist. In this cover, deHarak uses a photograph of Goodman, but plays with the positive and negative imagery, making it subordinate to the overall design. For at least one Columbia cover, Rachmaninoff's *Miserly Knight,* he won several awards, including ones from AIGA and the Art Director's Club. A deHarak trademark at Columbia was his

Designer: RUDOLPH deHARAK   Label: COLUMBIA Released: 1952

Designer: RUDOLPH deHARAK   Label: COLUMBIA Released: 1953

OPPOSITE: Designer: RUDOLPH deHARAK   Label: COLUMBIA   Released: 1951

ML 45

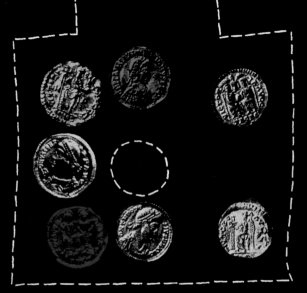

a columbia first performance

cesare **siepi** bass

the **miserly**

knight act 2

in the cellar

rachmaninoff

the little orchestra society
thomas scherman, conductor

arensky

variations on a theme by tchaikovsky
for string orchestra, opus 35a

columbia Lp
masterworks
originator of the modern long playing record

reinterpretation of the company's well-known LP logo. Here, he replaces the lettering with a hand-drawn or serifed typeface, whichever was appropriate to the cover he was doing. This attests to deHarak's anti-commmercial approach to design, something that Columbia's corporate offices would certainly not allow even by the late 1950s. In fact, deHarak's last covers were done for the label around 1954, at a time when the company was shifting to more commercial all-photography covers. DeHarak did other album covers during this period for Circle, a small jazz label founded by Rudi Blesh, and Westminster. At these labels his mature style was realized — bold shapes and color combined with new neutral typefaces like Berthold's Akzidenz Grotesk and, later, Helvetica. This style developed further in the 1960s with the many book jackets deHarak designed for McGraw Hill. The 1960s also brought his work into exhibition and museum design, starting with Montreal's EXPO '67 and later including the National Parks Service, the U.S. Postal Service, the New York Public Library, and the Metropolitan Museum of Art. In the late 1980s, deHarak was elected into the Art Director's Hall of Fame and received an AIGA Gold Medal. Throughout much of his career Rudolph deHarak has loved teaching, and taught design at Cooper Union from 1952 into the 1980s.[7]

Designer: RUDOLPH deHARAK Label: COLUMBIA Released: 1952

RUDOLPH deHARAK, 1954

OPPOSITE: Designer: RUDOLPH deHARAK Label: COLUMBIA Released: 1953

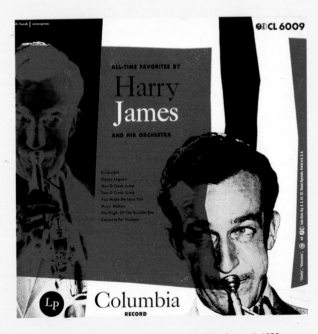

Designer: RUDOLPH deHARAK Label: COLUMBIA Released: 1952

CL 660

COLUMBIA

LP

after
hours
with

sarah Vaughan

after hours
street of dreams
you taught me to love again
you're mine, you
my reverie
summertime
black coffee
thinking of you
i cried for you
perdido
deep purple
just friends

Photo by: Hugh Bell

Designer: NEIL FUJITA   Photo: WILLIAM CLAXTON   Label: COLUMBIA   Released: 1954

Designer: BEN SHAHN   Label: COLUMBIA   Released: 1955

Designer: NEIL FUJITA   Photo: JAY MAISEL   Label: COLUMBIA   Released: 1956

OPPOSITE: Designer: NEIL FUJITA   Photo: HUGH BELL   Label: COLUMBIA   Released: 1955

Designer: NEIL FUJITA   Photo: ORMOND GIGLI   Label: COLUMBIA   Released: 1956

TONY

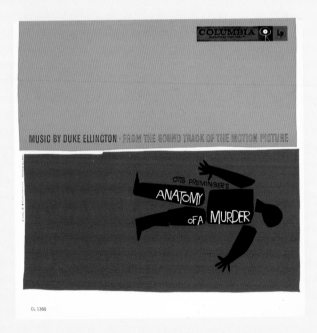

Designer: SAUL BASS   Label: COLUMBIA   Released: 1959

Designer: NEIL FUJITA   Photo: MARVIN KOHNER   Label: COLUMBIA   Released: 1956

Designer: NEIL FUJITA   Label: COLUMBIA   Released: 1956

PPOSITE: Designer: NEIL FUJITA   Photo: ARNOLD NEWMAN   Label: COLUMBIA   Released: 1956

Designer: NEIL FUJITA   Label: COLUMBIA   Released: 1958

Designer: UNKNOWN   Label: RCA VICTOR   Released: 1954

Designer: UNKNOWN   Label: RCA VICTOR   Released: 1954

OPPOSITE: Designer: UNKNOWN   Label: RCA VICTOR   Released: 1954

Designer: ROBERT JONES   Label: RCA VICTOR   Released: 1954

RCA VICTOR
LJM-3000

Brad Gowans

and his New York Nine

Poor Butterfield
I'm Coming Virginia
Jazz Me Blues
Stompin' at the Savoy
Singin' the Blues
Clari-jama
Carolina in the Morning
Jada

Brad Gowans, *Trombone*
Billy Butterfield, *Trumpet*
Arthur Rollini, *Tenor Sax*
Joe Dixon, *Clarinet*
Paul Ricci, *Bass Sax*
Joe Bushkin, *Piano*
Tony Colucci, *Guitar*
Jack Lesberg, *Bass*
Dave Tough, *Drums*

kysar

Designer: AUERBACH Label: RCA VICTOR Released: 1955

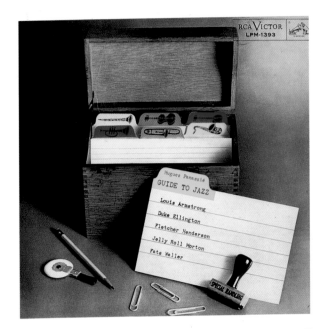

Designer: UNKNOWN Photo: ROY KUHLMAN Label: RCA VICTOR Released: 1956

Designer: UNKNOWN Label: RCA VICTOR Released: 1954

OPPOSITE: Designer: KYSER Label: RCA VICTOR Released: 1954

Designer: UNKNOWN Photo: MURRAY LADEN Label: RCA VICTOR Released: 1957

Designer: JIM FLORA   Label: RCA VICTOR   Released: 1954

Designer: JIM FLORA   Label: RCA VICTOR   Released: 1954

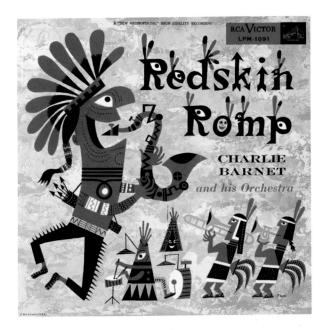

Designer: JIM FLORA   Label: RCA VICTOR   Released: 1955

OPPOSITE: Designer: JIM FLORA   Label: RCA VICTOR   Released: 1954

Designer: JIM FLORA   Label: RCA VICTOR   Released: 1954

Inside Sauter-Finegan

RCA VICTOR
LJM-1003
A "NEW ORTHOPHONIC" HIGH FIDELITY RECOR

HOW AB

AUTUM

SEPTEMBER'S

THE "THUNDISBRE"

10,000 B

FOUR HORSEMEN

WILD WINGS IN THE WOODS

WHEN TWO TREES FALL IN LOVE

OLD FOLKS

PENNIES FROM HEAVEN

EDDIE AND THE WITCH DOCTOR

NEW YORK....4 A.M.

FINEGAN'S WAKE

Designer: JIM FLORA   Label: RCA VICTOR   Released: 1954

Designer: JIM FLORA   Label: RCA VICTOR   Released: 1955

Designer: JIM FLORA   Label: RCA VICTOR   Released: 1954

OPPOSITE: Designer: JIM FLORA   Label: RCA VICTOR   Released: 1954

Designer: JIM FLORA   Label: RCA VICTOR   Released: 1955

YMA SUMAC

Capitol RECORDS

MUSIC
BY
MAISES VIVANCA

Legend of the Sun Virgin

Designer: UNKNOWN   Photo: TOM KELLY   Label: CAPITOL   Released: 1950

Designer: UNKNOWN   Photo: TOM KELLY   Label: CAPITOL   Released: 1951

OPPOSITE: Designer: UNKNOWN   Photo: TOM KELLY   Label: CAPITOL   Released: 1952

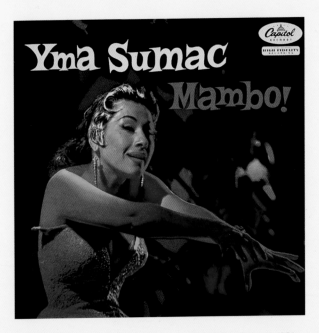

Designer: UNKNOWN   Photo: TOM KELLY   Label: CAPITOL   Released: 1954

DANNY KUAANA presents
holiday in hawaii
MAUNA KEA · LOVELY HULA HANDS · NOHO PAIPAI · KE KALI NEI AU · HILO HATTIE · E KUU LEI MY DARLING · KILIMA WALTZ · HE' UI
Capitol
RECORDS

Designer: UNKNOWN   Label: CAPITOL   Released: 1951

Designer: UNKNOWN   Label: CAPITOL   Released: 1953

Designer: UNKNOWN   Label: CAPITOL   Released: 1953

OPPOSITE: Designer: UNKNOWN   Label: CAPITOL   Released: 1950

Designer: VINCE   Label: CAPITOL   Released: 1950

Designer: UNKNOWN   Label: CAPITOL   Released: 1953

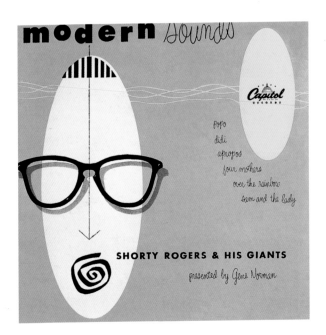

Designer: UNKNOWN   Label: CAPITOL   Released: 1950

Designer: UNKNOWN   Label: CAPITOL   Released: 1950

OPPOSITE: Designer: UNKNOWN   Label: CAPITOL   Released: 1954

Designer: GENE HOLTAN   Label: CAPITOL   Released: 1954

Designer: UNKNOWN   Label: CAPITOL   Released: 1956

Designer: UNKNOWN   Label: CAPITOL   Released: 1955

Designer: UNKNOWN   Label: CAPITOL   Released: 1955

OPPOSITE: Designer: McCAFFREY   Label: CAPITOL   Released: 1958

Designer: UNKNOWN   Label: CAPITOL   Released: 1957

DECCA

Designer: UNKNOWN   Label: DECCA   Released: 1954

Designer: UNKNOWN   Label: DECCA   Released: 1955

Designer: UNKNOWN   Label: DECCA   Released: 1955

OPPOSITE: Designer: ALEX STEINWEISS   Label: DECCA   Released: 1954

DECCA RECORDS
HI-FI

music by Elmer Bernstein from "The Man With The Golden Arm"

THE MAN WITH THE GOLDEN ARM

A FILM BY OTTO PREMINGER

Printed in U.S.A.

jazz sequences arranged and played by SHORTY ROGERS and His Giants with SHELLY MANNE

courtesy Atlantic Records   courtesy Contemporary Records

Designer: ALEX STEINWEISS   Label: DECCA   Released: 1955

Designer: UNKNOWN   Label: DECCA   Released: 1955

Designer: UNKNOWN   Photo: TONY SCOTT   Label: DECCA   Released: 1959

OPPOSITE: Designer: SAUL BASS   Label: DECCA   Released: 1955

Designer: UNKNOWN   Label: DECCA   Released: 1955

DECCA®
GOLD LABEL SERIES

33⅓ RPM
LONG PLAY
RECORDS

Richard Strauss conducts | **Ein Heldenleben**

op. 40
A Hero's Life

Bavarian
State
Orchestra

Erik Nitsche

Erik Nitsche was born in 1908 in Lausanne, Switzerland. Paul Klee was a family friend and influenced the young Nitsche to become an artist rather than enter the family business of commercial photography. Studying first at the Kunst-gerwerbeschule in Munich with noted typographer F. H. Ehmcke, Nitsche began his professional career in 1930. Within a year, he was working in Paris at an advertising agency in many facets of the design business, including illustrations and political cartoons for European weekly publications. In 1934, feeling the growing political unrest in Europe, Nitsche decided to leave for the United States. His friend Frederick Hollander, the songwriter who wrote "Falling in Love Again" for Marlene Dietrich, got him his first job designing stage sets for the musical *All Aboard* in Los Angeles. Hollywood was, however, too outgoing for the reclusive Nitsche, and he soon headed for New York. There he found work doing fashion layouts and covers for some of the top magazines of the day, including working with Alexey Brodavitch at *Harper's Bazaar, Town & Country, Vanity Fair, Stage, Arts & Decoration,* and *House Beautiful.* Nitsche's fashion work would ultimately lead to a job as art director for Saks Fifth Avenue in 1938. Always looking ahead, Nitsche tired of the fashion world by the early 1940s and took a job as far removed from the field as he could find: art director for *Air Tech* and *Air News.*[8] Around 1951, Nitsche added Decca Records to his list of clients, designing hundreds of covers for the label's classical artists. Nitsche's Decca work was unique in that he was the first to bring a decidedly post-war "Swiss" design sensibility to record graphics, long before it would become such a great influence in the 1960s. His design for Strauss's

Designer: ERIK NITSCHE   Label: DECCA   Released: 1951

Designer: ERIK NITSCHE   Label: DECCA   Released: 1953

OPPOSITE: Designer: ERIK NITSCHE   Label: DECCA   Released: 1952

ERIK NITSC

DECCA®
GOLD LABEL SERIES | 33⅓ LONG RECO

Walter Piston / Nicholas Lopatnikoff

sonata

for violin and piano

sonata No.2 op. 3

for violin and piano

Joseph Fuchs, violin – Artur Balsam, piano

DL 9541

Ein Heldenleben with its bold, delicate arrows and balance of two weights of Futura, appears ten years ahead of its time. In Weber's *Sonata No. 1*, a nineteenth-century pattern recalls the composer's era and is juxtaposed against a modern shape holding the type. Nitsche's Decca covers were also unique within the company, and were never used for popular music. Apparently, judging from the cover graphics, Decca's marketing approach to their popular artists was totally different. Most were blatantly commercial and lacked the sophistication that Nitsche lavished on the classical covers. Nitsche's work for Decca ended around 1954, when he began to concentrate on another account, General Dynamics. In 1955, he accepted a position as design consultant to the company. During the next ten years he designed for them an entire corporate identity, including posters, exhibits, and annual reports that would bring him to the forefront of corporate design. The death of General Dynamics's president in 1964 also meant the end of Nitsche's job. Turning his attention to book design, Nitsche produced a series of lavish pictorial history books in the late 1960s and '70s, as well a series of children's books. In the last fifteen years, Nitsche's projects included designs for postage stamps, special effects for films, magazine design, and book illustration. He died in 1998.

Designer: ERIK NITSCHE   Label: DECCA   Released: 1951

ERIK NITSCHE C. 1955

OPPOSITE: Designer: ERIK NITSCHE   Label: DECCA   Released: 1951

Designer: ERIK NITSCHE   Label: DECCA   Released: 1951

Designer: DAVID STONE MARTIN   Label: CLEF   Released: 1954

David Stone Martin was born in Chicago in 1913 and graduated from the Art Institute of Chicago in 1935. Martin's first jobs were in agencies sponsored by Roosevelt's New Deal, first as a supervisor for the Federal Arts Projects of Western Illinois and then as art director of the Tennessee Valley Authority. During this time, he also won several competitions for murals for public buildings in the South. In the early 1940s, Martin met and befriended artist Ben Shahn, whose work became a major influence on him. It was Shahn who convinced Martin to move to Jersey Homesteads, a community originally established through the New Deal. The community (later renamed Roosevelt) soon gained a reputation as an artist's colony after Shahn

Designer: DAVID STONE MARTIN   Label: MERCURY   Released: 1952

OPPOSITE: Designer: DAVID STONE MARTIN   Label: MERCURY   Released: 1950

FLIP

Collates No.2

Phillips

Supervised by Norman Granz

D.S.M.

CLEF RECORD

permanently settled there in 1939. During the war years, Martin, along with Shahn and William Golden (who later would design the famous CBS eye logo), was recruited into the Art Department of the Office of War Information, where he produced posters and artwork for the war effort. At this time, Martin also worked as "Artist and War Correspondant" for *Life* magazine. Like many other early record cover designers and illustrators, Martin's love of jazz was responsible for his first design job. Jazz pianist Mary Lou Williams, his close friend, persuaded the label she recorded for, Asch Records, to allow Martin to design her next album cover in 1944. Asch was a small independent label that produced jazz, blues, folk, and spoken-word recordings of such artists as Art Tatum, Josh White, Coleman Hawkins, Orson Welles, and Langston Hughes. Its owner, Moses Asch, who was also an art collector, liked Martin's first cover so much that he asked him to be the company's art director. For the success of his first covers and projects from other clients, Martin was presented the New York Art Director's Club Medal in 1946. Around this time, Asch issued the first recordings of jazz impresario Norman Granz's *Jazz at the Philharmonic* series, perhaps the most well known and popular of the albums the label released and responsible for Martin's affiliation with the man who would change his career. The *Jazz at the Philharmonic* was a series of live jam sessions presented for the first time on a concert stage. For the recordings of these concerts, Granz asked Martin to develop a logo that would differentiate his product from the rest of the Asch line. Martin's logo of a trumpet player (shown on p. 103) became one of the most famous logos in jazz, and one that is still in use today. In 1948, when Granz

Designer: DAVID STONE MARTIN   Label: MERCURY   Released: 1954

Designer: DAVID STONE MARTIN   Label: MERCURY   Released: 1954

OPPOSITE: Designer: DAVID STONE MARTIN   Label: CLEF   Released: 1952

MG C-078

COUNT
BASIE
SWINGS
JOE
WILLIAMS
SINGS

CLEF RECORDS SUPERVISED BY NORMAN GRANZ

muenster-dummel
HI-FI
recording

established his own labels, Clef and Norgran (later consolidated on the Verve label), he persuaded Martin to leave Asch and relocate to Los Angeles to illustrate and art direct the new company's covers. In Granz, Martin found an employer who encouraged him to take the same chances he did. Martin's sensitive line drawings, black and white or with vivid color wash backgrounds, evoked perfectly the avant garde or "pure" jazz that Granz became famous for producing. Like those created by Alex Steinweiss, many of Martin's covers did not have an actual image of the recording artist, but rather an abstract image that might recall the feeling of the music. Granz's unconventional formula for his labels proved to be a success. This success, however, led to Granz selling Verve to MGM in 1960, and the replacement of Martin's cover art with photography. Of the more than two hundred covers he designed for the Granz labels, his personal favorites were those he did for Billie Holiday from 1952 to 1957. Throughout his years as a cover designer, Martin always remained a freelancer; his other accounts included cover illustrations for *Time*, titles for CBS Television, posters for Broadway shows, book illustrations and covers, and movie titles including *Gigi* and *The James Dean Story*. From 1965 to 1968, Martin was an instructor at Parson's School of Design and the Art Student's League. His work has been exhibited at the Metropolitan Museum, the Art Institute of Chicago, the Brooklyn Museum, and the Museum of Modern Art. The first major exhibit of his cover designs was held in 1986 by the New York Public Library and the Museum of the Performing Arts. Martin continued his career as an illustrator, working on a series of musician portraits, until his death in 1993.[9]

Designer: DAVID STONE MARTIN   Label: CLEF   Released: 1955

Designer: DAVID STONE MARTIN   Label: CLEF   Released: 1955

OPPOSITE: Designer: DAVID STONE MARTIN   Label: CLEF   Released: 1955

Designer: DAVID STONE MARTIN   Label: CLEF   Released: 1953

Designer: DAVID STONE MARTIN   Label: MERCURY   Released: 1952

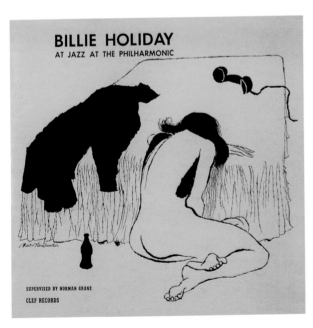

Designer: DAVID STONE MARTIN   Label: CLEF   Released: 1955

OPPOSITE: Designer: DAVID STONE MARTIN   Label: CLEF   Released: 1955

Designer: DAVID STONE MARTIN   Label: VERVE   Released: 1959

Designer: DAVID STONE MARTIN   Label: NORGRAN   Released: 1955

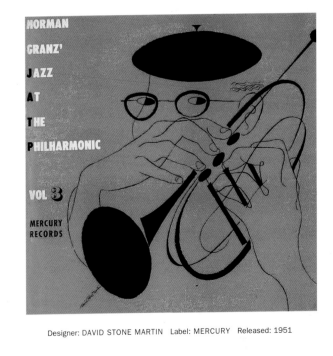

Designer: DAVID STONE MARTIN   Label: MERCURY   Released: 1951

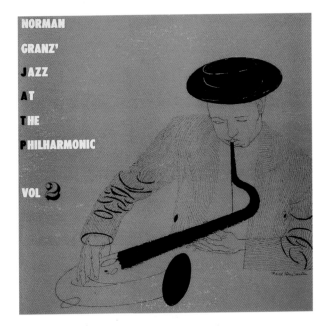

Designer: DAVID STONE MARTIN   Label: MERCURY   Released: 1950

OPPOSITE: Designer: DAVID STONE MARTIN   Label: CLEF   Released: 1952

Designer: DAVID STONE MARTIN   Label: CLEF   Released: 1955

COOL
VELVET
STAN
GETZ
AND
STRINGS

Designer: J. CHRIS SMITH   Photo: BURT GOLDBLATT   Label: VERVE   Released: 1958

Designer: JOSEPH YOUNG   Label: VERVE   Released: 1958

Designer: UNKNOWN   Label: VERVE   Released: 1956

OPPOSITE: Designer: MERLE SHORE   Label: VERVE   Released: 1959

Designer: UNKNOWN   Photo: MAURICE SEYMOUR   Label: VERVE   Released: 1958

Designer: BURT GOLDBLATT   Label: EMARCY   Released: 1954

Designer: UNKNOWN   Label: EMARCY   Released: 1955

Designer: UNKNOWN   Label: EMARCY   Released: 1954

OPPOSITE: Designer: FRED STEFFEN   Label: EMARCY   Released: 1954

MG 25196

just Patti

Everything I Have Is Yours

Don't Blame Me

Ghost Of A Chance

We Just Couldn't Say Goodbye

I'm Getting Sentimental Over You

Try A Little Tenderness

Under A Blanket Of Blue   Sweet and Lovely

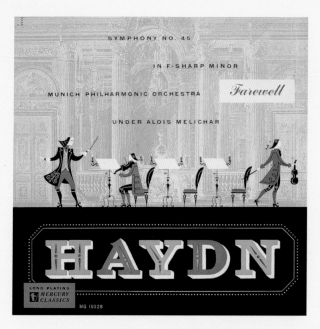

Designer: GEORGE MAAS   Label: MERCURY   Released: 1950

Designer: EMMETT McBAIN   Label: MERCURY   Released: 1958

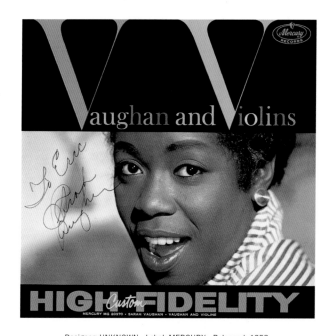

Designer: UNKNOWN   Label: MERCURY   Released: 1958

OPPOSITE: Designer: UNKNOWN   Label: MERCURY   Released: 1954

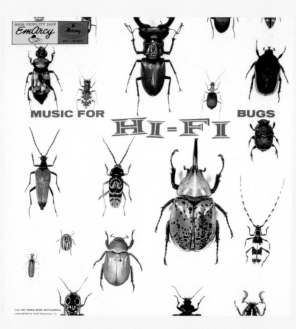

Designer: UNKNOWN   Label: EMARCY   Released: 1955

OSCAR PETTIFORD

BURT GOLDBLATT

BURT GOLDBLATT

Burt Goldblatt was born in Boston in 1924 and attended the Massachusetts College of Art, graduating in 1950. Originally a painter, it was Goldblatt's love of jazz that was the inspiration for his design career. Goldblatt designed his first cover for Columbia in 1951, the first of over three thousand covers created during his career. In 1952, he freelanced for Atlantic and Savoy Records and by 1953, he began his long association with Bethlehem Records, where he was the sole designer and art director. For Bethlehem, Goldblatt could make use of his many talents, not only designing every cover but creating all the illustration and photography as well. Goldblatt won many awards for his covers, including the Art Director's Gold Medal in 1956. Other accounts included promos for CBS Television and illustrations for *Harper's Weekly*. Goldblatt continued doing cover designs in the 1960s for Columbia, RCA, and Scepter before he gave up the record business in the 1970s to concentrate on book design and his career in fine art.

Designer: BURT GOLDBLATT   Label: BETHLEHEM   Released: 1955

BURT GOLDBLATT, C. 1955

OPPOSITE: Designer: BURT GOLDBLATT   Label: BETHLEHEM   Released: 1954

Designer: BURT GOLDBLATT   Label: BETHLEHEM   Released: 1954

BETHLEHEM BCP1022

MARIANO

BURT GOLD

Relaxin' with Frances Faye

Designer: BURT GOLDBLATT   Label: BETHLEHEM   Released: 1956

Designer: BURT GOLDBLATT   Label: BETHLEHEM   Released: 1955

Designer: BURT GOLDBLATT   Label: BETHLEHEM   Released: 1956

OPPOSITE: Designer: BURT GOLDBLATT   Label: BETHLEHEM   Released: 1955

Designer: BURT GOLDBLATT   Label: BETHLEHEM   Released: 1955

songs
by
Mabel
Mercer

VOLUME ONE

Little Girl Blue • Just One of Those Things
You Are Not My First Love • Remind Me
Feuilles Mortes • The End of A Love Affair
Hello Young Lovers • Sunday in Savannah
Ivory Tower • The First Warm Day In May

accompanied by
Sam Hamilton at the piano
with rhythm

BURT GOLDBLATT

ATLANT
ALS 402

ATLANTIC

RECORDS

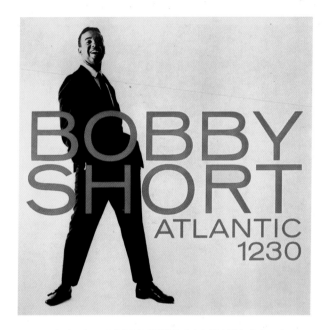

Designer: GUIDI   Photo: WILLIAM HELBURN   Label: ATLANTIC   Released: 1956

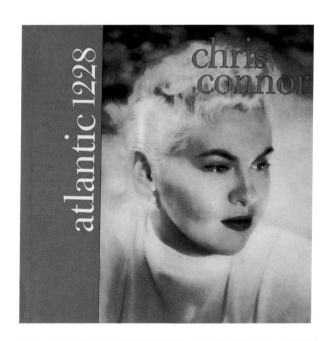

atlantic 1228

chris
connor

Designer: GUIDI   Photo: MARKUS BLECHMAN   Label: ATLANTIC   Released: 1956

OPPOSITE: Designer: BURT GOLDBLATT   Label: ATLANTIC   Released: 1951

VERNON duke PLAYS vernon DUKE
with vocals by Dorothy Richards
HUGUETTE FERLY
ATLANTIC ALS 407

Designer: UNKNOWN   Label: ATLANTIC Released: 1951

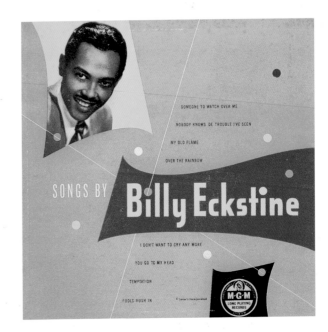

Designer: UNKNOWN   Label: M-G-M   Released: 1951

Designer: UNKNOWN   Label: M-G-M   Released: 1951

OPPOSITE: Designer: UNKNOWN   Label: M-G-M   Released: 1951

Designer: GEORGE MAAS   Label: M-G-M   Released: 1950

SONNY ROLLINS

blue note 1542

BLUE NOTE
THE FINEST IN JAZZ SINCE 1939

REID MILES

Reid Miles was born in Chicago in 1927 and grew up in California, attending the Choulnard Art Institute. In the early 1950s he left for New York seeking freelance work. Blue Note offered him a job in 1956, where for over fifteen years he would design almost five hundred covers, creating the look the label became famous for. In the 1960s, Miles held a succession of jobs at agencies and magazines, including art director for *Esquire*. By 1971, he turned his interests and career around to photography and television commercial production, working until his death in 1993.

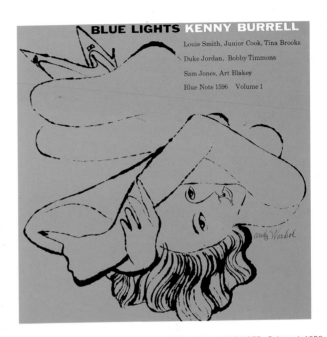

Designer: REID MILES   Illustration: ANDY WARHOL   Label: BLUE NOTE   Released: 1958

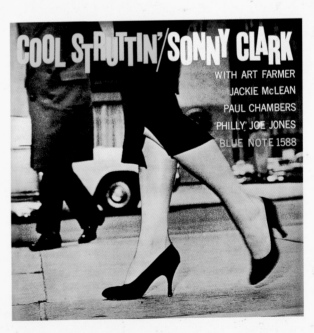

Designer: REID MILES   Label: BLUE NOTE   Released: 1958

OPPOSITE: Designer: REID MILES   Label: BLUE NOTE   Released: 1956

Designer: REID MILES   Label: BLUE NOTE   Released: 1958

Designer: ESMOND EDWARDS   Label: PRESTIGE   Released: 1958

Designer: UNKNOWN   Label: FANTASY   Released: 1951

Designer & Photographer: WILLIAM CLAXTON   Label: PACIFIC JAZZ   Released: 1953

OPPOSITE: Designer: BETTY BRADER   Label: FANTASY   Released: 1956

Designer: REID MILES   Label: PRESTIGE   Released: 1956

Designer: PAUL BACON   Photo: PAUL WELLER   Label: RIVERSIDE   Released: 1957

Designer: PINKNEY   Label: SAVOY   Released: 1950

Designer: GRAYSON   Label: ALADDIN   Released: 1952

OPPOSITE: Designer: UNKNOWN   Label: WESTMINSTER   Released: 1956

Designer: RUDOLPH deHARAK   Label: CIRCLE   Released: 1954

acknowledgments

I learned while choosing covers for this book that one's own collection is never complete. I am indebted to my friends and fellow collectors: Bob Belden, Barbara Carroll, Alan Eichler, Will Friedwald, James Gavin, Charles Granata, Steven Heller, Ken Kleman, Mark Murphy, and Morty Savada, who loaned me invaluable material missing from my own collection and always offered their support. Thanks also to the hundreds of record stores, antique shops, and flea markets I have haunted over the last twenty-five years. My thanks to Herman Leonard, Charles Peterson, Les Morsillo, and my sister, Lisa Kohler, for their photography; Steven Diamond and Ken Spole for their legal research; and the following record companies, estates, and individuals, who graciously allowed reproduction of their covers for this book: Milt Gabler at Commodore Records, Les Watkins and Arnold Levine at Columbia Records, Ray Tisdale at Capitol Records, Gregory Carapetyan at RCA Records, Paul Young and Sheryl Gold at Universal Records, Jonathan Lieberman at Polygram Records, Melinda Gaffin at Atlantic Records, Bill Belmont at Fantasy Records, Ken Cayre at Bethlehem Records, and the estates of Nat King Cole, Marlene Dietrich, Stan Getz, Teddy Grace, Carmen Miranda, Mel Powell, Billie Holiday, and Frank Sinatra.

Many thanks go to Alex Steinweiss, Jim Flora, Sydney Butchkes, Burt Goldblatt, and Rudolph deHarak, who spent many hours on the phone with me discussing their cover designs. Their work inspired me to begin this book. My sincere thanks to my publisher, Chronicle Books, my editor Nion McEvoy, creative director Michael Carabetta, Christina Wilson, and Patricia Evangelista for their interest and support. Also, thanks to Jeffrey Aronoff, Jean Conlon, Stephen Cipriano, Glyn Cunningham, Graham Marsh, Kenneth Silver, Edgar LaMance, Tom Nimen, Stephen Paley, Paul Ranson, Robert Richards, and my mother, Sue Kohler, for their support.

Last, I will always be grateful to Tony Bennett for writing such an insightful foreword to this book, and to Barbara Carroll, Rosemary Clooney, k.d. lang, and Jo Stafford for their generous endorsements.

THIS BOOK IS DEDICATED TO THE MEMORY OF JOE LOMBARDO.

Endnoted material in this book is as follows: 1. J. Kirvine, *Jukebox Saturday Night* (New Jersey: Chartwell Books, 1977), 72. 2. John Lahr, "Sinatra's Song," *The New Yorker,* November 1997, 80. 3. Steven Heller, "For the Record," *Print,* March/April 1992, 64–115. 4. Kirvine, 107. 5. Heller, 64–115. 6. Manek Daver, *Jazz Graphics: David Stone Martin* (Japan: n.p., 1991), 16–23. 7. Heller, "Rudolph deHarak: A Humanist's Modernist," *AIGA 14* (New York: American Institute of Graphic Arts, 1993), 10–23. 8. Heller, "A Contemporary Man," *Print,* January/February 1998, 104–220. 9. Daver, 22.

Holocaust Project

Holocaust Project

FROM DARKNESS INTO LIGHT

JUDY CHICAGO

WITH PHOTOGRAPHY BY DONALD WOODMAN

PENGUIN BOOKS

PENGUIN BOOKS
Published by the Penguin Group
Penguin Books USA Inc., 375 Hudson Street, New York, New York 10014, U.S.A.
Penguin Books Ltd, 27 Wrights Lane, London W8 5TZ, England
Penguin Books Australia Ltd, Ringwood, Victoria, Australia
Penguin Books Canada Ltd, 10 Alcorn Avenue,
Toronto, Ontario, Canada M4V 3B2
Penguin Books (N.Z.) Ltd, 182-190 Wairau Road,
Auckland 10, New Zealand

Penguin Books Ltd, Registered Offices:
Harmondsworth, Middlesex, England

First published in simultaneous hardcover and paperback editions by Viking Penguin and
Penguin Books, divisions of Penguin Books USA Inc. 1993

3   5   7   9   10   8   6   4   2

Acknowledgments for permission to reproduce artwork and reprint textual selections appear on pages 203–205

LIBRARY OF CONGRESS CATALOGING IN PUBLICATION DATA
Chicago, Judy, 1939–
Holocaust project: from darkness into light/ Judy Chicago; with photography by Donald Woodman.
p. cm.
Published in connection with a traveling exhibition launched at
the Spertus Museum in Chicago in 1993.
Includes bibliographical references.
ISBN 0 14 01.5991 6 (paperback)
1. Chicago, Judy, 1939– —Exhibitions. 2. Holocaust, Jewish
(1939–1945) in art—Exhibitions. I. Maurice Spertus Museum of Judaica. II. Title.
N6537.C48A4 1993
759.13—dc20   92–43297

Printed in Mexico
Set in Bitstream Transitional
Designed by Kate Nichols

Acknowledgments

Although I've done other major projects before, none involved the amount of travel, research, logistics, planning, or intensely focused work that the *Holocaust Project* exhibition and book entailed. My husband, Donald Woodman (with whom I worked closely), and I are deeply indebted to the board of directors of Through the Flower (the nonprofit organization that supports my art and vision) for its sponsorship and to its staff, particularly Jessica Buege. Many of the board members made personal contributions to the project or helped us raise funds.

We both wish to thank them, as well as Susan Grode for her special help. Mary Ross Taylor generously provided us with a nurturing place in which to live and work at very modest cost. Her beautiful house in Santa Fe was very important to us as we faced the darkness of the material, and we want her to know how much we appreciate her magnanimity.

Elizabeth Sackler joined Through the Flower's board in 1990, but before that time she aided Donald and me in obtaining our first grant and then provided us with substantial personal patronage, both financial and emotional. Her commitment to the project and to my art often sustained me through the many black days spent facing such overwhelming subject matter. We hope she will feel proud of what she helped us achieve.

Isaiah Kuperstein was our stalwart ally and mentor. From our very first meeting, he proffered assistance, information, guidance, comfort, support, and friendship. We cannot thank him enough. So many people have helped us, and we are grateful to Nancy Berman, Michael Botwinick, Konnilyn Feig, Rita Feigenbaum, Tom Freudenheim, Christie Hefner, Vera John-Steiner, Flo Kinsler, Gerry Margolis, Michael and Charlotte Newberger, Michael Nutkiewicz, Arlene Raven, and Joan Ringelheim for their help, interest, and advice. Adair Klein, the librarian at the Simon Wiesenthal Center, assisted us greatly in our photo research, and we are thankful to both Betty Levinson and David Hirsch of UCLA for their help in our film, video, and library research. Our rabbi and spiritual leader, Lynn Gottleib, first married, then educated and counseled us as we awkwardly made our way to a connection with our heritage as Jews.

Our therapist, Dr. Donald Fineberg, assisted us enormously in our struggle to maintain our married life while we coped with the many and often overwhelming pressures the project placed on us. Ginna Sloane, our graphic designer, provided essential and valued services, and we thank her. We are extremely grateful to the Spertus Museum of Judaica for offering institutional support and commitment to the philosophical goals of the art. We also wish to acknowledge the museum staff for their dedicated work.

The art itself could not have been created without the many people who were generous with their services. A special thanks to the always generous and stalwart Kate Amend, Bryan Cooke, Russell Elliott, Marty Horowitz, the team of Jim Kraft and Judy Booth, Helen and Marvin Leaf, my college soulmate Lanny Meyers, Juliet Myers, Steven Prins, my cousin Alan Schwartz, Matthew Sneddon, and Frannie Yablonsky. The talent and dedication of artisans like needleworkers Helen Eisenberg, Joyce Gilbert, Candis Duncan Pomykala, and Jane Thompson; welder Michele Maier; stained glass artisans Michael Caudle, Bob

Gomez, Dorothy Maddy, and Flo Perkins; and weaver Audrey Cowan have contributed greatly to the realization of our vision. Many of these people have worked with me before, often, as in Audrey's case, for many years. They have frequently faced considerable misunderstanding because of their decision to "volunteer." It has hurt us all that many people seem to be suspicious of our selflessness—theirs, Donald's, and mine. We have all worked voluntarily in the service of a large human task—that of transforming consciousness through art—and I am extremely indebted to all our colleagues. I am only sad that Dorothy Maddy did not live to see the installation of the stained glass piece she painted so beautifully.

This is not my first book, but in my opinion it is the best, thanks in large part to the staff of Viking Penguin, especially their outstanding production people, Kate Nichols and Dolores Reilly, my conscientious copyeditor, Bob Castillo, and my truly extraordinary editor, Mindy Werner. I also want to thank my long-time editor turned agent, Loretta Barrett, for her ongoing dedication, hard work, and integrity. And a special appreciation to Lisa Manziano for her dedicated work in preparing the manuscript.

Unlike many other artists, my art is primarily supported—not by the art world—but by a world-wide network of caring people. Their financial generosity has provided the resources for the *Holocaust Project*. Hundreds of people contributed money, and we thank them all and hope they will feel gratified when they see the show. We are particularly grateful to the Museum Educational Trust, the Threshold Foundation, the Streisand Foundation, the International Friends of Transformative Art, the Polaroid Corporation, and Fuji America for grants, materials, and support. Major contributors included (in addition to Elizabeth Sackler) William Turnbull (in memoriam); Stanley and Elyse Grinstein (whose generosity has been crucial to me for over twenty-five years); our new friends Evy and Marty Lutin and Spectra American Color Labs; and Ruth Lambert and Henry Harrison.

Other important donors were Bob and Audrey Cowan; my dear cousins Howard and Arleen Rosen and our very special aunt, Rosa Bergmann; Helen and Mel Eisenberg; and Sima and Morris Belzberg, Sallie Bingham, Judy and Al Glickman, Dr. Alfred and Cecilia Katz, Ann and Patrick Lannan, Reesa and Jerry Niznick, Cydney and Bill Osterman, Beverly and Lee Randall, Judy and Bob Rothschild, Rena Schulsky, Gilbert Silverman, Galen and Joseph Solomon, and Sylvia and Phil Spertus.

Finally, I want to thank my husband, Donald, who embarked on this long journey with me though we were barely newlyweds. Neither of us had any idea what difficulties and experiences we would share. I learned to admire my husband deeply for his strength, his talent, and his courage. Most of all, I could never have completed this project without him—neither aesthetically nor emotionally. The bonds we've forged during these years will, I hope, help sustain our marriage throughout our lives.

Contents

PART ONE

Awakening

I opened my door
and many, many crowded to come in
I therefore pushed back
the walls of my room
to welcome all my guests
And the room became the home
of my friends
and my room became the world.

—Amir Gilboa

first became interested in the subject of the Holocaust at, of all places, a 1984 Christmas party in Santa Fe, New Mexico, where I lived. I met a poet there named Harvey Mudd, who had just completed a long poem about the Holocaust. It was a topic that had interested him since childhood but one, I realized with shock, that I knew almost nothing about.

I asked to read Harvey's manuscript, which I found quite fascinating. He told me about the trip he'd made to Auschwitz and Treblinka in preparation for writing the poem, and I expressed surprise that he, a non-Jew, would have wanted to explore the subject of the Holocaust. He was equally surprised at my not understanding a phrase he'd used in the poem, *Arbeit macht frei* ("Work makes you free"); he explained—with some dismay at my ignorance—that this was inscribed at some of the concentration camps where, of course, thousands of people had been killed rather than freed by the numbing, dehumanizing work.

I began to wonder how I had come to be so illiterate on and unexposed to the subject of the Holocaust. In 1972, while traveling in Europe, I had visited the Anne Frank house in Amsterdam. When I saw the yellow star Jews had been forced to wear—with the threads used to sew it to the clothing still evident—I was stunned. But even that experience did not stimulate me to explore the Holocaust.

The subject had hardly been discussed when I was growing up, which, when I thought about it, I found baffling. I wondered why, despite having been raised in a politically active household and particularly in light of my father's avid interest in history and current events, the Holocaust had rarely even been mentioned.

Of course, I didn't know very much about Jew-

ish culture or history generally, despite my descent from twenty-three generations of rabbis, a long tradition broken by my father, who refused to go to religious school (*cheder*) as a child and, as an adult, exchanged the family calling for labor organizing and Marxism.

It was, however, probably inevitable that I would become interested in investigating my Jewish identity and exploring its influence on me. Although I was brought up in an assimilated, nonreligious household, I had always felt a certain pride in being Jewish, a sense that I was "special." This feeling was enhanced by my father's frequent references to our having "blue blood" because of our lineage. (I am descended on both my paternal grandmother's and grandfather's side—they were first cousins—from the Vilna Gaon, a famous eighteenth-century Lithuanian religious leader and renowned rabbi and teacher.)

For many years I had been focused on exploring aspects of my identity as a woman, and in the late 1960s I became curious about women's omission from history. As a young college student I took a course in European intellectual history, and in the first class the professor promised that, at the last meeting, he would discuss women's participation in European culture. I waited all semester for this lecture, only to be confronted finally with his curt summation of "women's intellectual contributions" : "they made none."

I was devastated by this for a long time, and the (still) widely held notion that no woman had achieved "greatness" undermined my self-esteem as I struggled to fulfill my ambitions as an artist. I had been a child prodigy and the school artist at an early age. My intellect was encouraged and my artistic talents fostered by my parents' liberal philosophy, which, I now realize, was grounded in the

traditional Jewish esteem for learning and scholarship, an esteem I enjoyed as a "smart" child. My gender didn't influence their belief in my worth, which resulted in my enjoying a solid sense of self and never experiencing the conflicts about my aspirations described in recent literature by other Jewish women.

I had always been encouraged to take myself seriously, and the political consciousness with which I was raised helped me identify sexism when I first encountered it in college. My childhood experiences, my father's passion for history and his belief that the world could be changed (which he passed on to me), helped me stand up to sexual prejudice, and I turned to history to see if my callous male professor's assessment of women was correct.

Long before women's studies courses existed, I spent years looking for books by and about women. Slowly, painstakingly, I pieced together a picture of female achievement that became the basis for *The Dinner Party*, a multimedia work that conveys a symbolic history of women in Western Civilization through a series of place settings. These place settings, executed in women's traditional crafts—i.e., china-painting and needlework—present images of women who contributed to our cultural history but who, instead of being honored, were ignored, maligned, or obscured by that history.

My goal with *The Dinner Party* was to teach through art, a goal shaped partly by my interest in medieval art—in which Christian dogma was transmitted to a wide audience through visual imagery—but also, I now understand, by my Jewish background. Our rabbinical tradition was combined with my father's (probably unconscious but deeply felt) belief in the Jewish concept of *tikkun*—the process of healing and repairing the world—and these were passed on to me. I was *expected* to participate in our family discussions—in the political conversations that filled our household—and, by implication, in the historic struggle for change that is part of both the American and Jewish democratic traditions and to which my father was deeply committed.

My mother's orientation was more toward the arts. A dancer when young, as an elderly woman in her eighties she entertained people in the retirement home where she lived by donning a multicolor dance skirt and performing Martha Graham–type modern dances. She encouraged my aspirations as an artist and, despite an extremely limited budget, found the money for me to attend art classes regularly from the age of five. Many of my mother's friends were in the arts at a time when the international art market was unimaginable, and they communicated the idea that art was about "truth and beauty" and had nothing to do with commerce. My goal was not to make money from my work but, rather, to be "in service" to art. It's an old-fashioned and generally scorned attitude today, but it's one in which I still passionately believe.

I brought this orientation to my thirty-year career as an artist and it greatly influenced, first, *my goals*, which include contributing to a transformation of consciousness through art; second, *my way of working*, which, because of the scope and purpose of my projects, often involves a collaborative process; third, *my methods*, which are based on egalitarian principles and respect for the talents of my collaborators; fourth, *my organizing*, first a local, then national, now international community of support, which was initially motivated by my encountering an absence of art world support, but which now allows my art to reach a wide commu-

nity of diverse people; and fifth, *my subject matter*, which, between 1968 and 1982, focused primarily on issues of female identity.

While working on *The Dinner Party*, it became clear to me that there was a dialogue going on inside the women's community (of which I was obviously a part) that was largely absent from the art community (of which I was also a member). One of my goals with *The Dinner Party* was to bring that dialogue out of its confines into a larger community and to thereby broaden the art audience and sensitize it to women's history—and I was determined to accomplish that through art.

When I began to explore the subject of the Holocaust, I discovered a similar dichotomy. Within the Jewish community, there is an intense dialogue about this subject and an understandable commitment to create monuments and institutions to commemorate it. But outside the organized Jewish community, there is incomplete knowledge, indifference, and ignorance about the subject of the Holocaust, a "blame the victim" attitude, a lack of understanding about the importance of confronting this subject, and/or the widespread attitude, "What does the Holocaust have to do with me?"

This is reflected in the art world, where, with rare exceptions, there are almost no major bodies of contemporary art about the Holocaust; certainly few that have grown out of the Jewish experience have successfully entered the mainstream of contemporary art. The art that is valued and preserved is ultimately a measure of what we as a society deem important. When there is an absence of images in our museums, it means that those human experiences that aren't imaged exist outside of what we (often unquestioningly) assume to be "universal." I have frequently been attracted to

iconographic voids, and addressing them has been one of the hallmarks of my work.

After *The Dinner Party* and based on the network of support that had grown out of it, I developed the *Birth Project*, a series of needleworked images exploring the subject of birth and creation, which relied on the collaborative methods I'd employed in *The Dinner Party*: people working with me, bringing their skills into the realization of my images. One of the aesthetic challenges of the *Birth Project* was to develop images in a visual vacuum. Generally, an artist works against the background of art history that is, of course, the history of iconography. Because much of women's experience *from a women's perspective* is absent from that iconography, there were few images of birth for me to draw on, and the ones that did exist derived primarily from nonindustrialized societies, which are very different from our own and in which, consequently, the birth process was more natural, less "medicalized," and certainly less male-dominated.

In order to create a range of images of birth, I had to draw on visual, written, and oral personal "testimony," as well as private records. I immersed myself in the subject of birth and made myself a vehicle for the information I discovered. The fact that I'd never given birth was, to me, an asset, though some people didn't think so and challenged my credentials. I tried to point out that in art direct experience is not always a prerequisite for making images; if it were we'd have no paintings of, for example, crucifixions. Not having given birth allowed me a certain distance from the experience, a distance that is often essential for the process of aesthetic transformation. Moreover, it is through art that the universality of unique human experiences is revealed.

As Joachim Cezanne expressed in his memoirs, art is the true, collective memory of the human race: "Where is yesterday and the day before yesterday? . . . In this picture, in these colors . . . a spirit emerges which is everywhere the same: memory translated into objective form."

By the time of my serendipitous meeting with Harvey Mudd at that party, I was engaged in private studio work again in order to create *Powerplay*, a series of works examining masculinity as a gender construct, in much the same way that, for the last two decades, I and other women had been exploring the meanings of womanhood, femininity, and female roles. My own development had led me to the point where I wanted to turn my gaze outward from my extended investigation of women—first to look at men, and then the world.

In *Powerplay* I examined the effects of power as it has been defined and enacted by men (who, for most of recorded history, have been in control of civilization's direction). These images explore the human consequences on men as a class for having borne the historic burden of power, as well as the ways men as individuals have been disfigured and dehumanized by the requirements of the male role.

My interest in issues of gender certainly prefigured my interest in the Holocaust. Most people have not paid any attention to the fact that the architects of the Third Reich were *all* men. It is true that there were women who participated and who, according to some accounts, even exceeded men in cruelty. But if one were to peruse the list of names of those who actually engineered the Third Reich and the Final Solution, no women's names would appear.

In referring to the Nazi march across Europe and the relationship between the concept of masculinity and fascism, Virginia Woolf wrote in *Three Guineas*:

As we listen to the voices we seem to hear an infant crying in the night, the black night that now covers Europe, and with no language but a cry. . . . But it is not a new cry, it is a very old cry. Let us shut off the wireless and listen to the past. . . . Whomsoever the city may appoint that man must be obeyed.

Who is that man? Woolf asks, and responds:

He is Man himself, the quintessence of virility, the perfect type of which all the others are imperfect and adumbrations. He is a man certainly. His eyes are glazed; his eyes glare. His body, which is braced in an unnatural position, is tightly cased in a uniform. Upon the breast of that uniform are sewn several medals and other mystic symbols. . . . He is called in German and Italian Fuhrer or Duce; in our own language Tyrant or Dictator. And behind him lie ruined houses and dead bodies—men, women and children.

And several decades later, in a visionary book entitled *The Chalice and the Blade*, Riane Eisler wrote:

In its faithful replication of rigid male dominance, authoritarianism, and a high degree of institutionalized male balance . . . the Nazi elite corps . . . were . . . living exemplars of "manly" virtues . . . and taught glory, honor and power by unleashing destruction and terror.

Various intellectual and aesthetic interests intersected when I met Harvey Mudd and learned about his work. My earlier research and my work on *Powerplay* had already given me insights into the relationship between traditional concepts of masculinity and Nazi ideology. My years of investigat-

ing women's history and experience had arisen partly out of my curiosity about the historic relationship between the powerful and the powerless, a grotesque form of which was enacted in the Nazi treatment of the Jews. Finally, I was becoming increasingly interested in my heritage as a Jew, and I was fascinated by the realization that I was so ignorant about an event as significant as the Holocaust. Moreover, I surmised that exploring the Holocaust would provide a unique opportunity to enlarge my understanding of both Jewish history and contemporary society.

At first I thought about illustrating Harvey's poem, and he and I had a few meetings to discuss this possibility. I thought that I had better do some studying before I attempted to create any images, something I customarily do before taking on a new subject matter. Over the years I had developed a process of immersing myself in a topic until I "discovered" the images I wanted to create. I had read about *Shoah*, the landmark nine-hour film about the Holocaust by Claude Lanzmann, and when it played in New York I decided to see it.

By then I had met Donald Woodman, a photographer and, like me, an assimilated Jew. We'd had a whirlwind romance and surprised everyone, myself included, by our rapid decision to wed. Donald had even less of a sense of Jewish identity than I did, and though he'd had a bar mitzvah, he remembered little about his Hebrew school education. Nonetheless, and somewhat irrationally, both of us wanted to be married by a rabbi. Because we are both uncomfortable with the patriarchal aspects of Jewish culture and the concept of a male God, we wanted to find a female rabbi, one who offered an egalitarian viewpoint and a wedding ceremony that affirmed both the woman and the man.

Donald felt strongly that if we were going to be married by a rabbi, we should explore Jewish tradition to see if there were any rituals we could incorporate to reflect our mutual values. These might best be expressed through a poem I wrote when I was working on *The Dinner Party*, a poem that informs my vision as an artist and is the "dream" of *The Dinner Party*: a world humanized through the introduction of what are sometimes called the "feminine values" of compassion and nurturance.

And then all that has divided us
will merge

And then compassion will be wedded
to power

And then softness will come to a world
that is harsh and unkind

And then both men and women
will be gentle

And then both women and men
will be strong

And then no person will be subject
to another's will

And then all will be rich and free
and varied

And then the greed of some will give way
to the needs of many

And then all will share equally
in the Earth's abundance

And then all will care for
the sick and the weak
and the old

And then all
will nourish the young

And then all will cherish
life's creatures

And then all will live in harmony
with each other and the Earth
And then everywhere will be called Eden
once again.

Donald and I used this poem on our wedding invitation and had it sung during the ceremony. It was later incorporated into new Jewish liturgy, and the rabbi who first included it told me that my poem expresses the ethical values of Jewish culture, values that, Donald and I slowly came to understand, had influenced both of us, though neither of us had connected these mutual values to our identities as Jews.

The learning experience about Judaism we were having in preparation for our marriage had stimulated Donald's interest in our heritage, and when I told him about my growing curiosity about the Holocaust, he decided to go to New York with me to see *Shoah*. In October 1985, we flew there to see the film. It totally overwhelmed us.

Sitting in that theater with Donald, it became clear that I couldn't illustrate Harvey's poem, that I'd have to find another path into this subject, one that could engage me as a Jew. Even though Harvey's work had grown out of a genuine interest in the subject, it was a reflection of *his* journey; I realized that I would have to take my own.

For years, my fundamental identification had been as a woman and I felt most closely aligned with other women. While watching *Shoah*, for the first time I experienced myself primarily as a Jew, bonded to the person beside me not by gender but by heritage. Issues were raised for me that I wanted to examine: What did it mean to be a Jew? How had it affected me and what had it meant to my family? I became determined to educate myself about not only the Holocaust but Jewish history and culture as well. On our way home from New York, Donald and I began to discuss the idea of working together on a project about the Holocaust. As the subject matter was vast and clearly very terrifying, I was glad to have a companion.

Between 1985 and 1987, Donald and I educated ourselves about the Holocaust. I immersed myself in a self-guided research and study program about both Jewish history and the Holocaust, compiling and studying an extensive library of books. We established and reviewed a collection of films and videotapes; traveled to UCLA and Yale to see taped survivor testimonies; visited Holocaust exhibitions around the country to understand how the subject was usually presented; looked at art about the Holocaust and met and corresponded with a number of scholars and people from various Jewish organizations.

We also slowly established a network for financial support and intellectual dialogue. When I had been working on the topics of women's history and birth, these had been largely unexplored, particularly as subject matter for art. By contrast, many people were engaged in work on the Holocaust and there was a lot of art on the subject, although most of it existed on the fringes of the contemporary art world. Donald and I felt it was vitally important to make contact with others interested in the Holocaust and to get feedback as we went along, something artists don't usually do. We published a series of newsletters about what we were doing, held slide presentations around the country, and also had small studio showings of the work as we went along. We encouraged dialogue, which sometimes resulted in our being challenged about our ideas, the connections we were making, our motivation and/or "right" to deal with this material—because we were neither survivors nor their children—and, of course, about some of the images. Many people had definite ideas about how the Holocaust "should" be dealt with, while others doubted that it could ever be the subject matter for meaningful art. We learned a lot from these discussions, and they resulted in our changing and expanding some of our initial ideas.

These presentations also helped to build funding for the project. The *Holocaust Project* was financed almost entirely by private donations, which paid for materials but did not sustain us personally during the eight years the work required. Basically, we lived from month to month and endured constant financial anxiety about whether we could raise enough money to go on. This financial insecurity was particularly hard to handle in the face of such grueling subject matter and the length of time we were immersed in the work.

We were vitally interested in seeing the ways the Holocaust was presented visually and looked at many exhibits. Usually the "story of the Holocaust" is depicted through text, photo-documentation, and artifacts. I found myself questioning whether any form of art could be more eloquent. But I soon decided that, as powerful as the photographs were, it was difficult for me to make a personal connection with pictures of piles of bones

or to visualize the abstract statistics and numbers (like six million) that were frequently repeated in Holocaust presentations. In my private studies, I was discovering that, if I transferred the facts or numbers into imagining how, had we lived in eastern Europe, Donald and I might have been caught in Hitler's net, I was more able to connect with the Holocaust as a *human* event—done *by* people *to* people.

I became convinced that painting could convey this human story and thereby provide a bridge between the abstraction of the statistics and the larger, universal significance of the historical event. But I intuited that in order for the paintings to be effective, they had to be rooted in historic reality, which was something that only photography could accomplish. Combining painting and photography seemed to present a unique aesthetic form for my intentions, and, of course, it was also a way to combine both my own and Donald's skills.

Donald had long been dissatisfied with some of the expressive limits of photography and was interested in expanding its parameters by combining our individual techniques. We spent a considerable amount of time searching for an appropriate surface: one that allowed for the integrity of each of our mediums, while permitting an integration of the two. Finally we discovered photolinen, a photosensitive material that accommodates both high-resolution photo printing and painting. Ironically, it was then available only from Germany.

In the *Holocaust Project*, as in all my previous work, I went from content to form: beginning with subject matter that interested me, exploring it, then slowly developing the appropriate visual methods through which it could be best expressed. But in this project I was faced with the problem of dealing with a subject matter fraught with extreme

anguish and pain. Moreover, Donald and I were in an early stage in our relationship when we decided to work together, and sometimes our personal struggles were clouded by the grief and confusion we both experienced in handling the subject matter.

Collaborating with my husband entailed a number of emotional as well as intellectual risks. It was difficult for us to learn to work together, and there were moments when we weren't sure if we ever could or if our relationship would even survive. Our different levels of public recognition also affected us. At one of my frequent lectures about my work, a woman in the audience asked me about our collaboration, inquiring how Donald dealt with the fact of my greater visibility. I asked Donald to respond to her. He said, "If I struggle with Judy for power, we fight. If I simply trust myself and her, we get along fine." The effort to learn not to compete or struggle but rather to support and trust each other and cooperate in our work has resulted in a sense of shared achievement that has greatly enhanced our respect for each other's individual talents and strengthened our marriage as well—but it hasn't been easy. I think the fact that we have different, complementary abilities has worked for us: Donald can't draw and I can't take photographs, and in this project we needed each other's skills.

It took a considerable amount of time for me to develop a tolerance for the Holocaust material. At first I couldn't read for more than an hour; it took a year before I could spend long periods systematically wading through the many written descriptions of deportations, mass murders, gas chambers, and crematoria. I'd fall asleep or read without comprehension, or, if able to take in the information, become depressed and/or suicidal. Only my commitment to the importance of our undertaking allowed me to persevere, and then I could do so only by maintaining a tightly disciplined work schedule and rigorous daily exercise.

After a while, I realized that some of my reactions grew out of the fact that my basic assumptions about people and the world were being profoundly challenged by the information I was encountering. I had always trusted people and believed the world to be a relatively fair and just place. Of course, I knew that terrible events happened, but I tended to see those as isolated phenomena. Confronting the Holocaust brought me face to face with a level of reality beyond anything I'd experienced before: millions of people murdered, millions more enslaved, millions made to suffer, while the world turned its back on the implementation of the Final Solution. I couldn't take it all in; it was too painful, and I was a long way from understanding what it meant about human beings and the world in which we live.

As we viewed one Holocaust exhibition after another and pored through the many books of art and photography available on the subject, we came to understand that the story of the Holocaust, as it is presented in America, is focused almost entirely on the Jewish experience, which, at first, was also what Donald and I thought we would do.

In 1987, after completing our initial study and research program, we made an arduous two-and-a-half-month trip through Germany, France, Austria, Czechoslovakia, Poland, and the then Soviet Union, visiting concentration camps, extermination and massacre sites, and seeing what little remains of eastern European Jewish culture. We completed our travel program with a visit to Israel in 1988, where we saw the country that survivors had built

and the monuments and museums they'd created.

Despite all my studies, nothing prepared me for what we encountered in Europe. In a way, we followed Hitler's tracks, covering thousands of miles and discovering enormous evidence of human suffering. The first camp we visited was Natzweiler, in the Alsace-Lorraine region of France. Dr. Konnilyn Feig, a Holocaust scholar who advised us on our itinerary, had suggested that we go there first because it was still pretty much the way it had been during the war.

One would have been hard pressed to find even the mention of the word *Jew* at Natzweiler, which shocked us because it was in such sharp contrast to the way the Holocaust is represented in the United States. It was extremely surprising to discover that throughout Euorpe, the story of the Holocaust was told so very differently from here. In western Europe the partisan struggle was stressed; in eastern Europe the Holocaust was presented as having been the result of capitalism and fascism, which, before glasnost, was regarded as having been banished to the West. In what was then the Soviet Union, the tragedy of the "Russian people" was presented, and until recently it was illegal to erect any monuments to the Jews. What became clear as we traveled was that the Holocaust was much vaster in scale and more complex than we'd understood, and our ignorance was even greater than we'd imagined.

One aspect of the Holocaust that I found monstrous was the scope of the slave-labor campaign. As the Nazis marched east, enormous numbers of people were enslaved and forced to labor in hideous conditions. In fact, Heinrich Himmler, one of Hitler's closest collaborators in the development of the Nazis' intended thousand-year Reich, imagined a permanent slave-labor system to support this plan. In Poland alone, millions of people were enslaved, and there, like everywhere, both women and men labored and died. Moreover, the degree to which women were arrested, enslaved, and murdered was not adequately reflected in any of the presentations of the Holocaust that we saw; the male experience was the focus of most of the exhibitions.

Although we did not intend to do a project only about women in the Holocaust, seeing the way women were omitted made us determined to structure our images so that they would be gender-balanced, which is how we believe history *should* be written. Later, when I did focused research on women's experience, I decided to do one image that examined the particularity of women's suffering in an effort to help balance the historical record.

One of the most astonishing parts of the trip was our direct confrontation with the destruction of our eastern European heritage; and for me it was making a deep personal connection with my ancestry in Vilna, the home of the Vilna Gaon. After weeks of seeing the remnants of Jewish communities, including descecrated cemeteries, boarded-up temples, and confiscated Jewish artifacts on display, we traveled to Russia, Latvia, and Lithuania.

In eastern Europe, Vilna was once such a great center of Jewish learning that it was referred to as the "Jerusalem of Lithuania." Before the war, 30 percent of the population was Jewish and there were hundreds of synagogues. At the time of our visit only one remained, which the small Jewish community was attempting to restore. To raise funds, they baked and sold *matzos* to their small community.

At sundown we went to the temple, having learned that we would usually find local Jews there in search of a *minyan* (ten men, necessary for the service). During our travels Donald was often asked to participate, while I, as a woman, was excluded because in eastern Europe the only form of Judaism practiced is Orthodoxy. This put me into a rage, of course, and reinforced my determination to demonstrate that the experience of Jewish women is also important to commemorate.

We got into a conversation with a young Jew who, though made uneasy by my gender, was impressed by my lineage. He took us to the site of my ancestor's home and school, both located near the corners of what were originally called Gaon and Jewish streets. These had been renamed and, like the town of Vilna itself (officially called Vilnius), reconstructed without any reference to the thousands of Jews who once lived there or their illustrious history. Then he took us to the Jewish cemetery, where the Vilna Gaon's tomb had been moved and restored after the war. Miraculously, our guide had the key, and as I stood inside, I thought about my father and wondered how he would have felt, had he still been alive, and about the long journey I had taken back to our roots.

I reflected upon the anger I'd expressed when I realized how women's history had been erased from our cultural memory, and I thought about how a people's identity and pride are largely determined by an understanding of their roots. At that moment some connection took place between my understanding of myself as a woman and what I was learning about being a Jew.

In exploring the Holocaust, I was learning about the tragic way Jews had been victimized, and this eventually linked up with my understanding of women's oppression. I realized that part of what had led me to the Holocaust was a deep, though previously unarticulated, interest in the "victim" experience and that my previous investigations of the ways women had been treated historically provided me with an unusual frame of reference for examining the Jewish experience of the Holocaust.

When we returned from our trip, I began to expand my investigation of Holocaust survivor literature by reading personal testimonies about the Armenian death marches, the Pol Pot massacres in Cambodia, and other genocidal actions of the twentieth century. I began to notice how similar many of these stories were to the Holocaust testimonies I'd read. What linked them, of course, was their *perspective*—which was from the point of view of the victim/survivor.

One could say that history, as it has been written, is the history of those in power, as they have been the ones in control of its writing. (This has been clearly demonstrated by watching the Chinese rulers rewrite the history of the 1989 rebellion in Beijing.) The history that has gone unwritten is that of those who have suffered the consequences of progress; of those who have been powerless to change the course of history; of those who have been the "victims."

It is not that the Jews have been the only target of genocide; according to my research, over 60 million people have died from genocidal actions in the twentieth century, which is sometimes referred to as "the age of genocide." Generally the victims have been voiceless—but not so the Jews. We have been able to articulate our experiences, and because we have been considered part of Western culture and grown powerful enough to influence it, we have often been heard. Jews, therefore, have been able to educate the world about our plight, even though we were unable to arouse sufficient action to avert massive destruction during the Second World War.

Other groups, less powerful and/or farther removed from world sympathy, have not been that fortunate; we know that many peoples and cultures have been persecuted, tortured, and virtually destroyed. But until the advent of the evolving global communications network, most of their stories haven't been known; or, like women, their experiences have been marginalized, left outside the mainstream of the historical record and our cultural iconography.

I was slowly making connections between different victim experiences and developing the concept of the Holocaust as a prism through which to view them; to put it another way, I began to perceive that the unique Jewish experience of the Holocaust could be a window into an aspect of the unarticulated but universal human experience of victimization. The problem was how to express that while honoring the particularity of the Holocaust as a historical event.

When I read Anne Roiphe's book *A Season for Healing*, I was struck by her reference to a comment made by Elie Wiesel during his Nobel Prize acceptance speech. Roiphe interpreted his message in words that moved me profoundly. We must, wrote Roiphe, "serve as carriers of empathy, as watchpeople for the vulnerable." Like women, Jews have been vulnerable during much of our history. Stateless and weaponless for a good deal of time, Jews were truly vulnerable, as the Holocaust clearly shows. Some people argue that it is this vulnerability that must be avoided, that Jews must be prepared to defend themselves at all costs. But I'm not at all sure that this is the primary lesson of the Holocaust. To me, one of the most important aspects of the Jewish experience of the Holocaust is that it provides us with a graphic demonstration of the vulnerability of all human beings and, by extension, of all species and our fragile planet as well.

My understanding of the Holocaust was dramatically broadened by examining women's experiences. As part of my commitment to redress the gender imbalance and male bias in both Holocaust and Jewish history, I undertook a study program with seven women writers and scholars, including Dr. Joan Ringelheim, one of the pioneers in scholarship on women and the Holocaust. One of the participants, the psycholinguist Dr. Vera John-Steiner, a survivor herself, helped me formulate a series of questions that were passed around the group in a series of round-robin letters.

One of the common themes in the women's responses was that of connection: the *connection of the Holocaust with other historical events*. This was dramatically different from most Holocaust literature written by men, which almost invariably stresses the uniqueness and mystery of the Holocaust. For example, Elie Wiesel wrote in a *New York Times* review of a 1978 TV docudrama on the Holocaust that Auschwitz "cannot be explained nor can it be visualized. . . . The Holocaust transcends history. Everything about it inspired fear and leads to despair. The dead are in possession of a secret that we, the living, are neither worthy of nor capable of recovering."

In sharp contrast to this now pervasive view in the dominant Holocaust presentations, Vera John-Steiner wrote in the round-robin:

The arguments in favor of seeing the Holocaust as uniquely Jewish cut away at our connectedness to other communities and other individuals who were also victimized by genocide and its legacy—mass murder. Focusing on the female experience

of the Holocaust helps us move toward, rather than away from, an understanding of our human connectedness and helps repair the human fabric of community.

Aviva Cantor, one of the co-founders of the Jewish feminist magazine *Lilith*, responded by arguing:

What made the Holocaust possible (and, some may argue, inevitable) is the fact of patriarchy, and the fact that partriarchal values dominate our society. . . . Patriarchy is rooted in the elevation of power to the highest value and in the struggle for it among groups of men and by individual men. Men seek power over each other, over women, over children, over animals, over the natural world, and justify this on grounds of utility. It is these values which have made the Holocaust possible.

Cantor's controversial but compelling view of the Holocaust as being rooted in this global structure of dominance and in a definition of power as power *over* others is one that might best be described as feminist, and it is this philosophical framework that provides the underpinnings for the *Holocaust Project*.

During the years of my Holocaust study, which continued during the six years it required to create the art, my ideas developed and deepened. By 1987 I was able to start making images. The first was a full-scale tapestry cartoon (the painting from which the weaver works). Woven by Audrey Cowan, my long-time collaborator, *The Fall* is a visual narrative that places the Holocaust in a historic context and makes connections between anti-Semitism and antifeminism, which often coincided in history and share certain inconographic and linguistic themes.

The Fall acts as the entryway piece into the 3,000-square-foot *Holocaust Project* exhibition, the concept for which unfolded slowly over the years. In 1988, in response to one of our newsletters, we received a letter of inquiry from Olga Weiss, the curator at the Spertus Museum of Judaica, a museum and college in Chicago. We entered into a dialogue with the staff about their interest in creating an educational context for the exhibition. The museum promised to explore the issues raised by the images and to provide a philosophical framework that would be consistent with the values expressed in the art.

In my previous exhibitions, related classes, seminars, and programs had developed spontaneously around the art, and these greatly amplified the impact of the work. The idea of institutional support for and help with educational programming was both appealing and appropriate. My vision of art is based on both expanding its accessibility and redefining the role of the artist. I have worked many years to reconnect art to the fabric of human life and community, from which it has become increasingly cut off.

Because the subject matter of the Holocaust is so painful, Donald and I decided on a modest, human scale for the paintings, so as not to overwhelm the viewer. We chose an altarlike format for the painting-photo combines, by which we intended a reference to the work of the painter Hieronymus Bosch, who, like Donald and me, expressed a worldview, though one quite different from ours. This multiple-panel configuration also provided a method of honoring the uniqueness of the Holocaust, as we always present it on separate or visually distinct panels—a metaphor for the fact that we are examining connections, not suggesting that the Holocaust is exactly *like* any other historic event. As Isaiah Kuperstein makes clear in a paper on the *Holocaust Project* commissioned by the Spertus Museum:

The Holocaust was an unparalleled event in human and Jewish history. Within the broad United Nations' definition of genocide as "acts committed with an intent to destroy, in whole or in part, a national, ethnic, racial or religious group" . . . the Holocaust was one of the most massive and extensive genocides ever executed. . . . It differed from other genocides in intentionality, planning, scope and implementation. Never before did a modern state implement a plan to kill every last person of a particular group—in this case, a Jew wherever he or she might be—simply for the "crime" of being born a Jew.

Donald and I created a singular method of combining painting and photography that involved a slow layering of the images, gradually transforming the photographs until they merged with the painted reality. I would often alter the photo with drawing or painting, then Donald would rephotograph it and transfer the manipulated image to the photolinen. In order to create a visual fusion between the painting and photography, I frequently incorporated sprayed acrylic, which can produce a quality similar to photo tones, and from time to time, we hand-colored the photographs or employed silk-screening. We tried to develop a different relationship between the painting and photography in each image, exploring varying methods of integrating them. Every painting was a visual, intellectual, and emotional challenge: how to deal with the difficulty of the subject matter (which became more formidable as we went along), express it, transform it, and unite the painted and the photographic elements into a whole.

When traveling in eastern Europe we visited many archives, examining and photographing hundreds of drawings by prisoners and survivors. Most of these were not sophisticated images but drawings, sketches, and notations done to "bear witness" to the horrific events that were taking place. Donald and I were deeply moved by these, and I was reinforced in my belief in the power of art and its potentially useful role in conveying an enlarged story of the Holocaust. I have drawn on these works, in much the same way we've used our photo archives, as both inspiration and studies for some of our art. I've done this consciously as a way to honor the artists, many of whom perished.

When we were in Israel we had a memorable Shabbat dinner at the home of Pinchus and Shoshone Freiberg. There were twelve people there: men and women from four different countries, of different ages, and mostly strangers. We all went around the table and told stories, and everyone *listened* for hours. For me the evening brought up not just feelings about my childhood but also the incredibly warm moments Donald and I had shared with Jews around the world. Being welcomed into Jewish homes during our travels gave us a profound sense of a global community and provided me with an idea for the last image of the project, an image of optimism and hope. Titled *Rainbow Shabbat*, the final work consists of three stained glass windows. The central window presents an image of the Shabbat as an international event of sharing across race, gender, class, and species. Shabbat ceremonies are traditionally begun with a prayer offered by a woman, and *Rainbow Shabbat* suggests reverence for the feminine as an essential step toward the humanization of our world—thereby uniting in one image my values as a woman and a Jew.

By the time I created *Rainbow Shabbat*, I had discovered that what it means to me to be Jewish relates primarily to my lifelong commitment to the ethical values of justice, so well articulated by Anne Roiphe, and that these values were deeply shaped by my heritage. The Jewish experience of the Holocaust certainly manifests the worst human beings can do, but within the Jewish experience there is also a vision of human beings at their best. During our travels, Donald and I were struck by the sense of connection we felt with Jewish families in different parts of the world. We realized that everywhere we went, we met Jews who were joined across geographical distances by a common belief in *tikkun*. This mutual adherence to a set of life-affirming ethical principles suggested a model for a new global community based on shared human values.

The long voyage Donald and I took helped me integrate my beliefs as a feminist with those I had, but didn't understand, as a Jew. Embedded in both perspectives, I discovered a set of positive values that have, I believe, if applied to the greater human condition, the potential for a profound change in the way we think and how we live. This hope is embodied in *Rainbow Shabbat* and was put into words by Robert Lifton in *The Genocidal Mentality*: "Each of us must join in a vast project—political, ethical, psychological—on behalf of perpetuating and nurturing our humanity . . . so that we clear away the 'thick glass' that has blurred our moral and political vision. We [thus] become healers, not killers, of our species." And, I might add, healers of our world.

The *Holocaust Project: From Darkness into Light* is an exhibition structured as a journey into the darkness of the Holocaust and out into the light of hope. It is based on the journey—intellectual, physical, and emotional—that Donald and I took, which is discussed in Part II of this volume. Part III deals with our struggle to transform that voyage into a body of art. Although the images were not created in a strictly linear fashion (sometimes we went back and forth, working on one, then another, based on the technical demands of the work), I have grouped them by year so that the reader will not become confused. The fourth—and, to my mind, most important section of the book—is a presentation of the art. The exhibition and the book are structured around our belief that you, our viewers and readers, will find as we did that confronting and trying to understand the Holocaust, as painful as that might be, can lead to a greatly expanded understanding of the world in which we live. We hope that this will contribute to a firm individual and collective commitment to take up the "vast project" of transforming ourselves and "nurturing our humanity," thereby creating a more peaceful, equitable world.

PART TWO

Journey

The world is ruled by neither
justice nor morality; crime is not
punished nor virtue rewarded, one
is forgotten as quickly as the
other. The world is ruled by power.

—Tadeusz Borowski

In October 1985 I began my Jewish Journal (I had been keeping a personal journal since 1971) in a yellow notebook on lined paper. I had purchased it in order to record my investigation of the Holocaust and my inquiry into what it means to be a Jew.

1985–1987

1985

October

I am in New York with Donald, my soon-to-be husband; we came to see the nine-and-a-half hour film *Shoah*, by Claude Lanzmann. It was a very thought-provoking film, and at the end of the two days required to view it I realized that I couldn't illustrate Harvey Mudd's poem; rather, I need to make my own journey into this subject. It is not only that his poem isn't the right vehicle, but also the fact that he is not a Jew.

It was interesting to see *Shoah* with Donald, who, like me, *is* Jewish. It was one of the few times in my adult life that I had an experience in which my sense of self was not gender-based. As Donald and I sat together in the theater, sharing this confrontation with what had happened to the Jews during the Holocaust, I felt bonded with him *as a Jew*. This was a new experience for me and one I want to explore.

I told Donald that I realized I couldn't work with Harvey, and we began discussing the possibility of working together on the subject of the Holocaust. As we are both equally ignorant about this subject, as well as Jewish history, we'll be starting off on equal ground.

New York, NY

November

Since seeing *Shoah*, beginning to think about my Jewishness and learning about the Holocaust, I keep asking myself certain questions. When I am shocked by human behavior, as I was by the revelations in *Shoah*, I realize that it's because I start from the assumption that human beings are basically good or at least benign. When confronted by what people did to each other in the Holocaust—if I maintain my assumptions—then I cannot comprehend the Nazis' actions. But what if my assumptions are not true? What if human beings are not "good" at all but are actually capable of an enormous range of behaviors, most of which are held in check only through social structures and institutions? Strange that I had never thought about all this before.

So now I ask, as if for the first time, how do people become so dehumanized that they can throw large numbers of babies into fire pits or gas thousands of people at a time or push even *one person* into the fire? Where does this behavior come from?

I plan to spend the next year slowly reading, thinking, and preparing to collaborate with Donald. It's interesting: I've never started something I wanted to work on so slowly, but the horrors of the material are such that I have to go at a snail's pace or I shall surely go mad.

Santa Fe, NM

I've taken a break from the Holocaust material because I want to concentrate on the joy of planning our wedding. Donald and I have been studying with our rabbi, Lynn Gottleib, as we have decided to incorporate Jewish rituals into our wedding ceremony. Rabbi Lynn will perform a contemporary and equalized version of a traditional ceremony that will include a modern purification ritual and a *bedekken* rite, in which the groom visits the bride before the ceremony to lift her veil and say the vows privately. We're going to compose vows that are meaningful to us and then create a personal *ketubah* (marriage certificate). We are building the ceremony around my poem about the merging of masculine and feminine, emphasizing the meaning of our merger on a symbolic as well as a personal level: a fitting way to start the New Year, as our wedding will be on New Year's Eve.

This is my third marriage; my first ended in tragedy, my second in divorce. I'm nervous, but maybe three's a charm. Each of my husbands were Jewish, but this is the first time I've been married by a rabbi. Somehow it seems appropriate, as we begin to learn about Jewish history, that Donald and I are claiming some of the positive, spiritual aspects of our tradition by incorporating them into our marriage ceremony.

Santa Fe, NM

December

Donald and I have come to Chicago to celebrate my Aunt Enid's eightieth birthday. She is my father's sole surviving sibling and the only one to whom I was ever close. We brought my mother from Los Angeles and on Friday gave a party for her, which was attended by some of her oldest friends. Because I've known almost everyone at both events for many years, thoughts of my childhood were inevitably stirred up.

Watching my mother with her friends, most of

whom are Jewish, was like time-traveling: There they were, eating, talking, smoking, and carrying on at top volume, just as they had when I was young. I remembered how passionately my parents and some of these same liberal friends had once believed that "talking" counted. And how they talked—about ideas and feelings and the world and, of course, politics—and here they were, still talking like that after so many years!

My childhood was filled with discussions like these, discussions that taught me to believe that ideas could change the world and that the course of history could be altered, which I still believe.

On the other hand, everyone spent so much time at the party reminiscing. It made me wonder: When is it positive to examine the past and when does it become suffocating and entrapping? I can remember as a young girl wanting to escape from family attachments and everyone's constant recitation of family memories. Had I also wanted to run away from my Jewish identity? Had they?

It's all wrapped up together somehow: my childhood, my family, my Jewishness, my wanting to learn about the Holocaust, and trying to claim parts of my heritage in our wedding ceremony. Donald's first wife wasn't Jewish and he never felt much sense of any Jewish identity. In fact, a lot of people are surprised to learn that he *is* Jewish. But I knew from the moment we met.

Chicago, IL

1986

January

On Tuesday evening, December 31, Donald and I were married in a very personal version of a traditional Jewish wedding. As is customary, we slept apart on Monday night and on Tuesday afternoon performed a contemporary version of the *mikvah*, or ritual cleansing.

At 8:45 P.M. on New Year's Eve, I walked into the bedroom of the friend's house where we were to be married and where our family, close friends, and rabbi were all waiting. I sat veiled on a chair alone; the room was very quiet. As the minutes passed I became more and more agitated; I was waiting for Donald to enter the room. Suddenly I felt the tension in the room shift, and I knew he had arrived. The hairs on my neck stood up; I felt his presence intensely.

I guess I should discuss why I, a twentieth-century feminist, would participate in a ceremony that includes veiling, which in many traditional societies is certainly associated with some extremely oppressive customs, like purdah and dowries and of course, women's second-class status.

As part of my research I had been reading a book called *Holy Days*. The author, Lis Harris, became interested in a Brooklyn Hasidic community whose wedding customs include the *bedekken* ceremony. According to Harris, many Hasidic customs have been misunderstood; some of their marriage and sexual rituals are derived from a belief in the sacredness of the sexual bond and are supposedly intended to enhance the erotic connection. Certainly, our ceremony was nothing if not erotic. When Donald walked over to me I was trembling. When he lifted my veil I beheld him—in his white tuxedo with a white floral wreath on his head—transformed from Donald into *my groom*. He was radiant—and I guess I must have been too.

Donald took my hand, and together we walked over to the rabbi, to whom Donald handed our illuminated *ketubah* (which we had spent two days working on). After reading and signing our vows, Donald dropped the veil back over my face and we were carried in on chairs to the festive music of a traditional klezmer band. I waved my handkerchief wildly (traditional in Hasidic ceremonies) and the rabbi chanted and ululated in the ancient woman's vocal sounds of celebration. Once we were standing under the *huppa* (marriage canopy) and facing Rabbi Lynn, she began to chant. Her voice seemed to come up from the depths of her being as she gave the blessing she had written—a blessing that was completely in keeping with the values we were trying to express through the rituals we had chosen or created. These rituals helped me bond with Donald, and even though we had both been married before, we felt that this was the first time that the wedding ceremony became a transformative event.

After joyous dancing, many toasts, and a wonderful New Mexican meal, Rabbi Lynn reassembled everyone at midnight, at which point she blew the *shofar* (ram's horn), traditionally done on Rosh Hashana to commemorate the Jewish New Year and thus very fitting. We all offered blessings, continuing the theme of merging masculine and feminine values in order to bring harmony and balance to the universe.

Santa Fe, NM

February

Three weeks after our wedding, I was hit by a pickup while running. Taken to the hospital in an ambulance, I was in intensive care for two days and in the hospital for a week. I lost half my body's blood in internal bleeding and had to be transfused with two pints of blood—apparently I almost died. Now I am recovering, and Donald is in a state of shock.

Santa Fe, NM

ABOVE: Dancing at our wedding

RIGHT: Artist unknown; wood inlay
(Collection: Chaim and Gita Barjman, Kovno, Lithuania)
When we saw this charming work showing a traditional
Jewish wedding, we were reminded of the rituals we had
drawn upon for our own ceremony.

March

Slowly we're picking up our lives and I've begun to read and study again. But if I spend too long with the Holocaust material, I become emotionally devastated and full of despair. It's just so painful to keep reading about death, destruction, and human suffering, but at the same time I feel compelled to go on. When the material becomes too unbearable I go into the studio. I've been working on a series about the accident, which is giving me the opportunity to try out ways of combining my drawing and Donald's photographs. We've been recreating the accident, and I'm using the photos of the reconstructed event and my battered body as the base for the drawings. This is a good exercise in working together as well as in dealing with subject matter that's quite raw (to say the least). It's also giving us the chance to deal with our myriad of feelings about the accident.

Santa Fe, NM

April

Audrey Cowan, my long-time weaving collaborator, Donald, and I went to UCLA, my alma mater, where they have an archive of more than a hundred hours of survivor tapes. Audrey is also interested in the subject of the Holocaust. She has indicated that if I were to include any weaving, she wants to do it.

In *Shoah* most of the interviewees were men, so I wanted to view tapes of women survivors to see if their experiences were any different. We saw a number of tapes, three of which were riveting. At first I had the same problem I had with *Shoah*, wanting to go to sleep and having trouble paying attention; but I got up and moved around the viewing room and watched the videos standing up (which I couldn't do during *Shoah*), and that helped. In general there was one significant difference between the interviews with the women and those of the men in *Shoah*: The women consistently emphasized family connections. There was one story about a young woman who rode in the railroad cars with her mother standing on her toes so that she could keep her feet warm.

Several of the women emphasized the importance of female bonding and women helping and protecting each other. There was also a lot of discussion about resistance, which I found interesting. We frequently encounter the attitude, even among our Jewish friends, that the Jews were "willing" victims, but that is not at all the story as presented by the survivors themselves. Instead they described many forms of resistance, from small gestures (that were death-defying in that if they were caught they'd be shot) to active fighting in the ghettos.

I was curious about the sexual abuse of women, but there was only one reference to it. Audrey thought it was because the women were too embarrassed to mention it; but after listening to the tapes I think that it was such a common occurrence that the survivors didn't even think of discussing it, and/or the interviewers didn't bring it up. (I later found out that it was *not* an issue raised by the interviewers—even in more recent video interviews made when rape was already a subject of much public discussion.) One woman did refer to the Nazis regularly raiding the barracks of the concentration camp, raping the most beautiful women, and then shooting them. But until I began asking some of my survivor friends about this, I rarely heard a survivor talk about herself being sexually abused. I believe this omission reflects a consistent male bias in the way the Holocaust has been approached and presented.

Anyway, we watched and heard the testimony of a number of women; the most compelling was that of a woman from Bialystok, Poland. Her town was invaded and bombed by the Germans early in the war. Though still a young girl, she was forced to witness two thousand men being rounded up and then burned alive in the temple. She described German soldiers taunting and persecuting helpless old men; houses set on fire with people still inside; people fleeing and screaming in general pandemonium; the community gradually narrowed and fenced in; and Jews forced to wear yellow stars. But according to her, Bialystok was "lucky," as the Germans needed Jewish workers in the wool, furniture, and fabric centers; therefore the ghetto was maintained longer than it was in most other towns.

This woman and her family hid in a secret room in a house with some other people, among whom was a mother and child. When they heard the Nazis outside the door, someone pushed a pillow over the baby's mouth (so that it wouldn't cry and give them away) and held it so long that the baby died. The mother went insane, which, according to this survivor, happened to a lot of people.

She survived, she insisted, either "by accident" or as a result of a series of "coincidences," something we heard again and again by others, some of whom expressed a sense of guilt for being the only member of their family *to* survive. But the major theme in her narrative was *terror*: the terror she felt and the incomprehensibility of what she, a mere child, had witnessed. Trying to imagine how she could have dealt with such overwhelming horror made me feel desperately sad.

The last tape was of a woman from a small village in Germany. She was eleven years old when she was rounded up with hundreds of other people from her home town and sent to a ghetto, where she saw SS men kill her brother in front of her eyes. She was one of only seven survivors of the original 1300 villagers.

She witnessed mass exterminations, babies smashed against walls in front of their mother's eyes, and other events so ghastly she couldn't speak through the tears. During the killings she witnessed, people kept screaming that it was essential for the survivors to tell what had happened, which was what, she stated, had sustained her. She had dedicated herself to "bearing witness," though she too insisted that it was only "coincidence" that had kept her alive. No one took any credit for their survival by suggesting that they had had more strength, cunning, or determination than others; again and again, we heard that their survival was due only to luck.

The German woman was sent to Auschwitz, where she was "selected" for the gas chamber, but there was a lot of confusion and she managed to hide in a pile of dead bodies and was "miraculously" rescued by some other girls, who got her into a line where people were being sent to work camps. She was in seven camps over a five-year period. "After the liberation, I was like a stone." That's about how I felt after days of seeing tapes of these people and hearing their stories, which are, I'm told, quite typical of the experiences of survivors.

Los Angeles, CA

We're back home after a very tiring but informative research trip to Los Angeles, New York, and Washington, D.C. The work we did moved me forward conceptually quite quickly—too quickly in a way, as I still have so much old work to finish here. I need to slow down, though I find myself incredibly drawn to this material.

In Los Angeles we went to the Martyrs Memorial and Museum (a survivor-founded space) and the Simon Wiesenthal Center and were given a tour by their respective directors. The survivor museum is simple and straightforward, which reinforced my sense that Holocaust material needs to be presented simply. Both museum directors were very helpful, and Michael Nutkiewicz of the Martyrs Memorial referred us to a man in Washington,

D.C., named Isaiah Kuperstein, whom we've now met. He's the education director of the Holocaust museum being planned on the Mall. Mr. Kuperstein helped me understand what a large network of Jewish organizations and groups involved with the Holocaust exists around the country. Nonetheless, he recommended that we work independently because he perceived correctly that, as artists, we need to remain free to pursue our own path, whatever that turns out to be.

During our discussion Mr. Kuperstein mentioned that Jewish survival over the centuries has been partly the result of the Jews' ability to organize. Given my own history, this was a very illuminating thought. It made me wonder if there were any connection between my decision to organize a women's art community (which I did in order to survive) and my Jewish heritage.

While examining exhibitions on the Holocaust, I began to notice that there didn't seem to be a lot of information about women and that most of the bibliographies I consulted included many more references to men's writing than to women's. I started asking around and was finally referred to Dr. Joan Ringelheim in New York, who is apparently doing work on women and the Holocaust. I've also made contact with Dr. Konnilyn Feig, who teaches at San Francisco State University and is, I'm told, knowledgeable on the subject of women and the Holocaust. I'm hoping to meet with her when I go to the West Coast in October, and I'm also planning to try and contact Dr. Ringelheim.

Santa Fe, NM

May

I've started reading a book of Holocaust stories introduced and annotated by Elie Wiesel. I really don't understand his insistence that the experience of the Holocaust stands out as a totally singular event in history. I think it's important to see it as an *aberration in the history of human cruelty*: The Nazis went too far, much too far, but there have been many, many cruel events in history.

I got the most wonderful letter from Isaiah Kuperstein; it was in response to both our meeting and my having sent a follow-up packet of info and slides of my earlier work. The letter was warm, emotional, and direct; I thought about the Jewish museum administrators we'd met. There is a quality in all of them to which I really responded, a quality I've observed in many Jewish men I've known and which my father also had: a high moral purpose combined with a deep, emotional capacity.

Maybe it was because the Jews didn't have a military for so many centuries that they could devote so much energy to culture, ethics, philosophy, and religious study. When Jews came to America and became secularized, they brought all this cultural richness to the arts—to literature, music, visual art, and the sciences. Perhaps our achievement suggests how much a people can do if their money and energies are not squandered on defense.

The other night, Donald and I watched a film that was made right after the camps were liberated: horrifying footage, difficult to look at, but compelling in the sense that all Holocaust material compels. To look at it is to look at human beings doing their worst to other human beings.

Santa Fe, NM

We're going to Germany—for only a few days, but I'm totally freaked out about it. There is a big celebration around *The Dinner Party*, organized by a group of women as part of their effort to get it exhibited there. The only time I was ever in Germany was *before* I'd done any investigation of the Holocaust. Years ago, when my second husband and I drove through the country and stopped for just an hour, I was shocked by the fact that I became extremely upset. For the brief time we were there, I was acutely aware that I was a Jew.

Now I feel compelled to figure out how to integrate my developing Jewish consciousness into the structure of *The Dinner Party* events being planned there. Perhaps I can participate in the memorial they're planning about the burning of witches during the Middle Ages (85 percent of whom were women) and relate that to the more recent burning of the Jews. I think I'll prepare something to read. I certainly intend to begin my lecture on *The Dinner Party* by discussing the place setting for *Judith* and to thereby assert my Jewish identity right from the start. It scares me, but so did the first talk I did years ago about my struggles as a woman artist— and this is just another step in being who I am.

Santa Fe, NM

June

I'm on the plane back from Germany. It was totally different from what I'd imagined. I spoke with Isaiah Kuperstein before I left and told him how anxious I felt about going there. He told me to try not to have preconceptions but rather to open myself to the experience, which I tried to do.

I had planned to read the statement I'd written at the Memorial to the Witches, but the festival organizer was very controlling and rigid and didn't want me to do that. I don't know if she was afraid I'd disrupt "her" festival or if there was something anti-Semitic going on. Instead, I integrated my comments into my public lecture at the point where I discussed the witch hunts and *Petronilla de Meath*, who, on *The Dinner Party* table, symbolizes the way witches were persecuted during the Middle Ages.

The seemingly sympathetic response of the seven hundred people in the audience made me feel better. Though feminist consciousness in Germany is way behind that in America, the political consciousness is so much higher. The audience response seemed to convey a real understanding of the political issues involved in my work and an apparent empathy for my feelings as a Jewish woman coming to Germany.

We made a trip to Essen, Isaiah's home town, where the only German museum concerned with the Holocaust is housed; this, of course, reflects the denial that is practiced there. Our guide, the woman who's the German coordinator for *The Dinner Party*, had been born and raised in Frankfurt. She refused to tour the exhibit with us, saying only that her father had been in the police force during the war and the subject upset her. The exhibition, which is in the Old Synagogue, a beautiful building that is slowly being restored by the town, chronicles the history of the Jews in Essen and tells of their extermination. Its primary function is to educate young people about the Nazi past and to help them deal with it.

Both Donald and I found the exhibition very moving, particularly as it involved seeing photos of events that had gone on in this very town; we could look out the window and see the same streets. I wrote to Isaiah about the experience and about my discovery of how Hitler had subjugated large parts of Europe, in addition to trying to murder all the Jews. It was this context of oppression, force, and overall brutality that I didn't understand before. I must study more about the whole history of anti-Semitism so I can relate the

This magnificent synagogue at Essen, built between 1911 and 1913, was destroyed during Kristallnacht.

The restored temple is now used as an exhibition hall. It was reopened on the anniversary of Kristallnacht in 1980.

Final Solution to a broader historic framework.

The trip to Germany was positive in the sense that I was able to get over my fear and see Germans as people, but I still found it unnerving to be there. I wonder if other Jews who visit feel the same way.

On the plane home

August

I sent Isaiah the statement I had prepared for the Memorial to the Witches, in which I raise the question of the relationship between the burning of witches and of Jews. He wrote back, warning me not to make facile comparisons. I replied, thinking he'd find my response thought-provoking, but so far I've heard nothing from him. I hope he won't find my ideas threatening, as so many men do. They seem to assume that men's experience constitutes the universal and that including—much less focusing on—women is an intellectual distraction.

The research has been very difficult lately. The other day I became so depressed that I found myself trying to figure out how to "off" myself. Did I have enough pills? Could I do it so it would be done before Donald came home and tried to stop me? If I feel so much despair just *studying* the Holocaust, imagine what the Jews in Auschwitz must have felt. I can't fathom having the will to go on under such circumstances. I can hardly handle it as it is—but I must.

Santa Fe, NM

September

It's a good thing I have a long history of doing disciplined work, for it is the only thing that allows me to get up and face the next day. It's helped that we went on a trip. We've been traveling and studying a number of Holocaust museums and presentations around the country. There's an attitude in many of them, particularly the audiovisual presentations, that really distresses me. It's a sort of incredulous tone: like "How could this have happened in such a civilized world?"

Donald and I had the same tendency when we started, but by now our thinking has evolved somewhat. You'd think people steeped in the subject would be able to move beyond the initial horror and help the audience reach a greater understanding. I hope that the work we do can clarify the reality of the world that produced the Holocaust. More and more, I'm coming to believe that confronting the Holocaust can lead to knowledge about the true nature of the world in which we live: a world with a thin veneer of "civilization," beneath which there is a different, more primitive morass.

One thing that is strange to me about the development of this project is that I'm verbalizing more than I've ever done before when embarking on a new subject. It seems necessary, however, as we're trying to build support—both financial and intellectual—and I will certainly have to have many discussions with Donald as we go along. We have had some already, but none quite as intense as when we were in Chicago a few weeks ago. We went to Maxwell Street, which used to be the old Jewish market. I had never gone there when I was a child, but I have memories of references to it that were quite shaded, in that the voice tone of the person speaking seemed to drop, suggesting something shameful; at least that's how it appeared to me when I was a child. Perhaps what was really going on was the usual attempt by a younger generation (my parents and their friends) to separate from the Old World, which Maxwell Street clearly represented.

The area certainly wasn't what I expected, though we did find a little of the old flavor of Jewish life. I felt shy and also, I realized later, unaccustomed to just hanging out and starting up conversations.

Donald was taking pictures, but he wasn't sure if he had gotten anything worthwhile. We are still a long way from knowing how to collaborate; that will take time, I'm sure. I'm used to establishing the ground rules and having other people help me. But Donald and I have to learn how to work together in a way that allows both our voices and perceptions to mingle.

Santa Fe, NM

I subscribed to a new liberal Jewish magazine called *Tikkun* and found the first issue very moving. The lead editorial, by Michael Lerner, discussed how deeply embedded in Jewish tradition is the idea that "this too shall pass"—something my mother used to say when I was young, which drove me wild. At the time I felt as if she were discounting my feelings, and maybe she was. But after reading the editorial, I could see the phrase in a more philosophical way. It is more profoundly expressed in the Jewish belief that history *can be changed*, which accounts for the strong liberal and radical traditions in Jewish thought. *Tikkun* is taking a very clear stand on the idea that Jewish tradition is one based on human rights, which struck a chord in me. The editorial also brought up a lot of feelings from my childhood, which I wanted to write about. Had I always known I was Jewish? Yes, I think so, though I probably wasn't too clear about what that meant: We didn't keep kosher, go to temple, or celebrate most of the Jewish holidays. Our main connection to our Jewish tradition was through my grandmother Cohen, my father's mother, who lived on the west side of Chicago in a "real" Jewish neighborhood, to which we made regular trips on the streetcar. My grandpa, the rabbi, had died before I was born. My father was the youngest "of ten children, nine of whom were living," as my grandma used to put it. He had two older brothers and I have no idea why they weren't chosen to carry on the rabbinical tradition; maybe because my father was the brightest member of the family, or so everyone said.

Our family (my mother, father, me, and later my brother) would go to my grandma's house—usually on holidays, though no explanation was given or celebrations performed. We'd eat traditional Jewish food, prepared by my old maid Aunt Molly, who was the one who lived at home and cared for her mother. My grandmother was a rather atypical Jewish matriarch: thin with white hair, usually dressed in black, sitting with a large stack of Yiddish newspapers, smoking asthmatic cigarettes (which in those days contained cannabis), surrounded by a cloud of smoke and the distinct odor of what I now realize was marijuana. She ruled her remaining children with an iron glove; they all called her *every* day, no matter where they were.

The older aunts had been born "over there," and when the family came to America, they settled in Cedar Rapids, Iowa, where my grandfather became the local rabbi. Years later, when I had a show and gave a lecture in Cedar Rapids, I went to the temple over which my grandfather presided.

While growing up I was often told that my talent had come from my grandfather. While in Cedar Rapids I searched out a drawing he had done called *Praying Hands*, which, incredibly, was still there. It was clear from the drawing that, wherever my talent had come from, it hadn't come from him. At the time I saw it, however, I had no idea

that the image signified the rabbi class from which I am descended.

All my memories of Jewish holidays were of boring, empty rituals, except for the good food and the sense of family that ended with my father's death when I was thirteen. As for religious life, I'd experienced none at all. In fact, one could probably say that in my parents' house the only "religion" was politics. As soon as I was old enough I began to stay up at night to listen to the discussions, which were almost always led by my father. He believed in equal rights for women and always encouraged my female cousins to participate. Thus as a child I saw women (or girls, in that case) accepted for their ideas and acting as if they had every right in the world to engage in intellectual life.

The passion of these dialogues shaped my ideas about the human condition, and their implied notion of *tikkun* was embedded in my earliest memories. That is why the editorial in *Tikkun* affected me so profoundly: It identified and clarified what had been the earliest context of my life. My father may have rejected the rabbinical pulpit, but he was, I suddenly understood, Jewish to the core. Though unstated at the time, his worldview, his values, his political ideals were clearly rooted in the concept of *tikkun*, and he not only passed those on to me but expected me to enact them in my life as well.

Then I began thinking about how, when I was a child, we celebrated Christmas, though we weren't allowed to have a tree, which I could never understand. We had raucous, festive parties where different members of the family would arrive carrying mounds of cheap presents. We abruptly stopped celebrating Christmas when I was about eight years old, taking up the custom of Hanuka, but it was never the same.

As I read about Jewish history I wondered

whether the shift away from Christmas, coming as it did in 1946 or 1947, had anything to do with the Holocaust and my parents having to face their Jewishness in a rather overwhelming way; I'll have to ask my mother. In fact, I need to ask my mother *many* questions.

It's interesting to examine my childhood again, this time with some consciousness of being Jewish, which I didn't have when I wrote *Through the Flower*, my autobiography. I believe I can sense a shadow over my childhood: unsaid things, strange statements that I didn't understand but, if I can remember them, will probably provide me with a lot of insight into my parents' state of mind as second-generation Jews.

For years it seemed to me that my mother suffered from a kind of Jewish paranoia, which, now that I begin to study history, is not as farfetched as I once thought it was. America stands between younger Jews and the long historic experience of being persecuted, exiled, and finally murdered. But it's not so long ago and Europe not so far away that, to my mother's generation, it wasn't still real. Still, I wonder: How could my family have celebrated Christmas while European Jews were being herded onto trains and carried unknowingly to total dehumanization and death?

Santa Fe, NM

October

We saw a film called *The Partisans of Vilna* on Sunday. The same thing happened to me that happened while watching *Shoah* and the survivor testimonies: I had this terrible urge to go to sleep, as if my system didn't want to deal with the information. I fought it off, however, and managed to get into the film, which I found somewhat didactic but inspiring nonetheless. It demonstrated that the Jews, in contrast to the oft-repeated idea that they went like sheep to the slaughter, had in fact—in Vilna as in many other places—stood up to the Nazis; and in this case they saved the town, if not its Jewish population. Since members of my family came from Vilna, the film was particularly meaningful to me.

Generally, when I asked myself the question "What would I have done?" in response to the Holocaust, I saw no answer. The film provided me with one: I'm quite sure I would have become a partisan, a resister, a fighter; at least that's what I hope I would have done. Many women fought side by side with the men, as well as participated in the resistance movements in many other ways.

The film triggered a lot of feelings, especially when we walked past the theater where we'd seen *Shoah* last fall. The memories are still so vivid—not just of the film itself but of standing in line for tickets; waiting for the bathroom with children of survivors and hearing their stories; going around the corner for coffee during intermission; all the smells of that neighborhood; and Donald and I sitting next to each other, hands clasped, discovering something about our common heritage that, as Donald says, helped bind us together.

New York, NY

Audrey is having a dinner party for us to help build support for the *Holocaust Project*. Some of the people who are coming keep kosher, so Audrey hired a Jewish caterer. I went with her to plan the menu. The woman was quite cold when we arrived, but then Audrey told her I was an artist and made me tell her what I was doing; she immediately warmed up. At first I was uncomfortable with Audrey "blowing my cover," but as I told her later, the kind of dia-

logue that ensued was exactly what I couldn't initiate on Maxwell Street. Audrey said she'd had a feeling the woman was a survivor, and she was right.

There she was, sitting right next to us in this little restaurant. She looked old enough to be my mother, but she was really close to my age. She was wearing a strawberry-blond wig (she was Orthodox) and kept smiling at us in this uncanny way as she recited her tale. She began by tearfully thanking me for deciding to deal with the Holocaust and for "telling her story." It made me feel even more anxious about being able to do an adequate job. I have so much more to learn; I am not a survivor and art has its limits. But her words moved me and made me even more determined to try.

Then, with a frozen smile on her face, she recounted her experiences: how she had lost everyone in the camp, how she was "miraculously" saved, but how the hurt she carried with her had caused her to act in ugly ways. When the camps were liberated she was only nine years old and totally alone. She returned to her home in Czechoslovakia to find a Gentile woman standing in her mother's kitchen, kneading dough on the breadboard her mother had used to make *challah*. She threw the woman out and brought another woman to live with her, the same one who had previously hidden her family in an (unsuccessful) effort to save them from the Nazis. The woman took care of her for two years, during which time she was, she said, terribly antisocial and hostile. She fought with her classmates and beat some of them up; she just couldn't function within the framework of "civilized behavior."

This was the first time I ever heard a survivor speak about madness, rage, hostility, and antisocial or disordered behavior. She recounted how she was returned to the refugee camp at Bergen-Belsen af-

ter two years, then sent to a relocation camp, from which an American-Jewish woman took her to America to live with her. The terrible pain inside her, however, had never subsided. How could it? she asked.

She spoke of her children and how life-affirming they were for her. But at the same time, even with them she had had trouble, especially with her daughter. Without any apparent emotion, she recounted a story about how, when her daughter was nine years old, she made her dress up in her grandmother's clothes, as if she were trying to bring her own mother back from the dead.

Then she spoke about cooking: about cooking the way her mother had, of thereby trying to honor her own past in some way. I had never been in a situation quite like this before. When we watched the survivor testimony at UCLA, as moving as it was, there was an emotional distance because it was on video. Here there was no distance. I could *feel* the woman's hurt and realized how wretched it must be to have such a large shadow on one's life.

Los Angeles, CA

While I was in Los Angeles I spent an afternoon with my mother, making an audiotape dealing with her feelings about being Jewish and her knowledge of the Holocaust. I also asked her about her mother, Bertha. I don't know that much about my mother's family; my father's family had always been more of a presence in my life. It turns out that my maternal grandmother came from Vilna; in fact, she'd come to America alone, which I guess was somewhat unusual for young women at the end of the nineteenth century. She was an educated woman who had had an unfortunate arranged marriage in the United States, and her life hadn't worked out very well. When I knew her my grandmother was a small, birdlike woman who always seemed frightened. Whatever independence she had once possessed was long gone; washed away, I imagine, by the sadness and disappointment of her life.

The most fascinating part of the afternoon had to do with the whole issue of Christmas. I asked my mother about it and she told me why we'd celebrated it and why we'd stopped. When she was growing up her family lived in a Gentile neighborhood and her mother didn't want her kids to feel excluded when Christmas rolled around, so she filled their stockings with oranges and other treats.

When my parents married they were quite close with my Aunt Enid and her family, who lived nearby. My mother asked my father if she could buy the kids presents for Christmas, and when he said he didn't care, she did. That activity seems somehow to have evolved into big family parties after I was born. I told my mother I thought it was peculiar, and she admitted that after the Holocaust she began to feel uncomfortable about our celebrating Christmas and we stopped—though at the time she never told us why.

As to the Holocaust, she said that because my father avidly read *everything*, he had followed the rise of the Reich during the 1930s and knew a lot about what was happening in Germany. I asked why, despite their political activism, they did not mobilize around Jewish issues of any kind. Neither of them, my mother responded, "liked" the politics of the Jewish organizations; as for Zionism, my father had dismissed Israel as a "potential powerkeg."

When I asked her about their silence regarding the Holocaust, my mother explained that the prevalent attitude during the 1940s was that Jews should remain quiet. She said that she had gone to a discussion at the local temple in 1939 about what was happening in Germany. At the end of the

evening, the rabbi put his finger to his lips and said: "But we must say *nothing*, or it will happen to us!" My mother, apparently like many other American Jews, followed his advice—which, I must say, I find utterly baffling.

Shortly after this conversation with my mother, I met yet another Gentile who, like Harvey Mudd, had more knowledge about the Holocaust than I. At the beginning of this week, while I was in Benicia, California (where the headquarters of *Through the Flower*, the corporation that supports and sponsors my work, is located), I spent an incredibly intense evening with Dr. Konnilyn Feig.

Konnilyn learned about the Holocaust when she was twenty-two years old and living in Montana, where she grew up. She set out on her own to learn about "man's inhumanity to man" (is there an equivalent term that includes women?). Konnilyn became a student of the Holocaust, and her work led her to a commitment to Soviet Jewry, particularly to the women, with whom she's quite involved. She goes to Russia regularly and works to bring Jews out of the Soviet Union. I learned a lot from her and now want to read her book, *Hitler's Death Camps*.

On the plane home

November

I spent the day reading Konnilyn's book and watching educational videos for children about the Holocaust that Isaiah made as study guides. Last night, after reading Konnilyn's book for an hour, I developed an irrational urge to make chicken soup from some leftovers. So all day I've been reading, watching videos, and making chicken soup, which seemed to provide a positive, though short-lived, antidote to my feelings of despair.

Donald and I have been discussing a trip to the concentration camps next year. We both feel that we have to travel there physically and Konnilyn's book provides a very good guide. She has offered to advise us on our itinerary, which I'm planning to take her up on.

Santa Fe, NM

I spent several hours yesterday talking to my Aunt Enid about our family and her feelings about being Jewish. In the process I discovered that her three oldest sisters were born in a town called Kovno—not in Vilna at all, which is somehow what I thought; just goes to show how cloudy the information about our family was.

Interestingly, neither my Aunt Enid, my mother, nor I have any memories of having been discriminated against *as girls* in our family (even though Aunt Enid was brought up in an Orthodox family)—despite all the rhetoric in feminist circles about the patriarchal character of Judaism. Maybe this was because both my grandmothers were from relatively wealthy homes and were educated. As for me, of course, my egalitarian upbringing was a result of my parents' liberal beliefs.

Talking with my Aunt Enid about anti-Semitism and discrimination brought me in touch with some childhood experiences I'd never even thought about. I realized I'd had two or three bouts with anti-Semitism as a teenager, but I had no context for them. Most of the Jewish kids in my neighborhood ended up at a predominantly Gentile high school, where many of us were in the honors class. Our home-room teacher made a nasty comment one day about Roosevelt and the "Jewish conspiracy." As the class was 95 percent Jewish, we all stood up and walked out. The issue of anti-Semitism, however, was never discussed—not in class and not at home.

When I was on the student council there was a statewide meeting of council officers. I stayed in a hotel room with some girls from southern Illinois. They asked me if I'd take off my clothes, as they'd never seen a Jew and wanted to see if I looked "different." Then, as I thought about it, I remembered anti-Semitic phrases scrawled on the wall of my high school. My class was the first with a high percentage of Jewish students, and I guess that stimulated some rather nasty responses from some of the students.

I must have pushed all these events out of my consciousness and rationalized them by thinking how "stupid" these people were. I can see now that this was a defense and that I had never really dealt with what had occurred, nor had my family. These memories are making me think about the whole issue of deception—my parents' and my own.

When I met with Dr. Gerald Margolis, the director of the Simon Wiesenthal Center in Los Angeles, he spoke about how getting deep into Holocaust material can result in the realization that reality is nothing but a "tissue of lies." This chilling phrase haunts me, particularly now that I've begun to think about self-deception and deceit. Learning about the ways in which the Nazis deceived the Jews shocked me: telling them they were going to a resort, taking all their money, then packing them into cattle cars headed for the camps and, once there, telling them that they were headed for the showers. People deceiving others like that challenges all my basic assumptions. I've always just accepted that people *are telling me the truth*, which now seems to be an utterly naive assumption. In fact, if I think back over my life, I realize that many people have, in fact, lied to

me. So why have I been so innocent and trusting?

My surprise at this probably comes out of the fact that I was so protected as a child: from my father's death, from the reality of female oppression and Jewish persecution. And I guess that spending so many years in my studio, grappling with the problems associated with making art, hasn't dramatically altered my childlike approach to the world.

Chicago, IL

I'm reading Robert Lifton's *The Nazi Doctors* and somehow finding it easier to plow through after reading the Feig book. Konnilyn's book was so clear; it helped me understand the structure of the different types of camps and sites—concentration camps, slave-labor camps, and extermination sites (like Treblinka or Birkenau) where the Final Solution was carried out.

Her book left me enlightened but terribly depressed; understanding the level of manipulation and dishonesty used by the Nazis led me to the upsetting conclusion that there is never any assurance that people are telling the truth. As incredible as it may seem, I never realized that people are often motivated by a whole combination of factors that are foreign to me: jealousy, narrow self-interest, a lack of self-knowledge, ulterior motives, bad habits, bad communication skills—on and on.

Lately I've been thinking about deception and the hideous ways in which the Nazis lied to the Jews. I can't comprehend how one person could tell another they were going to the showers when, in fact, they were actually going to be killed. I was brought up to believe in the value of the truth and I've always been a truthful person. Deception makes me feel *very* insecure; my trust—one of the most basic principles in my interactions with other people—has been ripped away, and thus my reality

foundation shudders. Can I rebuild it with the understanding that people *may not* be telling the truth? I don't know. I have always seen the world as innocently as a child (and one who had never thought about Auschwitz, that's for sure); and now Auschwitz (as a metaphor for Nazi evil) is forcing me to lay aside childish notions and face a level of human reality so much more complicated than anything I've ever comprehended before.

Santa Fe, NM

I just finished the Lifton book, which made me think about the fact that almost none of the writing I've examined so far confronts the fact that the Holocaust and all genocides, in fact, have not been enacted by *man*, as these writers keep saying, but by *men*. Women may have *participated* but they have never *initiated* this kind of destruction. Lifton comes close when he says that "*man* [or men] *kills to assert his life power*," which is intimately tied up with the whole notion of "masculinity" and the concept that man is created in God's image. This really places a terrible burden on men to seem *Godlike*—i.e., omnipotent.

As Lifton writes in *Nazi Doctors*: "One can reach the state of requiring a sense of perpetual survival through the killing of others in order to re-experience endlessly" what he refers to as "the moment of power." This requires a "hardening of the self" that, he says, "is related to cultural principles of masculinity."

Santa Fe, NM

December

I just read *The Painted Bird*, by Jerzy Kosinski, which I found both fascinating and disturbing; it's as if his life was so bizarre that literature cannot express it. The book is allegedly based on his child-hood experiences; his parents gave him to someone for safekeeping during the war and he became stranded and was forced to wander around by himself in order to survive. As a child he witnessed events beyond what most children I know ever witness: rape, murder, and unbelievable brutality. He recorded it all in a series of images that are so graphic they are horrifying to read.

Kosinski bombards the reader with descriptions that are practically obscene. Though I could barely stand to read the book, I forced myself through it. He pushes the boundaries of what is permissible to express, which I found fascinating. On the other hand, I found the book almost pornographic in the psychic violence of the images, and upsetting because Kosinski's conclusions about human beings are so terribly sad: i.e., his notion that freedom comes only from being *absolutely alone*.

One reason it was so upsetting is personal: I'm trying to really open up and collaborate on this project, which I find somewhat threatening in that it cuts down the level of absolute psychic privacy I've always maintained. In addition, I'm searching for how best to deal with this subject matter aesthetically, and *The Painted Bird* challenges me and makes me wonder how far I need to go in order to express the obscenity and violence of the Holocaust. Being so graphic scares me, as it has to do with letting go on a level beyond what I've ever done before. Moreover, I'm afraid that what I'll create will be ugly. That's why *The Painted Bird* shook me up. It *is* ugly—the imagery is bestial and unsparing—but I guess I respect him for refusing to compromise the subject matter *at all*.

Santa Fe, NM

I've been reading Martin Gilbert's *The Holocaust*. It chronicles the "extermination" process in endless particulars and identifies by name the people who were murdered, which makes the killing even more real. Gilbert discusses in detail the implementation of the Final Solution in many towns, including Vilna, Kovno, and Riga—the three towns where my grandparents were from. Though they all came to the United States in the late nineteenth or early twentieth century, they must still have had some family there. It suddenly struck me that when I was growing up I was told that we were from Latvia and Lithuania, which, according to my parents, *"didn't exist anymore."* I imagined that somehow they had been wiped off the map. But reading the Gilbert book brought home to me that some of my relatives might have been in those very countries that "didn't exist."

It is hard for me to imagine the agony of "six million Jews," but one person—like my second cousin—is different: I can imagine her screams, feel her pain, identify with her circumstances, and weep for her death. What must it have been like for my maternal grandparents and my father's mother when they found out? Did they know about people from their home town being slaughtered while they were safe here in the United States? Why is it more meaningful when someone who suffered is *someone in your family* or *someone you might have known . . . or been? Because you can imagine it!*

I am seized by a terrible anger at the complicity of my own family: Why didn't they tell me the truth about Jewish persecution, the history of our people and the Holocaust? Was it too terrifying to think that if their parents hadn't left, we'd have been victims too? I want to raise my father from the grave—my radical, "truth-telling" father—and ask him why he wasn't truthful about this. I shake

with rage and despair at the distancing from our heritage embodied in the statement "We come from Latvia and Lithuania, but they don't exist anymore."

Santa Fe, NM

1987

January

This year Donald and I tried to celebrate Hanuka. Donald got a small menorah and birthday candles, which we lit every night. It was embarrassing because neither of us knew what we were doing; Donald doesn't remember anything from Hebrew school and can't really make a prayer, and all I remember is a children's song. The best part was making up a personal prayer of some type each night that had to do with the symbolic aspects of the holiday and of light. I can't really relate to the destruction of the Temple of Jerusalem, which, on one level, is what Hanuka is said to be about. I can, however, identify with the concept of celebrating the "eternal light" of knowledge and fidelity to the universal principle of justice, which Rabbi Lynn suggested as an alternative concept.

Donald got me a Jewish cookbook for the holidays, which has mostly resulted in his cooking *gribines* (fried chicken fat and onions), which he loves. He says they remind him of his maternal grandmother, who seems to have been the person he was closest to when he was growing up.

Along with reading, I have also been working in the studio, finishing some images from my last series, *Powerplay*. I can see now how my interest in the Holocaust was inevitable and logical after all my previous work. For years I've dealt with women as "victims of power" and explored our oppression, survival tactics, and triumphs (often derived from the very basis of our oppression). Then I turned my attention to the "oppressors"—i.e., men, their actions, and the price they pay for their privilege and power. Now I am approaching an experience where power and powerlessness were most dramatically played out. And it is the relationship between power and powerlessness that ultimately defines the nature of civilization.

I see now that this is a very complex issue: People go through different stages of power or powerlessness as they move through life. Moreover, how we experience these stages is shaped by geography, gender, class, race, economic status, education, et cetera. Even in the most emancipated situations, of course (e.g., a white, healthy, upper-middle-class American male, who typically embodies our image of power), powerlessness is sometimes unavoidable—in childhood and old age, as well as in sickness and some personal circumstances. The way one is treated when one is powerless is a measure of the humanity (or lack of) in the family, community, and, ultimately, in the society.

I've been thinking about how Hitler's Germany made explicit many of the implicit attitudes in Western civilization: i.e., only *some* people are "fit to live," while others are irrelevant or destructive to the "health" of the society. Variations of this theme are played out today in many forms all over the world: in South Africa, where many Afrikaners unconsciously see themselves as "fit to live" and the blacks as entirely dispensable, except when they are needed to help whites survive; in India and other still traditional cultures, where female infanticide and suttee are the manifestations of this inarticulated idea of who is "fit to live."

In the United States, of course, whites slaughtered thousands of Native Americans in the name of "manifest destiny" and insist that they "discovered" America. The reality of Native American existence was not only ignored but discounted by defining them as "heathens." Hitler articulated the concept, but it is everywhere on the globe. It helps explain the lack of concern for children, the shameful treatment of old people—all of whom are implicitly, if not explicitly, considered not "fit to live," either before they become "adult and powerful" or after that stage of their life is past. My mind is working steadily on these ideas, but they are new to me and, therefore, still somewhat garbled.

We have decided we must go to Germany (East and West), Austria, Czechoslovakia, Poland, and, if possible, travel into the Soviet Union. I feel somewhat unsure about the value of going to Russia, but Donald insists it's important. We also plan to visit the areas my grandparents and Donald's paternal grandparents came from, though I can't imagine what we'll find there.

Santa Fe, NM

We have done several presentations about our project for some of the people involved in developing Holocaust museums here in Washington and in New York. We did what we set out to do: let them know that we are involved in a project on the Holocaust and that we want to establish a dialogue. This will allow us to communicate with them as we go along, draw on information from their extensive archives, and, hopefully, stimulate their interest in exhibiting the work later on.

It has been a difficult week, and I feel like my nerves are rubbed raw; I hate all this talking—I'd rather paint. But I believe that it's important to connect with the people who are involved with the institutions devoted to preserving the memory of the Holocaust—both because they are the logical places to show the work and because they have been working on this subject for a longer time than we have and can teach us a lot.

One question I'm pondering is how to avoid presenting just one loathsome image after another, something a number of other artists have done. Someone on the staff of the Washington Holocaust Museum told us that they get endless slides showing "the horrors of the Holocaust" and that this approach simply won't work: Who would want to look at it? The question is, Can one make any art on this subject sufficiently compelling that it *can* be looked at?

Washington, DC

In discussing the issue of not wanting to present "the horrors of the Holocaust," Donald and I also began talking about how we are beginning to realize that we see the Holocaust quite differently from many other people engaged in work on the subject. We have an evolving sense of how it relates to some of the larger issues of the history of Western civilization: patriarchy, concepts of power, dominance, and the rule of force.

Placing the Holocaust in the context of a global structure of power, for example, seems a more comprehensive approach than we've seen and one that distinguishes our viewpoint from that of most of the members of the Holocaust community. We had originally planned to follow the fairly conventional "story of the Holocaust" as it is presented in most documentary exhibits, but after our discussions with Isaiah I'm not so sure, particularly now that we see how much our philosophical views differ from those of the mainstream. Generally, everyone tells the story the same way: There is an endless recitation of facts and no real discussion of the larger meaning of the events.

Isaiah said that this "documentary" approach is the way the Holocaust has been presented in the United States and Israel for forty years. The trouble is, one's mind simply blurs after a while: How many facts can one take in? This person was killed in such and such a way; this town was "liquidated" with all the gory details; this family was separated and its members subjected to these indignities before they were gassed—and on and on. But what does it all *mean*? How could it have happened? What does it tell us about our *social values*, our *real* feelings and behaviors? And *why the Jews?*

This question is something my research is providing some insight into. The establishment of Christian society (and many societies, in fact) was built on the destruction of everyone who believed differently. The holy wars, the Inquisition, and the burning of witches and heretics were all part of the effort to rid Western culture of dissident voices and impose Christianity. Many parts of Europe were forcibly Christianized and people "chose" to convert under considerable pressure. Most Jews, however, continued to live, albeit insecurely, as Jews in a Christian world.

We've remained "different" throughout thousands of years; surviving in the face of persecution, prejudice, and oppression; and have (until recently) done so without a nation-state and without the use of force. The change brought about by the creation of Israel may protect the future of Jewry, but it also raises a number of serious questions. Does the existence of a nation-state *require* a military to protect it and inevitably lead to a people becoming oppressors of others?

Then there are other questions: Why have Jews been hated? Is it the fact that we remind society that it is possible to be different and *to survive* despite society's teachings that one must conform? Is it that we repeatedly transcended the limits set for us by society? Where does the hatred come from? Is the Holocaust a direct outgrowth of the patriarchal mind and, if so, how did it develop? Are the oppression of women and Jews linked in any way and, if so, how? Are the Jews the only people who've been subject to extermination policies? If so, why? If not, what other historical genocides relate to the Holocaust? Questions, questions, and more questions; the deeper I get into this material the more questions I have.

Elie Wiesel has said that "the imagination of the Nazis (the perpetrators) was stronger than that of the Jews (the victims)," but really, that's true and not true. In the end the Jews' capacity for survival *was* stronger than the Nazis' will to destroy us; that has always been one of the Jews' strengths: our ability to survive. Even though Jewish culture was in tatters and Jewish survivors still carry shadows on their souls, we Jews *have* survived, and by telling our story and rebuilding our culture we will have ultimately *triumphed.*

The story of the Holocaust is usually told so that it leads up to the establishment of the state of Israel. I want our images to end in a sense of triumph also, but I'm not sure that I should express this only through references to the creation of Israel, as much of an achievement as that is.

On the plane home

February

I spent another interesting evening with Konnilyn Feig, who went over our planned itinerary and made some changes, suggesting that we go to Natzweiler, in the Alsace-Lorraine region of France, where the camp is still very much like it was during the war. She thinks we should spend more time in the Soviet Union and she insists that we go to Nuremberg, where the anti-Semitic laws were drawn up and where, at the end of the war, the Nazi war trials were held. Regarding the trials, Raul Hilberg, one of the most significant Holocaust scholars, claims that two million people were involved in implementing the "war against the Jews." If that is true, it makes the Nuremberg trials of a few individuals seem somewhat ludicrous—but how do you try two million people?

Audrey, Donald, and I spent another day at UCLA. In the morning we saw this incredible anti-Semitic propaganda film made in 1941 called *Jud Suss.* A period piece, it was both effective and horrifying. For a while Audrey was actually convinced the film was "true," which suggests the level of falsehood a well-made work of art can create. To dismiss it as propaganda is to miss the point, which is that the dominant viewpoint can be so overpowering that it can be construed as truth—in art as well as in politics.

We then had lunch with some distinguished Holocaust scholars at UCLA and a survivor named Sam Goetz. He was instrumental in getting the documentary video program of survivor tapes underway. His gentleness, humility, and generosity were quite touching. Afterward, we watched his tape and were struck with what he had endured, which made us marvel at the dignity with which he conducted himself. His demeanor was in such stark contrast to that of the caterer I'd met. I guess there are different types of survivors: those filled with bitterness who never recovered from their experiences and those who were able to transcend their suffering, transforming it into deep empathy, compassion, and grace.

Los Angeles, CA

This is the first time I've spent so much time on the organizational and preparatory aspects of work *before* making the art; it's strange, but essential. The setting up of a framework that will support this project is a slow, arduous process.

Sometimes I experience waves of anxiety that I'll never be able to create art, but I'm trying to trust myself and this unfolding process. It's not that I haven't been on a trip full of discovery and unknown experiences before and succeeded in making art out of it. It's just that this process is different, as it has to be because the context is so different.

We're working against a background of a large, extensive Jewish network and years of scholarly work on and investment in the subject of the Holocaust. We're trying to plug in to that context so that we can become educated, build support for our work, and also find help in exhibiting it.

Santa Fe, NM

We've been buying a lot of books, and today a shipment arrived from a Jewish bookseller in New York. As I was cataloging them, I examined some of the volumes. One was on art from the concentration camps; people worked on scraps with any kind of materials they could find. They scratched, carved, and drew on anything, trying desperately to "make something from nothing," to express some part of their experience and thereby grasp some meaning from the daily degradation they faced.

Yesterday I spent $185 on art materials and didn't even think about it; today I feel humbled by the fact that so many people like me—people with

talent, with the need to create, with the capacity to express themselves—were denied what is so basic to my survival and my identity. For one moment I experienced their deprivation and the starvation of their spirits; I felt terribly sad.

Santa Fe, NM

This morning I read *This Way for the Gas, Ladies and Gentlemen*, a book of stories by the Polish writer Tadeusz Borowski, who was enslaved at the I.G. Farben rubber plant at Monowitz. Because they'd stopped killing Poles at Auschwitz shortly before his arrival, he survived. The stories are incredible, some of the best writing about the Holocaust I've encountered, other than the more recently published collection of stories by Sara Nomberg-Przyfyk, *Auschwitz.*

Borowski never really seems to have escaped the experience. He killed himself at thirty, without having written his planned "great novel," in which he intended to use the concentration camp as a metaphor for the reality of the world. This was one of his great insights:

You know how much I used to like Plato. Today I realized he lied. For the things of this world are not a reflection of the ideal, but a product of human sweat, blood and hard labor. It is we who built the pyramids, hewed the marble for the temples and the rocks for the imperial roads. . . . We were filthy and died real deaths. . . . What does ancient history say about us? SILENCE! The reality of human existence is not recorded . . . only the reality of those who benefited from the labor of the mass of human beings.

Santa Fe, NM

March

Only six weeks before we leave for Germany; it becomes more real every day. In the meantime I'm reading like mad. I went through a book by the father of a local art dealer who was a medical officer in the liberation army. He was at Dachau and the experience apparently scarred him for life; yet his writing was totally objective and distanced. Nowhere did he mention how traumatized he was—and, more important, *he never mentioned he was a Jew.*

Then I started reading a much-touted book about Treblinka but found it, like a lot of the early postwar literature, very dated. There's a big difference between earlier writings on the Holocaust and the more recent material like *The Nazi Doctors* and Claudia Koontz's *Mothers in the Fatherland*, which I'm reading now. Like the Lifton book, the latter reflects more recent thinking as well as feminist history and theory. The Koontz book presents *both* men and women participating (albeit differently) in the development of the Third Reich.

Sometimes I wonder about historic voids and how one doesn't notice them until they begin to be filled. The Koontz book is a good example of that. All the historic imagery about the Nazis is male, even though women participated in and supported the Nazi party, especially at the beginning, when their organizing and fundraising was essential. As in so many political movements historically, both on the left and the right, once the movement was established women were no longer needed and the MEN ONLY sign was prominently displayed.

Nazi women, at least the early leaders, were certainly not interested in "home and hearth" but in playing prominent roles in those social areas they thought of as part of the "feminine sphere." This involved, in addition to motherhood, teaching, social work, volunteer work, nursing—all the "womanly arts." These women believed that it was impossible to wrest power from men and that instead of fighting the "futile feminist fight" (their view), women should accept patriarchy in exchange for protection and should, because they accepted patriarchy, be allowed to enjoy the many freedoms available within the female sphere. Imagine their surprise when, once on stable political ground, the men made it clear that they had no intention of allowing women even the female sphere, unless it was male dominated.

The book is interesting, both in terms of my search for imagery and women's long and sometimes misguided methods for reaching some measure of power. It's almost as true of the right today as it was of the Reich then: Women who accept patriarchal values ultimately find themselves constrained or betrayed by the men whose efforts they support.

Santa Fe, NM

I just finished reading a book by Marilyn French called *Beyond Power*. It is not specifically about the Holocaust, though there are numerous references to it. Rather, it's about patriarchy, a kind of historic and literary analog to my *Powerplay* series. The history French chronicles closely parallels the history symbolized by *The Dinner Party*, and the similarities between our worldviews was very gratifying to me. But more important, her investigation of patriarchy and patriarchal values provides an important context for understanding the Holocaust. For, as she says, the line between the suppression and the extermination of a people is not as clear as some like to think.

If I seem to be jumping around in my reading,

it's because I feel compelled to look at this subject from many points of view. First, I wanted to simply explore the information, which resulted in my need to compensate for the male bias in that information by trying to understand something about women's experience. Then I wanted to get some sense of the experience. Then I wanted to get some sense of the experience of Germans themselves, including reading *Mothers in the Fatherland* and other books, notably one I'm reading now about day-to-day life during the Reich. (I'm not so interested in focusing on the Nazis; for me they are simply the most dramatic example of those who've been "disfigured by power," something I explored in *Powerplay*. But I am fascinated by why women colluded in their power.) Also, I felt a need to see the whole experience of the Holocaust in the framework of the history of patriarchy, something the French book allowed me to do.

I feel impatient that I'm not coming up with images, but the material is so complex; it's like wading through mud and trying to "have an idea." I have *some* ideas in my mind but I'm afraid to commit them to paper yet.

We've been listening to Polish and Russian tapes, trying to get some sense of those languages in preparation for our trip. However, I'm so bad at languages that I got totally discouraged and am planning instead to make flash cards with all the basic phrases, which I hope will allow us to communicate in a rudimentary way.

Santa Fe, NM

We just watched *Triumph of the Will* by Hitler's favorite filmmaker, Leni Riefenstahl, which I had never seen. It was very interesting, given what I've been reading lately. It is, of course, a paean to patriarchy and nationalism. At one point one of the

Nazi leaders says to the masses of assembled Nazi youth that there is no class or caste system in the Reich. This is totally ironic in that he is addressing only young Aryan men and, of course, has a concept of a world where women's purpose is only to produce more "pure white youths."

It's hard to look at the film without seeing parallels to patriarchal structures all over the world; the Marilyn French book is acting on my consciousness. And of course, *Triumph of the Will* was made by a *woman*, one completely in thrall to patriarchal values.

And suddenly, I've begun to draw. It just started to happen today; they are only line drawings, but it's a start!

Santa Fe, NM

April

When I was in Los Angeles last week visiting my mother I had this terrible thought: I realized that she—too old, sick, and fragile to work—would have been deemed "unworthy of life" by the Nazis. Wondering how they managed to excise any feelings of sympathy for the weak from their emotional makeup suddenly produced an enormous wave of compassion for my mother. It was as if thinking about the Nazis' utter lack of sympathy triggered a flood of feeling. I simply cannot imagine how they could close themselves off sufficiently to commit mass murder. It is an emotional hurdle I can't get over; I can't picture doing it, no matter how I try.

In a week we leave for Germany to install *The Dinner Party*, and then we start our travels. We've been preparing for it for so long it's hard to believe it's finally here. My studies and readings have finally helped me take an intellectual step. I no longer look at the Holocaust as I did when I began. Now I see it in a larger context: as one of the most graphic demonstrations of the injustice inherent in the global structure of patriarchy and the result of power as it has been defined and enforced by male-dominated societies. As Virginia Woolf put it, fascism can be construed as "masculinity gone mad." Now I've come to the point in my thinking that only *being* in the places where the Holocaust took place can lead me farther along.

Santa Fe, NM

We're on our way to Frankfurt, Germany, to install *The Dinner Party*, and then we'll travel to camps and sites. I feel that this trip is somewhat like a rite of passage. I became quite terrified on Monday because it was suddenly real; we are actually going to travel through the "landscape of the Holocaust."

Travel Itinerary

1987	Site	Location
May 4–5	NATZWEILER*	France
6–7	Nuremberg	Germany
8–10	DACHAU	Germany
11–13	MAUTHAUSEN, GUSEN	Austria
	EBENSEE	Austria
14–16	Vienna	Austria
17–20	State Jewish Museum of Prague	Czechoslovakia
	THERESIENSTADT	Czechoslovakia
21–23	AUSCHWITZ	Poland
24–29	MAJDANEK	Poland
30–June 2	TREBLINKA	Poland
	Warsaw	Poland
June 3–6	Leningrad	Russia
7–8	Riga	Latvia
9–10	Kovno	Lithuania
11	Vilna	Lithuania
12	Return to Warsaw	
13–14	STUTHOF	Poland
15–22	RAVENSBRUCK	Germany
	SACHSENHAUSEN	Germany
	BUCHENWALD	Germany
23–25	BERGEN-BELSEN	Germany

*Names in all caps refer to camps and/or extermination sites.

I just read psychiatrist Victor Frankl's *Man's Search for Meaning* and found it fascinating. Based in part on his experiences in Auschwitz, he developed the philosophy that the essential need in human beings is for a sense of *meaning* in life, which, he argued, could be found even in suffering. Since the concentration camps created extreme suffering, it was possible for him to explore this idea both personally and from a professional perspective.

Thinking about this book did bring me to ask yet again: What *is* the meaning of the Holocaust? Some Holocaust scholars insist that it has *no meaning*, but I can't accept that, as I believe all historic events have something to teach us, if only we're open to the

don't understand is how the Jews went "like sheep to the slaughter." They are being entirely ignorant of the circumstances and unaware of how they themselves would probably have acted in a situation where they were being so thoroughly deceived.

Working here has challenged my assumptions about Germans. It made me realize that there is no special taint in them that mark them as "crazed animals" or "monsters"; they seem no different from the French or the Dutch or even we Americans. Whatever it is that contributed to the Holocaust, it doesn't seem immediately apparent in the German character.

Frankfurt, Germany

May

I have heard the sound of trains going by every day I've been here; I keep thinking of *Shoah* and the interminable sound of the trains carrying more and more people to their deaths. I wish I could find a comparable visual image—one that would convey the same sense of the way the activities of the Holocaust took place as part of everyday life. The trains passed carrying their human cargo; the prisoners walked or took streetcars to and from the work camps, which were often down the street and practically next door to spas or resorts. In fact, it could all be going on right now: The trains I hear *could* be the cattle cars. I could "know" what was happening and "not know" it all at once.

Another damn train is going by. I'm getting to the point where I can't *bear* the sound of them anymore. I'll be glad to leave!

Frankfurt, Germany

Natzweiler, the first concentration camp we've actually seen, loomed up like a colossus in the fog. All

the reading I've done didn't prepare me for it: the rows of barbed wire; the dank, cold, humid air; the seven-kilometer road the prisoners had to walk up (which they first had to build); and the nearby hotel-bar in Struthof, three kilometers from the camp. Directly across from this inn was a bathhouse, converted at some unknown time into the gas chamber for the concentration camp.

It was so foggy we could barely see the camp or the museum, where there was hardly even a mention of the word *Jew*. This shocked us, because in the United States the Jewish experience is the one primarily emphasized. Here there are frequent references to the French "martyrs and patriots" who had died during the war. The French let the re-

mains of this camp disintegrate for twenty years before they decided to memorialize the shameful era when the Vichy government gave over so easily to their German "oppressors."

We drove through the ancient town of Natzweiler and wondered if the villagers had watched the prisoners struggling up the hill. Everyone must have seen them as they walked from the railroad station to the camp. Did anybody care?

As we ascended the mountain, up and up the winding roads, we entered a place where "anyone could do anything"—and *did*. I saw and felt EVIL for the first time. I never understood that word, or related to it. But today I smelled it, smelled how evil human beings can be. It was in the air, in the dampness, and it was in the twisting streets up which the prisoners marched.

I am already overwhelmed on Day One of the Trip; no amount of study is the same as standing on the soil where these terrible deeds were done.

Alsace-Lorraine, France

After seeing what the weather was like yesterday, how cold and rainy it was even in May, we prepared ourselves better today. But no matter how many layers of clothes we wore, the wet, damp rain soaked us and the horrors of the concentration camp chilled us spiritually. After six hours of retracing our steps from yesterday, we drove home in total silence with the car heater going full blast.

At the hotel I plunged into a hot bath, scrubbing every inch of my body to try and remove the stain and the smell of the camp. But as I submerged my body in the water, I kept seeing pictures of the women's bodies in the tubs they used to pickle them after their deaths. Their bodies were then sent to the nearby University of Strasbourg for "study."

We first went to the railroad station where the trains full of "deportees" (as they called them here; each country has its own euphemisms) used to pull in. I stood at the station in the rain, wondering how it must have felt to be crowded in one of the railroad cars as it pulled up to the station.

Then we drove slowly up the serpentine mountain roads, stopping so that Donald could photograph, trying to create a sense of the environment: the mountainous countryside and the small villages nestled into the hills. There was the pleasant sense of a centuries' old peace here, in dramatic contrast to Germany, where all the traditional architecture had been bombed away. As we entered the town of Natzweiler we stopped—this time to photograph one of the many crucifixions that guard the entrance to most of the houses. It made me feel creepy to see them; as if beneath the surface of the ancient calm of this village, there still seethed superstitious fantasies about Jews as Christ-killers.

We continued up the twisting, turning road until we came again to Struthof, where the seemingly innocuous inn had been a Nazi hangout during the war. We wondered if people had actually sat on the patio, drinking their aperitifs, oblivious to the people awaiting their deaths or the horrible screams of those who realized it wasn't showers that awaited them but gas.

My image of the lovely French countryside began to crumble as I looked around at some of the older people having lunch and wondered what they'd been doing during the war. Had they continued eating their large midday meals, impervious to what was happening across the street or three kilometers away?

Then we went back to the camp, which, despite the pouring rain and heavy fog, we toured for

Inn at Struthof, used both now and during the war. Across the way is the converted bathhouse.

Crematorium building at Natzweiler

Crematorium oven
When I lay on the shovel that carried bodies into the crematorium, I realized that, had I lived in Europe during the war, this would probably have happened to me. (Donald is too young.)

hours. The French began transforming it into a "monument to the Resistance movement" in the 1960s. The crosses on the houses in the town were mirrored in the rows and rows of crosses on the hillside at the camp site.

We went to the crematorium; entering it was like descending into Hell. First I, then Donald, lay upon the long shovel that carried the bodies into the flames. The oven was like a terrible inversion of the X-ray machine I'd recently been in for a CAT scan—modern technology used by the Nazis for methodical killing.

One thing that, in my ignorance, I had never understood was that Jewish tradition prohibits the cremation of bodies. I realized with shock that Jewish bodies being burned was yet another form of abuse in the horrendous series of violations to which Jews were subjected.

Near the crematorium there were rooms to store bodies, rooms for experiments and vivisection, rooms for waiting "patients." I thought: If only those rooms could speak. Even mute, they were powerful and overwhelming testimony. And the smell! Everywhere was the odor of human flesh, which decades of cleaning and whitewashing could not remove. It made us both sick.

A hotel near Natzweiler, France

We're in Nuremberg—where it began with the Nuremberg laws restricting Jews, and where it ended with the trials of Nazi war criminals. We went to a German restaurant yesterday, an old beerhall-type place. Both Donald and I felt oppressed by it; we chattered on, probably because we were afraid of the anguish we felt: the pain of *being* in Germany as Jews and letting ourselves know, feel, and experience this place, like no other place, where the Holocaust was born.

The more I understand, the less I understand. I turn again and again to Wiesel for help, even though I don't always agree with what he says. But one remark of his was quite illuminating in terms of my inability to understand the perpetrators. I have written that I cannot inflict pain knowingly on others because I am a feminist and a conscious woman, and then I came upon Wiesel's statement that "the Jews were told they were forbidden to diminish freedom. *They were forbidden [by Scripture] to inflict pain.*" Thus I find that I have carried a dual commandment, as a *feminist* and as a *Jew*. What an interesting revelation!

Nuremberg, Germany

Historic photo of Nazi rally at Nuremberg Stadium

Audrey Cowan at Nuremberg Stadium, 1987
Audrey Cowan, my long-time weaving collaborator, accompanied us on the first part of our trip. The deserted stadium provided few hints about the enthusiastic crowds that had filled it in support of Hitler and the Third Reich.

It's Mother's Day in America and at the concentration camp at Dachau it was a Day of Remembrance. This included an emotionally moving, commemorative ceremony for the twentieth anniversary of the Jewish memorial and, after that, a hideous international ceremony full of militaristic overtones, focused once again on the "patriots" of the Holocaust. The Jews played a small part in that ceremony, but the earlier one was another matter.

There were a few hundred people gathered in front of the memorial, 90 percent of whom were survivors. A cantor sang the *Kaddish* (memorial prayer); old men *davened* (prayed); old women wept; and an intense emotional quality filled the air. I stood in the midst of them, crying and feeling overwhelmed.

Suddenly I realized that, during all the weeks we've been in Europe, we haven't seen *any* Jews until today. We finally met a Jewish couple, the Snopkowskis, through the USIA (the United States Information Agency, which has been very helpful to us with our trip). The husband's a survivor, the wife a converted Jew, and together they run an organization in Munich that holds Jewish cultural events. They told us about their long struggle to have the Jewish memorial built, a struggle that mirrors the one in which German homosexuals are now engaged.

While we were at Dachau there was a demonstration of about one hundred people carrying signs with pink triangles—the despised "mark" of homosexuality in the concentration camps. Apparently there's been a great deal of research recently on the experience of homosexuals in the camps, but we were told that there is a lot of resistance to any formal commemoration, particularly among some of the Jews in the United States. I wonder why.

Sign at the entrance to the concentration camp at Dachau
Situated right next to the town, the historic marker refers to the area as a twelve-hundred-year-old "artists' centre . . . offering a splendid view over the country." Someone had scrawled above it: "HAVE YOU NO SHAME?"

Survivor at Dachau, 1987
This survivor, who attended the ceremonies on the Day of Remembrance, stands on the site of the razed barracks.

What a different experience Dachau was from Natzweiler. It's all cleaned up and antiseptic here; most of the original buildings have been razed. The ovens at Dachau, in contrast to those at Natzweiler, are clean, polished, and utterly spotless. The camp is adjacent to the city of Dachau, where there were a large number of satellite work camps scattered throughout the town during the war. The prisoners actually rode the streetcars to and from work dressed in their prison garb. Dachau was one of the earliest concentration camps, and at least at the beginning, because inmates were communists or political activists, many of the antileft townspeople felt they'd gotten what they deserved. But by the end of the war, when the crematoria were burning constantly and the smell of human flesh filled the air, it's hard to believe the Germans' assertion that they didn't know what was going on.

Munich, Germany

We crossed over into entirely new and unfamiliar territory today. I've never been east of Germany before. One thing became crystal clear: A number of the camps were located in obscure areas where people still lived in semifeudal ways and thus had many fears and superstitions (including, I guess, how Jews killed Christ).

Because they were out of view, away from "civilization," these camps in particular allowed the most brutal aspects of human nature to thrive. *ANYTHING WAS PERMISSIBLE!* I suppose that the potential for barbarity is there in many of us, but the Nazis, who strategically positioned the camps in remote locations, promoted the acting out of unimaginable atrocities.

Bad Ischl, Austria

Crematorium building at Dachau, thoroughly
cleaned up and landscaped

LOWER RIGHT: Dachau at Liberation, 1945

Survivor Max Mannheimer at Dachau, 1987

Today we were at Ebensee, site of one of the numerous satellite work camps of Mauthausen, which was clearly one of the most hellish places on Earth. Prisoners were literally worked to death, dying of exhaustion sometimes only three days after their arrival. I really didn't understand before that most of the camps we've heard about were only the center or "mother" camp of whole networks of work camps; some, like Ebensee, were actually larger than their "mother" camp (I hate the use of that term, as if "mothering" had anything to do with the Nazi system of terror).

We drove to this nice, quiet subdivision, built on the grounds of the former camp, and went to see the cemetery that commemorates those who had died in the war. It's peaceful, modest, and full of plaques honoring different groups who were victimized, including, though not emphasizing, the Jews.

Then we walked up above the houses, looking for the slave-labor tunnels we had read about. They were mostly used for weapons production and had been closed off after the war. Suddenly we found them, buried in the side of a hill, set against the gorgeous alpine landscape. One of them was partly open; the wooden slats barring the entrance had been forced open. Ignoring the signs in German forbidding entry, we started inside, completely unaware of what we were going to see.

It was cold and damp, even on this warm, sunny day, and our eyes gradually became accustomed to the darkness. The tunnel must have been two miles long and connected to others in the mountains, all apparently built by prisoners working with primitive tools. When the Allies destroyed their above-ground munitions factories, the Nazis began

Ebensee, Austria, 1987

The entrance to the work camp at Ebensee was marked by this arch, which now graces a subdivision. In the course of our travels we became aware of how concentration-camp architecture had been incorporated into the contemporary environment.

Historic wartime photo, taken three weeks after the freeing of the camp, depicts entrance to slave-labor camp at Ebensee

Hillside, Ebensee, Austria, 1987
The tunnels are blocked off but this fence was partly torn down, which allowed us to enter.

Historic photo showing the underground tunnels in operation

Drawing done secretly by the French prisoner Bernard Aloebert shows workers being forced into tunnels

PRECEDING PAGE: **Inside a tunnel at Ebensee, 1987**
Built by the prisoners with primitive tools, the tunnels went on for miles inside the mountain.

building armaments deep inside the mountains, with a vast network of forced labor. Now, forty-five years later, nothing grows here—as if the terrible deeds done inside these walls prevent the growth of any life at all.

Neither Donald nor I had really understood the slave-labor aspect of the Holocaust; it was only when we stood inside that cave that we began to comprehend what it meant in human terms. *Evil* was the only word I could think of, *overwhelming evil.* "Everything is understandable," I kept saying. But this—was this understandable? The Nazi march across Europe was like the Crusades, the Inquisition, any of the hideous religious wars of days gone by, vanquishing the "heathens" and making slaves out of all those they conquered. *But was this understandable in modern times?*

These Nazi madmen had set out to vanquish the world, but they weren't conquering foreign lands; they were conquering Europe, their own continent, and they were murdering Jews as they went. I suddenly realized that the "liquidation" of the Jews was only part of this madness. Himmler stood on a mountainside here and thought this would be a good place for arms factories, "manned" by thousands of slaves from the countries they were overpowering. He envisioned a permanent slave-labor force in service to the Reich. To him these people counted for nothing; they were only *a means* to an end.

I am completely undone. It boggles the mind. Wiesel is right: It's incomprehensible.

Bad Ischl, Austria

We're staying in a posh Austrian hotel, where we checked in yesterday—or crawled into, is more like it. The contrast between our level of physical comfort and what we're seeing is unnerving, to say the least. Yesterday we visited Mauthausen, which, in keeping with its intended permanence, was built like a fortress. Here and in the adjoining network of labor camps it was death by exhaustion, desperation, or starvation. The principal work site was the quarry, where men usually labored for no more than three months before they died.

As we walked down the road toward the quarry, built by hand by the workers with stones from that very place, I felt like we were walking on bodies.

Mauthausen, the fortress-like camp built from stones quarried by slave labor

We went down the 186 handmade steps to the pit, the source of so much torture and suffering. As we descended, my mind was filled with images of the workers we had seen in photographs and drawings: days of staggering up the steps in wooden clogs with the terrible weight of large blocks of stone on their backs; then pitifully meager rations and sleepless nights, three men to a small wooden bunk, lying under the cramped bodies of those who screamed in their tortured sleep. There was not one moment of relief, privacy, or pleasure for those who were housed there.

Linz, Austria (Hitler's birthplace)

I got totally drunk Wednesday night and all night I dreamed I was trapped inside barbed wire. The next day, when we visited the memorial site at Gusen and then went back to Mauthausen to photograph, I acted really badly toward Donald. I just couldn't take any more horror. I began to see it everywhere: in the trees, where I envisioned people being shot; in the pastoral landscape, where I imagined Jews fleeing and being refused sanctuary. It was as if the surface of reality had been peeled back and all the horror revealed. I felt like my skin was crawling.

Now we're in Vienna and I feel better. We had a nice dinner last night and took a long walk back to the hotel. Today we have an appointment at the government archives to look at some art done by prisoners, and then we plan to take the weekend off, which we both need.

Vienna, Austria

We have begun to see a lot of art on this trip that depicts *exactly* what life was like in the camps. I was afraid that only photographs could provide a sense of the reality of the Holocaust experience. But at the archives in Dachau and here in Vienna, we've been seeing a considerable amount of visual

Interior square, now empty
and mute

Historic photo showing Mauthausen
full of prisoners

Victor Siminski, *In the Gas Chambers*, 1944,
35.5 cm x 61 cm
There is a story in the guidebook at Natzweiler about the camp commandant, Kramer, who after gassing a group of women and listening to their screams, looked inside the gas chamber and saw their dead bodies covered with excrement. He is quoted as saying: "I felt no emotion when performing these acts for I was brought up like that"—i.e., to "be a man," to feel nothing.

Peephole into the gas chamber
Companies competed for the contract to build equipment for the gas chambers and crematoria. The successful enterprise displayed its name on this peephole.

Gas chamber today

ABOVE: Quarry steps at Mauthausen, 1987
Climbing the quarry steps was difficult for many of the tourists there. Most of them couldn't even imagine the conditions under which the prisoners worked.

ABOVE LEFT: Wladyslaw Siwek, *Przy łopacie (with the Spade)*; watercolor

LEFT: Historic photo depicts prisoners carrying quarried stones up the stairway known as the "death stairs"

work done by prisoners that "bears witness" to their experiences in as poignant a way as I could ever imagine. This reinforces my belief that I *can* play a role in expressing this material through my art. What is interesting is that the prisoner art *expands* the experiences represented by the photographs; but what the photos make clear is that the drawings are "true." I guess that's why I decided to combine painting and photography. While photography can establish the veracity of the subject, only painting can provide a means of transformation. But at the moment I feel like I can't do much more than make chicken scratches in my drawing book, which, nonetheless, I carry with me wherever I go.

Vienna, Austria

Bronisław Latawiec, *Beati qui moritur*, watercolor

Ellie Lieberman, *Die SS quält*, 1943

We arrived in Prague last night and walked around town and over to the old Jewish area. There are still a considerable number of buildings and synagogues once belonging to the Jewish community, which dates back more than a thousand years. Now the buildings house innumerable Jewish artifacts and works of art that are part of the State Jewish Museum of Prague. When the Nazis arrived they slowly liquidated the Jews and their property. Most of the people were sent to Terezin, a fortified town sixty kilometers away, which the Nazis converted into what they called a ghetto but was really a concentration camp.

Terezin had two parts: the old town, Theresienstadt, which was turned into a "Jewish ghetto," and a small fortress that functioned as a camp for political prisoners and some Jews (both were built by the son of Maria Theresa of Austria and named after her). But Theresienstadt was an unusual camp; it was intended partly as a "showplace" to demonstrate to the world that the "grotesque stories" about Nazi treatment of Jews were not true. Though Jews died from despair, starvation, and disease, they were not "exterminated" in Theresienstadt but transported later, primarily to Auschwitz.

During their stay they were encouraged, within limits, to pursue cultural activities, though that was only to support the facade that Theresienstadt was not a doorway to death but a "model ghetto." Meanwhile the Nazis confiscated Jewish property and used the closed buildings to house the Jewish art and artifacts that were being sent to Prague from all over Europe. (Some of these toured the United States in the marvelous *Precious Legacy* exhibit.) The Nazis had a plan to create a museum to commemorate the "extinct race" of Jews, where these collected possessions would demonstrate our

Fritta/Fritz Taussig, *The Shops in Terezin*, 1943; India-ink pen drawing, 57 cm x 84.5 cm, #SJM 174.160
One of the most hideous aspects of Theresienstadt was the level of deception practiced by the Nazis. They forced the prisoners to participate in a bizarre hoax for the International Red Cross, aimed at demonstrating how "well" they were being treated. After the visit, a propaganda book was produced, showing the "humane" conditions there.

"strangeness" to future generations, who, of course, would know no living Jews. German officers (living in confiscated Jewish apartments) furnished their places at minimal cost with carpets, furniture, and other valuables from these storehouses of collected Jewish goods. Oddly, for a culture committed to not "polluting" itself by trafficking with Jews, the Nazis did not seem to object to living in Jewish homes, walking on Jewish carpets, or eating off Jewish plates.

After the war a few thousand survivors of the once-flourishing Jewish community of Prague returned. The Czech government gave them back their belongings and their buildings, but there were not enough Jews, nor did they have sufficient financial resources to be able to maintain the community. Instead, they took what they needed personally in order to reestablish their lives and, in the 1950s, gave everything to the state, which set the buildings up as museums.

One of the sites, the old Jewish cemetery, contains an absolutely astonishing collection of tombstones; they say that nearly 100,000 people are buried there, some graves dating back to the Middle Ages. It is an amazing place, absolutely bursting with tradition. The tombstones seemed to say "Here

I am, a person of worth." There are thousands of markers, each carrying inscriptions in Hebrew, each containing the ideas of the deceased or the grief of the survivors.

Then I saw a tombstone engraved with praying hands: the symbol of the rabbis and spiritual leaders of the communities. I remembered the drawing of praying hands I had seen at the temple in Cedar Rapids, Iowa, done by my grandfather when he was a rabbi there. No one had told me what the symbolism was. Now I knew that it was the sign of my ancestry, the *Kohanim*, and noted that the image was inscribed on many of the tombstones.

It was *so* painful to see the buildings, the property, the streets, and the artifacts of Jewish culture—and no Jews; just a few old folks eating a kosher lunch in the town hall, a kosher meal brought from hundreds of kilometers away, since there are no kosher restaurants in Prague. *No kosher restaurants* in a town that had once been home to thousands and thousands of Jews. And now there are these daily tours: hundreds of people from the Eastern bloc countries streaming through the buildings; most of them probably never met any Jewish people.

The sadness in my heart is great. I fully comprehend the meaning of the words the "destruction of European Jewry." Here in Czechoslovakia, as in Austria and Germany, it is nearly *Judenrein* (free of Jews).

Prague, Czechoslovakia

On top of the pain of what we're encountering, there's the general bleakness and depression of eastern European life. Everywhere it's gray and chilly with oppression. Never having been in an eastern European country, I didn't know what to expect—and it's only going to get worse as we go farther east. Next we go to Auschwitz, which seems like going to the very center of Hell.

Prague, Czechoslovakia

Historic photo depicts Jews arriving in Theresienstadt in 1942

Helga Hošková-Weissová, *Bialystok's Children Arriving in Terezin,* 1943; colored-pen drawing, 17 cm x 24 cm, 29.VIII. 1943

Prague today

In the Jewish section the town hall (pictured here) contains two clocks, one with Jewish numerals which runs backward. The thousand-year-old community was almost entirely destroyed during the war.

Dr. Galsky, former head of the small Jewish community

The steel doors protect the Torah from fire in the Old-New Synagogue (Altneuschul), which is supposedly the oldest standing temple in Europe.

Jewish curators working in one of the Prague synagogues
sorting Jewish property confiscated by the Nazis, 1942–1943

ABOVE RIGHT: **Looking at stored paintings**
Dr. Bedrich Nosek, head of collections at the State Jewish Museum of
Prague, showed us the stacks of paintings by Jewish artists, most of whom
had been killed by the Nazis. The government does not have enough
money to properly care for or exhibit most of the work.

FACING PAGE: **One of the oldest**
Jewish cemeteries in Europe

Except for
the Barbed
Wire it looked
almost like a
normal town

Donald and I were totally flabbergasted by the enormous scale of the Auschwitz installation, which covered eighteen square miles and comprised three separate sites. Auschwitz itself was shocking by its seeming normalcy; it looked almost like Lowell or Lawrence, the nineteenth-century factory towns we had recently visited in Massachusetts. Nearby Monowitz had housed the Farben rubber factories, which employed prisoner and slave labor during the war and are now used by the Poles as petrochemical plants. The third site was Birkenau, one of the extermination sites for

Jews and Romanies. Some people were "selected" for work details when they arrived there, but most, especially women with children and the elderly, were immediately dispatched to the gas chambers and crematoria.

Auschwitz now contains a series of exhibitions in the very barracks where prisoners once lived, and there was a scale model of one of the four crematoria. It made it clear that they were actually like giant processing plants—except that instead of processing pigs they processed people who had been defined as pigs. The Nazis had cunningly ap-plied the assembly-line techniques of the Industrial Revolution to the Final Solution; everything was engineered with maximum, but entirely dehumanized, efficiency.

My studies were teaching me that one of the essential steps in being able to "process" human beings was to dehumanize them, reduce them to "things" that are seen merely as means to an end. Ghettoization, starvation, filth, and brutality took their toll on the Jewish people, and the Nazi propaganda machine, which continually described Jews as "vermin" or "pigs," convinced the body politic that it could only be "healed" by getting rid of the Jew. Contemplating the model of the crematorium at Birkenau, where the Final Solution was implemented, I suddenly thought of the "processing" of other living creatures, to which most of us are accustomed and think little about.

I had learned that during the Industrial Revolution pigs were the first "things" on the assembly line. I began to wonder about the ethical distinction between processing pigs and doing the same thing to people defined as pigs. Many would argue that moral considerations do not have to be ex-

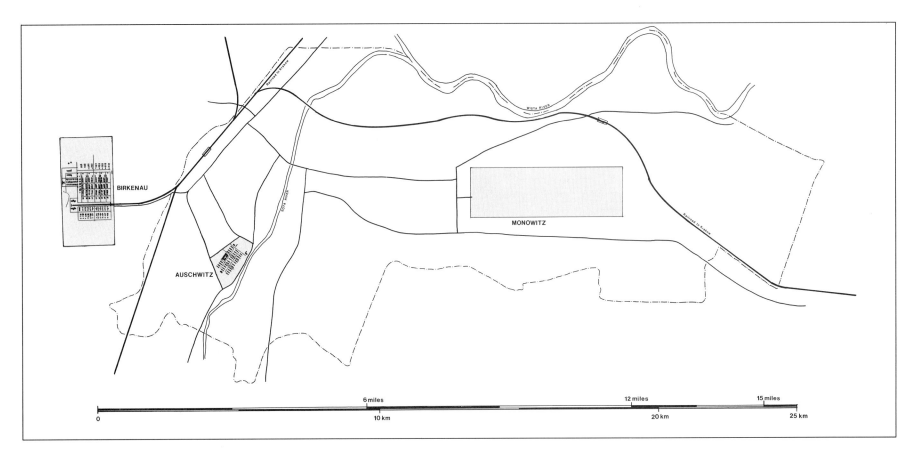

Map of Auschwitz, Birkenau, and Monowitz: The installation comprised eighteen square miles and was entirely fenced off.

Historic photo shows I.G. Farben Rubber Works in Monowitz during the war

tended to animals, but this is just what the Nazis said about the Jews. Others argue, or believe subconsciously, that animals exist for human use. They assume that people are more important than other species and are horrified when human beings are treated like animals.

Confronting how the Nazis "processed" human beings, we were, of course, revolted; but what was so unnerving about being at Auschwitz was how oddly familiar it seemed. Some of the things the Nazis did in the camps are done all the time in the rest of the world. The "processing" methods used at Birkenau were a grotesque form of the same modern technologies upon which we all depend. Many living creatures are crowded together in despicable quarters; transported without food or water; herded into slaughterhouses, their body parts "efficiently" used to make sausages, shoes, or fertilizer. Some people on the planet are "selected" for good educations, jobs, and privileges, while millions of others starve. Many people work at slave wages while others profit from their work. It's monstrous to realize, of course, but suddenly something inside me went "click."

I saw the whole globe symbolized at Auschwitz, and it was covered with blood: people being manipulated and used; animals being tortured in use-

---

Artist unknown, drawing shows prisoners being marched into Siemens plant

One of the Siemens stores today
Siemens provided the electrical installations for the concentration camps and staffed some of its production lines with camp inmates. It employed many prisoners, transporting them from all over to work in its plants. Siemens is now the second-largest electronics company in the world.

View of ramp at Birkenau today,
where selections took place

Mieczyslaw Koscielniak,
Panorama obozu w Brzezince
(Panorama of Birkenau)

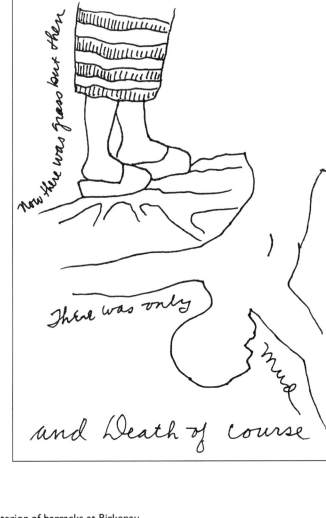

Now there was grass but then
There was only
mud
and Death of course

ABOVE LEFT: Interior of barracks at Birkenau, which was heated by only one small wood-burning stove

LEFT: Janina Tollik, *Ulica w obozie kobiecym* (*The Street in the Women's Camp*); watercolor

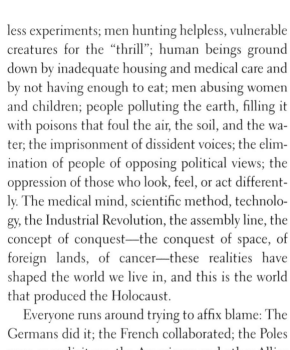

less experiments; men hunting helpless, vulnerable creatures for the "thrill"; human beings ground down by inadequate housing and medical care and by not having enough to eat; men abusing women and children; people polluting the earth, filling it with poisons that foul the air, the soil, and the water; the imprisonment of dissident voices; the elimination of people of opposing political views; the oppression of those who look, feel, or act differently. The medical mind, scientific method, technology, the Industrial Revolution, the assembly line, the concept of conquest—the conquest of space, of foreign lands, of cancer—these realities have shaped the world we live in, and this is the world that produced the Holocaust.

Everyone runs around trying to affix blame: The Germans did it; the French collaborated; the Poles were complicitous; the Americans and other Allies were indifferent. The list continues, trying to assign blame for something for which no one is to blame, but for which all human beings are responsible. *As a species, we are responsible for what we've done to each other, the Earth, and its creatures.* The Holocaust can be seen as the logical outgrowth of the rule of force, dominance, and power. It doesn't even matter which gender did it, though it falls on men. Would women have done any differently? Who knows? The question is, can we see what we've done and change what we do? If not, the Holocaust of the Jews will, without any doubt, become the Holocaust of the world.

Now that this stupefying reality has become apparent to me, I am faced with a major problem. Making art about a subject as overwhelming as this

one is turning out to be is going to take an exceedingly long time. But I don't want to spend too many years on such dreadful material—it takes all the joy out of life! I miss our cats and our house and our life at home very much now. As we drive east and deeper and deeper into both Holocaust territory and the gray oppression of socialist societies, I feel my grasp on sanity faltering. Can I hold on to myself, deal with these terrible truths and find meaning in this world now that I see it clearly in all its horror? We still have six weeks to go and Russia ahead of us. I'm tired—not ready to go home yet, but very, very tired.

Krakow, Poland

Remains of one of the crematoria at Birkenau

One crematorium was blown up in a carefully planned though ultimately unsuccessful act of resistance by a *Sonderkommando* team—prisoners who were entrusted with certain important camp duties. The others were dismantled by the Nazis in an effort to destroy the evidence.

We've met a number of people here in Krakow. At the U.S. Embassy, we spoke with the acting director of the new Jewish-Polish Institute they're organizing, as well as Henry Halkowski—a *young* Jew, something extremely rare in Poland. Now that all the Jews have been wiped out, the Poles are beginning to study Jewish history, partly with an eye on the tourist dollars that this will bring in. The Holocaust and Jewish culture are becoming big business on an international scale. It's really appalling. Most of the people involved in the museum work, scholarship, and growing dialogue on Jewish issues (both here and throughout eastern Europe) are non-Jews, of course.

Henry, who wants to live some kind of Jewish life in Poland, has had to teach himself what he could about Jewish culture from a few old and musty library books. His knowledge is very spotty and he seems very isolated. He showed us around the old Jewish ghetto and then didn't want to part with us. Last night, when we stumbled into the dining room at nine o'clock after twelve hours at Auschwitz, he was waiting for us. We bought him dinner, but the effort to relate to him after such a grueling day was almost too much for us.

Krakow, Poland

Maybe we're becoming accustomed to concentration camps. Majdanek was just the "usual" configuration, though huge (despite the fact that only 20 percent of the planned structures were actually built during the war). It was intended to be a permanent SS work camp (with auxiliary camps) providing slave labor. Unfortunately for the Nazis, the Russians liberated it in 1944 and their plans were thwarted.

In a way, though, the environs around Lublin are more upsetting than the camp. Jews once lived

Abandoned and desecrated synagogue in Krakow

Detail of cemetery wall constructed from vandalized gravestones

everywhere—but no more. They were rounded up and killed in the local cemetery, in the nearby woods, and, of course, in the extermination camps. Now the whole area is *Judenrein*, and in place of the Jews are the Poles—many of whom seem brutal, uncouth, and coarse and have provoked an unaccountable hatred in me. I know they'd been victimized by the Nazis as well, but still, they occupy the houses of, were enriched by the property of, and now study the culture of the murdered Jews.

Lublin, Poland

Tour buses at Majdanek outside of Lublin, Poland, 1987
Like Auschwitz, Majdanek is on the tourist route. There was something terribly unnerving about seeing all the buses lined up.

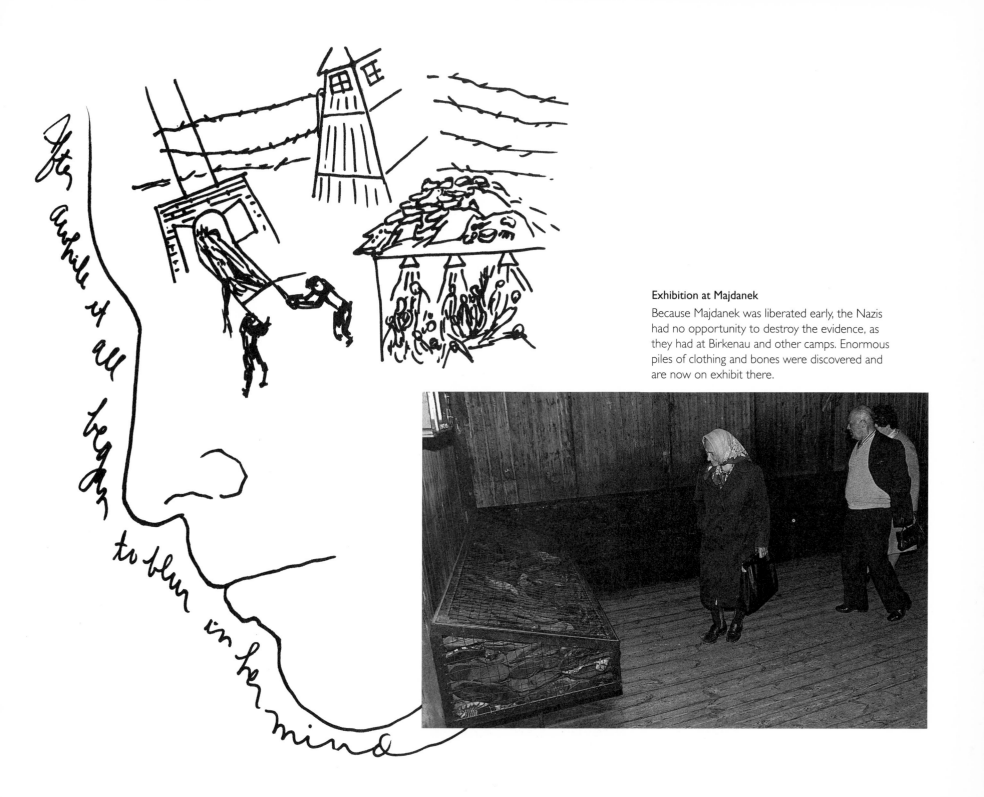

It all began to blur in her mind

Exhibition at Majdanek

Because Majdanek was liberated early, the Nazis had no opportunity to destroy the evidence, as they had at Birkenau and other camps. Enormous piles of clothing and bones were discovered and are now on exhibit there.

As Harvey Mudd said in his long poem, Treblinka is
the saddest place in the world. It is out in the middle of nowhere; the Nazis chose the site well. The
people who lived here probably neither knew nor
cared about what was going on, although I've been
told that the smell of burning bodies could be dis-
cerned for miles around. We'd thought that the
markers commemorating the crimes of this extermination camp were all inscribed with the names
of the Jewish communities whose residents were
murdered here. The names of a few towns were
carved on some of the larger stones, but most of
them were blank, as blank as the stares we received
from our guides at Auschwitz when we mentioned
that we were Jews.

And even though most of those killed at Treblinka were Jewish, there were no Stars of David or
any reference whatsoever to the Jewish victims in
any of the literature. Realizing that even in death
Jewish identity was being destroyed, I burst into
tears, and during our entire stay at Treblinka I just
cried and cried.

Treblinka, Poland

There are 17,000 stone markers at the memorial at
Treblinka, most of them uninscribed. They surround a
forty-foot obelisk.

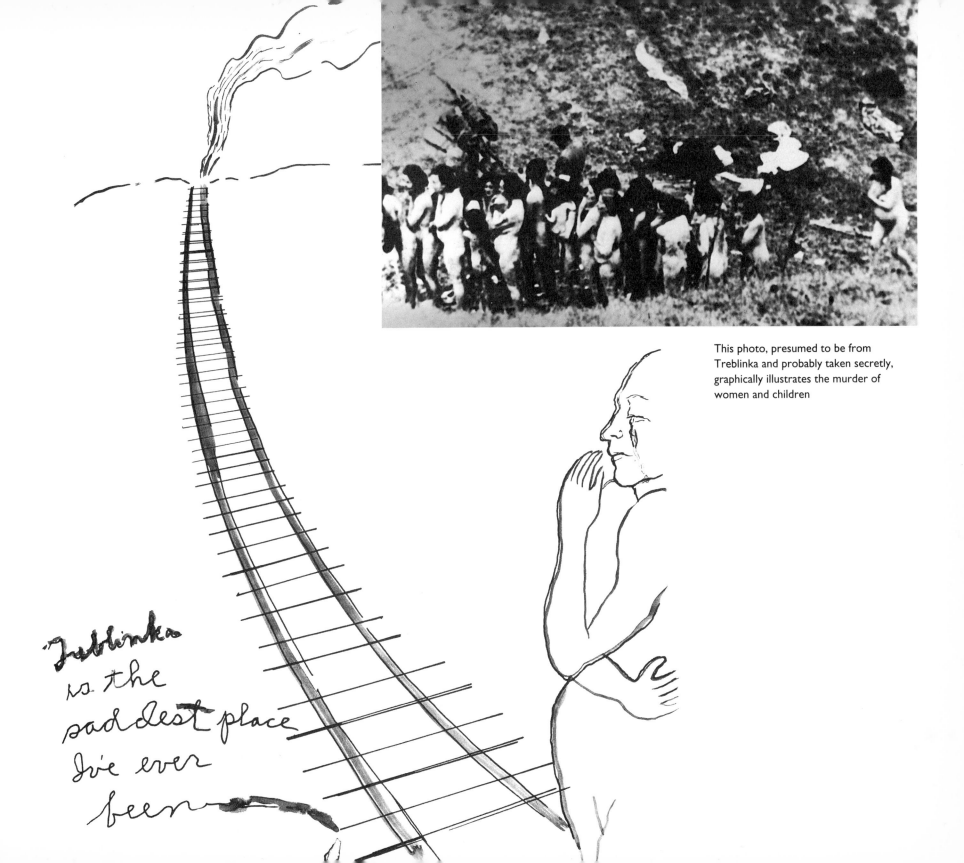

This photo, presumed to be from Treblinka and probably taken secretly, graphically illustrates the murder of women and children

"Treblinka
is the
saddest place
I've ever
been"

Warsaw is not as bad as I'd imagined it would be. Although the postwar architecture is dreary, the streets are broad and full of trees and the city seems quite lively, given the standards of eastern Europe so far.

We wandered around the old Jewish ghetto, which was destroyed by the Nazis. There's almost nothing left to see in terms of what Jewish life was like here. At least in Krakow and Prague, remnants were still evident.

We spent a day in the archives of the Jewish Historical Institute and saw an incredibly powerful series of more than one hundred and fifty drawings by a Gentile, Joseph Charyton, done ten years after the war. He documented what he had witnessed: the rounding up, torture, and murder of all the Jews in his town in images that are vivid and profound.

On Wednesday we fly to Leningrad.

Warsaw, Poland

ABOVE RIGHT: Josef Charyton; from a remarkable series of drawings

RIGHT: All that remains of the Warsaw ghetto

June

We're back from the USSR, staying near the border between Poland and East Germany. I did not bring my journal or sketchbook to the USSR because I'd been frightened by things people said. Several people suggested that we might be harassed at the border and that our personal materials might be confiscated. I didn't want to lose all my notes and drawings, so I left them in Warsaw.

As it turned out, the customs agent went through everything in my carry-on bag including the catalogs of my work that I'd brought to give away. Then our compartment on the train was brusquely searched on our way back from Vilna to Warsaw, where we picked up our car. The soldiers even looked under the seat cushions, though I have no idea what they were hunting for.

Nonetheless, our ten-day trip to the Soviet Union was absolutely fascinating. The people we met were incredibly generous, sharing time, information, and their hearts. The way we were welcomed into Jewish homes everywhere we went gave us a real sense of belonging to an international community.

We had been given the name of Boris Kalman, a *refusnik* in Leningrad, whom we finally reached by phone. We had to call from an anonymous pay phone blocks away from the hotel, then meet him at a subway stop. We walked with him to his apartment, where he beseeched us to keep quiet until we were safely behind the door.

He conveyed a lot about the history of Jews in the Soviet Union and put us in touch with Jews in

Warsaw cemetery, which is slowly being restored by the small Jewish community

At first, we thought Leningrad was very beautiful ... like Venice... and it is. But then we wondered: What happened to all the JEWS?

Passport of *refusnik* Boris Kalman, which refers to Judaism as a nationality, like Latvian or Georgian

Temple gate at Leningrad (now St. Petersburg), 1987

When we asked for directions to the synagogue at the hotel, we were sent to a Russian Orthodox temple. After wandering around the neighborhood, we finally stumbled upon the Jewish synagogue, which was locked.

Latvia and Lithuania. In Riga we met a wonderful *refusnik* and his family, who gave us a very welcome home-cooked meal, a lot of information about what had befallen the Jews of Riga, and a tour around the remains of the former ghetto, where, as we had come to expect, there was no mention of Jewish history.

From there we went to Vilna, in Lithuania, where we had an amazing experience. At the synagogue we met a young Jew, Jacob Schekter, who, like Henry Halkowski, was entirely self-educated in Jewish religion, history, and culture. Although there are millions of Jews in the Soviet Union, they were only allowed to practice privately. Before *glasnost*, any attempt to extend Jewish life into a public sphere was met with harassment, punishment, and even imprisonment. Nevertheless, there were thousands of Jews who were insisting on their right to know their own history and publicly acknowledge their identities. Meeting some of them was an inspiring experience.

Jacob showed us around the former ghettos and took us to the site of the home and school of the Vilna Gaon. He then took us to the Jewish cemetery, where he miraculously produced a key to my ancestor's tomb. As I stood inside the mausoleum,

ABOVE RIGHT: Entrance to Salapilis, outside Riga
The enormous "official" monument at Salapilis commemorates the suffering of the Latvian people. No mention is made of the Jews or the complicity of the Latvians. The phrase on the wall reads: "Behind this wall, the Earth moans."

BELOW RIGHT: Jewish memorial
Jews erected this small memorial at an obscure site outside Riga. Although it was illegal to use Yiddish, they did so, unveiling the monument in the presence of Western media in an effort to guarantee its safety.

Interior of Vilna temple, which is being painstakingly restored

Trying to capture my feelings when we saw the tomb of the Vilna Gaon, which had been moved and restored after the war

I wondered what my father would think if he could see me there. It had indeed been a long journey from the ignorance of my childhood to that moment when I fully connected with both the richness and the sadness of my personal heritage as a Jew.

Vilna, Kovno, and Riga: towns where the population had been almost 40 percent Jewish and where now there is almost no evidence of Jewish life or history. In all three cities, as in Babi Yar and too many other sites, the Jews had been massacred. When the Nazis invaded Russia, they simply rounded up the Jews as they went—sometimes killing them immediately, other times ghettoizing them first, then marching them to the woods where, in two or three days, tens of thousands would be murdered in cold blood.

In Latvia and Lithuania, as in Poland, the local populace, supervised by the SS, actively participated in the killings. That's why it was so difficult to deal with all the sorrowful memorials to the "patriots" of those countries. Not that the Slavs, the Poles, the Lithuanians, the Latvians, and others did not suffer under the Nazi regime. But they also collaborated in the destruction of European Jewry and the subsequent distortion and eradication of the history of what had taken place. By the time we went to Ponar, the woods outside Vilna where thousands of Jews had been massacred, our sorrow was so great it was hard to bear.

All in all, the USSR was an entangled experience: fascinating, frustrating, confusing, thrilling, painful, informative, and puzzling. Now I want to read historical books, fiction, and everything I can get my hands on. I feel so frustrated that I can't get any literature here in the East except propaganda or "accepted" material. It's amazing how little I, a "red diaper" baby, actually know about life in the Soviet Union.

The path into the forest of Ponar, where the Jews of Vilna were destroyed—and, with them, the thousand-year tradition of European Jewry

---

The train ride from Vilna to Warsaw was the reverse of the trip taken by the Jews who had been transported to their deaths. At the border between the USSR and Poland we, like they, were stopped for hours while the wheels of the train were changed to accommodate the different-size tracks. I've never read anything about that; imagine how terror-inspiring it must have been.

Tomorrow we leave this dreary country and drive to West Berlin. Then we cross over to East Germany to see Ravensbruck, Sachsenhausen, and Buchenwald.

Gdansk, Poland

Today we went to Ravensbruck, the only women's concentration camp (there were, of course, female slave-labor camps). The exhibition at Ravensbruck was very poignant: something about the scale of the women's clothing and the small objects they'd made, many of them embroidered pieces for their children.

I was wild to get into the archives, and at first the officials said we could see them the following day. We went back with our guide (you're not allowed to travel without one in East Germany), only to be informed we'd made the trip in vain. It was primarily a question of bureaucracy, or at least that's what they implied. But I was horribly disappointed at not being able to investigate the sole women's archive.

East Berlin, Germany

Because we couldn't get into the Ravensbruck archives, we spent most of the day at Sachsenhausen,

Sign on road near
Sachsenhausen
showing route of
death march

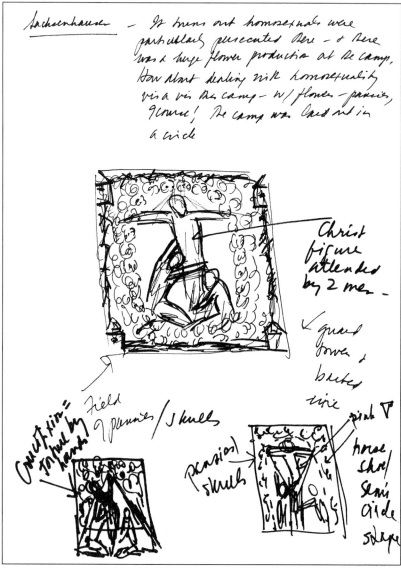

Historic photo of
death march

the camp where many homosexuals were imprisoned, tortured, and/or worked to death. The camp had a reputation for having beautiful flowerbeds, tended, of course, by the prisoners.

By now all these camps are blurring: the barracks, the guard towers, the barbed wire. And the stench: It's probably something we imagine, but they all seem to smell like burning flesh.

East Berlin, Germany

It rained again today, which it's done throughout the trip—in fact, almost every day we've visited a concentration camp. I *hated* Buchenwald. It's been completely rebuilt, with these absolutely Nazi-like monuments and oppressive architectural structures that make the entire place seem utterly surreal.

The exhibits present a barrage of antifascist, anticapitalist propaganda, implying that all Germans were members of the resistance and that "all the Nazis had emigrated to the West." And of course they barely mention the word *Jew*.

One of the museum curators showed us around the archives. She had assembled a considerable amount of prisoner art for us to examine, some of it quite good. The work demonstrated that here, as in many of the camps, there was an ongoing struggle to maintain a cultural life—which was a form of spiritual resistance, as art often is.

Weimar, Germany

Back in the West with a great sense of relief. Bergen-Belsen is definitely the best memorial site we've seen; it was established by an association of Jewish survivors, who formed an organization after the camp was liberated. For five years Belsen served as a refugee camp for Jews. It was, as one survivor put it, the last *shtetl* in Europe. Unlike most of the

BELOW: *In Memory of the Millions*, 1987; photography, sprayed acrylic, and oil on photolinen, 12" x 16"

This was our first effort at combining painting and photography on photolinen.

other memorials, it has no hidden agenda—except to honor the dead.

West Berlin, Germany

July

We're home; I'm exhausted. I can't believe we made this trip. It is as if we descended into a deep, dark place and came out of it into the light. I wonder if the fights Donald and I had related to the stress of the trip. Now that I'm on the other side of it, I can't believe I/we survived. It's Independence Day—how fitting to return today. As I said to the immigration clerk when he asked for my passport, "How about if we just sing 'America the Beautiful'?" This trip certainly taught us how lucky we are to live here.

Santa Fe, NM

1988

November

I've been in the studio for months and didn't really want to leave, but our travels would not have been complete without a trip to Israel, where neither of us had ever been. People told us that we couldn't imagine what it's like being in a country that is almost all Jewish. And they were right: It *is* astonishing. We're staying in an apartment in the Old City, which is full of young, born-again American Jews. The first evening we were here we went out to dinner with two of them. The young man refused to shake my hand, which aggravated me. He explained that he wasn't "prejudiced against women" but was only "following God's law." I said I couldn't accept that God wanted

View of Jerusalem showing Old City between the Jewish cemetery (in the foreground) and the new, white city (behind)

him to do something that made me feel like a piece of dirt.

The next day we toured the Old City and went to the Western Wall, which was both overwhelming and unsettling. We were surprised by the number of soldiers everywhere and greatly moved by the tiny *kvitels* (messages to God) pressed into the cracks of the Wall. It was, however, distressing to realize the strict segregation of the sexes. On the men's side there's a lot of joyful praying, especially on Shabbat; but on the women's side it's silent and subdued. Moreover, they all seem to accept praying to a male God, which many of us American women can no longer do.

Then we visited the Hasidic section of Jerusalem, and Donald and I couldn't believe our eyes. When we were in Vilna, Warsaw, or Prague, we had to try and imagine what Jewish life had been like. We had no idea that the old *shtetl* existence had been recreated here in Israel in areas like Meah Shearim. It is full of men in dark clothes and women wearing "modest dress"—a euphemism for, to my eyes, unattractive and body-concealing garments. What really got to me were the women with shaved heads. As Donald remarked, it's a pretty direct way of depriving women of their identity.

Jerusalem, Israel

Today we wanted to walk around the Muslim section of the Old City but couldn't, because there was a strike and everything Arab was closed. Instead we went back to the Hasidic area of town to shop on the pretext that we wanted to start accumulating gifts to take home. In actuality, we wanted to wander around, because the fundamentalist aspect of Jewish life was totally unknown and utterly fascinating to us. It raised a lot of questions; I'd never found fundamentalism the least bit interesting in its Christian or Muslim guises. So why were we so mesmerized by the Jewish version of what, to us, is an antiquated and oppressive lifestyle, especially for women?

While we were there I was accosted by a young Hasid who was upset that I was wearing jeans (rather than a long skirt) and no scarf. The guy said that "unlike Russia, Israel is a free country but it was 'disrespectful' of me to appear in modern garb." I tried to point out that I had worn the same outfit in the USSR and no one had hassled me there, but it was to no avail.

Jerusalem, Israel

The women sit in tunnels, isolated from the men's section by an iron gate and curtain

Underneath the buildings adjacent to the Wall, 1988
Among the Orthodox Jews of Israel, men and women are strictly separated and many activities are virtually closed to women.

Streets of Vilna, Lithuania, 1987

Streets of Meah Shearim, Jerusalem, 1988

I am sitting in the car in the rain in Meah Shearim, waiting for Donald to finish photographing. I feel ridiculous; in order to blend in this time I wore a long dress and a scarf. As soon as I put on these clothes I immediately felt subdued, as if I were "disappearing" into my "uniform"—and this even with a scarf that doesn't completely cover my hair and a dress that, compared to what the women here wear, still has a lot of individuality.

Jerusalem, Israel

Today we toured Galilee, driving through Haifa and Akko, stopping in Safed, a lovely old Sephardic community that is now an art colony. The old town of Tiberius, which I adored, was built by the madman Herod. It is a very old cabalistic center, and there are many beautiful historic sites here, including a number of old Sephardic temples.

Before leaving Jerusalem we went to the home of Pinchus and Shoshone Freiberg for Shabbat. We had a terrific evening: a real sharing, despite everyone trying to convince us to move to Israel and make *aliyah* (become Israeli citizens). I confessed to many of the conflicts I've been feeling about the terrible contradictions here: the oppression of the Palestinians; the resurgence of traditional religion, with its patriarchal nature intact; the second-class status of women; the general sexism; and, of course, the military presence everywhere. I've come to understand its necessity but it still unnerves me, particularly seeing schoolchildren on field trips accompanied by men with rifles.

The evening also stimulated memories of my childhood, as well as the incredibly warm moments

The entrance to Meah Shearim, which bears a sign warning women about appropriate dress

we'd shared with Jews in Germany, Czechoslovakia, Latvia, and Lithuania. It gave me such a sense of international community, as well as the idea for an image of the Jewish Shabbat experience as a metaphor for human sharing on a global level.

Tiberius, Israel

Yesterday we spent the day at Yad Vashem. I had a long discussion with the museum director about the trivialization of the Holocaust, an issue that keeps coming up in discussions with many members of the Jewish community when the idea of comparing the Holocaust to any other historic event is suggested. It's an important point for Holocaust scholars and I have to find a way to deal with it, although outside the Jewish community people make these types of comparisons all the time, sometimes quite inappropriately.

We saw some incredible examples of micrography (the art of tiny writing), which is used in *mezzuzahs* (small parchment scrolls inscribed with a biblical passage and affixed to the doorposts in Jewish homes) and *tefillin* (little boxes that hold Old Testament writings, which are bound to the forehead and left arm during morning prayer). I was especially struck by a micrographic image of Jerusalem, where what appeared as a drawing was actually a letter to be read. I've always been attracted to coded or disguised visual forms, and I found micrography absolutely fascinating the first time I encountered it a few years ago in an exhibition about Jewish folk art. I even got a lesson in it from Jacob el Hanani, an artist and modern-day micrographer in New York. Micrography is the only craft actually invented by Jews and not adapted from their host country. I'd like to find a way to incorporate it into some of the images.

Jerusalem, Israel

Tel Aviv, 1988

We spent the day sightseeing around Tel Aviv, which is a big, secular city, in great contrast to Jerusalem, where there's such a strong religious presence. Today we read an article in the *Jerusalem Post* that gave the U.S. election results; there was a list of all the Jews who'd been elected to office, something I've never seen in America. All this "Jewish consciousness" sometimes gets to be just too much.

Tomorrow we go to the Diaspora Museum, and soon we'll be going home. We've certainly traveled a lot of miles on our Jewish quest.

Tel Aviv, Israel

The Diaspora Museum, which tells the history of the Jewish people, was truly remarkable: in scale, concept, and diversity. It enriched our understanding of the grandeur of Jewish history and reinforced our hard-earned sense of pride in our heritage.

Tel Aviv, Israel

Ancient olive groves in the verdant valley of Galilee

December

I keep thinking about Israel; our experiences there raised many questions that I haven't yet resolved. On the one hand, there was something very appealing about the sense of "belonging," which makes me want to go back. But I'm not sure whether I believe in the whole notion of statehood; and if not, what's the alternative? How can a people have an identity and a sense of security without resorting to being an armed state? Does one have to become an oppressor in order to protect oneself from oppression?

When I shared my conflicts with Michael Nutkiewicz (one of our advisors who'd become our friend during the course of the project), he responded by saying that "Israel would evolve into the Zionist ideal of a democratic, egalitarian country that many of us long for." I hope he's right.

In the meantime I am eager to get back into the studio and make the images that are now filling my mind. This has been a long and arduous education—physically, emotionally, and intellectually—and one that I hope Donald and I can fully translate into a meaningful body of art.

Santa Fe, NM

PART THREE

Transformation

Study of the Holocaust, the ultimate realm of
death, is in a profound way also the study of life,
for it exhibits the extremes of human nature. . . .
By itself, the Holocaust is an unmitigated disaster;
it is only the application to it of the intelligence and
the imagination that can transform it into tragedy,
that is, an event upon which some pattern of
meaning, however grim, can be imposed.

—Yehuda Bauer

Our travels dramatically broadened and deepened our understanding of the Holocaust, which resulted in our enlarging our goals and expanding the focus of the art we wanted to make. By the time we returned from Europe, I was ready to start working in the studio. I had many ideas, beginning with *The Fall*, the large tapestry that places the Holocaust in a historic context. Because the weaving required five years, I could not include photographs of the finished work in the book. Instead, I have reproduced the painted cartoon and a detail of a completed section of the tapestry.

The concept for the exhibition, which, in addition to the tapestry, contains twelve painting-photo combines and the stained glass pieces (the logo and *Rainbow Shabbat*), evolved slowly over a span of almost six years: from the summer of 1987 until early 1993. During that time I continued doing research, always moving out from the base of the Holocaust. For example, when we approached the subject of children, I reviewed the literature on the experiences of children in the Holocaust, then expanded my historic research to examine the conditions under which many children presently live. I did this type of investigation for each of the subject areas that we explored; our conclusions are best transmitted through the art reproduced in the last section of the book. They say that a picture is worth a thousand words, and Donald and I spent so many years on the art because we believed it was the only form through which our ideas could be fully conveyed.

Along with my studies, artmaking, and writing, Donald and I worked with the Spertus Museum and other institutions to develop the exhibition tour and related programming. We did ongoing fundraising, sent out regular newsletters, and continued traveling in order to expand our image research. We also gave slide presentations about our work, both in the studio and around the country. The logistics of a big project were familiar to me, although in the past I'd had a large staff; this time there was primarily only Donald and me. Moreover, as the years passed, I became quite exhausted by the material and the struggle to transform it into art.

We'd originally planned to complete the *Holocaust Project* by 1990, but it became clear within a short time that the work was going to be exceedingly protracted. Each image required months and sometimes years of development, including focused research, photo tests, drawings, and scale models. The finished works demanded considerable emotional stamina to execute, as well as uninterrupted time. Between paintings, I tended to catch up on the nonartistic tasks that are essential to a complex project and also to prepare myself psychologically for the next image. I would accomplish this by taking breaks from my arduous daily painting schedule, working instead on research and doing visual notations and preliminary sketches in order to develop a clear idea of what I next wanted to create.

The long process of translating the information, our experiences, ideas, and perspective into a body of art is described in this section of the book. The images are grouped in the sequence in which they were created, which is different from the way they're presented in the exhibition. In the show they are installed in subject-matter areas, but I couldn't reorganize my journal writing to accommodate the philosophical structure of the exhibition.

The Fall

1987

July

'm working on *The Fall*, after having done studies and a small scale-model drawing. I've been slowly enlarging the image. Now I'm working at two-thirds scale, solving some of the visual problems: The content was all there, but what works at six inches doesn't work at six feet, so I needed an intermediary step before starting the full-scale cartoon.

I thought a long time about the narrative structure of this image. I wanted to start with a representation of "the battle of the sexes" as a metaphor for the historic defeat of matriarchy and the rise of patriarchy. The work will then visually chronicle the conquest of women and nature and the gradual development of male-dominated religion and society and then explore some of the tragic consequences of the Scientific and Industrial revolutions. I want to demonstrate visually how assembly-line techniques, originally used to "process" animals, were eventually applied to human beings. I'm also trying to portray the historic overlaps between antifeminism and anti-Semitism in a second strata of iconography emanating from the center image.

I chose tapestry, which I believe is the perfect technique for this subject matter, because I want to emphasize how the Holocaust grew out of the very fabric of Western civilization. I particularly like the irony of using a modified Aubusson method of weaving, because women were excluded from the High Renaissance Aubusson and Gobelin workshops.

Santa Fe, NM

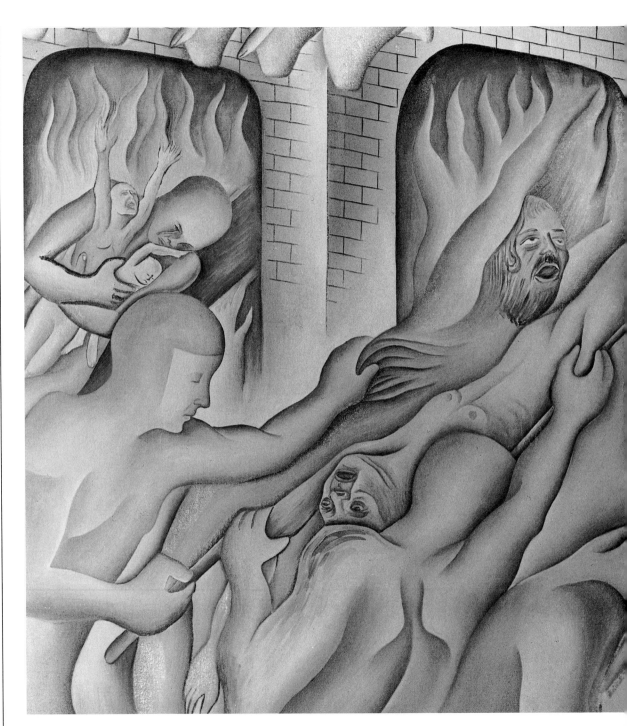

Detail, lower right section of cartoon for *The Fall* (see COLOR PLATES 1 and 2)

October

I've been working for months on the full-scale painted tapestry cartoon, and the end is not yet in sight; at least another ten days before the spraying and flat painting are done and I can start the oil painting. I keep changing the date for Audrey to come here to work with me. We have to choose thread colors for some preliminary weaving tests and also do a black-and-white line drawing that she can stitch to the warp as her weaving guide. The cartoon is going well, though a terrible sadness sometimes overtakes me as a result of being with the darkness of the subject matter. The only thing that helps is my belief that the story I'm telling in this work is, if not literally, then at least symbolically true.

In the early mornings I continue my research. I'm making my way through *Operation Reinhard*, a very painful book on the hideous plan used to implement the Final Solution at the death camps of Treblinka, Belzec, Chelmno, and Sobibor. It's so hard to read that even with my hard-won level of tolerance, I can only bear forty-five minutes a day.

Santa Fe, NM

Audrey was here for a few days to help me with the cartoon, but I doubt that it will be done before Thanksgiving, despite the fact that I'm working long hours, six days a week. I had to make some changes in order to accomodate the technical limits of weaving, but even so I've given Audrey a formidable challenge.

I've stopped reading for a while; that book on the Nazi killing operation at the extermination camps really depressed me. And I couldn't

Detail, *Pergammon Altar* (Staatliche Museum, Berlin, Germany)

I based the first section of *The Fall* on the famous *Pergammon Altar*, which, like other friezes of the Greek period, presents the mythological battle between the Amazons and the Giants—an image that many feminist scholars believe to be based upon the struggle between ancient matriarchal, goddess-worshiping cultures and the emerging patriarchal, Indo-European warrior societies that overpowered them.

Study for *The Fall*, 1987; ink on paper, 8" x 11"

Spraying the cartoon for *The Fall*, Summer 1987

The central image in *The Fall* juxtaposes a reinterpretation of Leonardo's *Vetruvian Man* with a
representation of the Scientific Revolution in the
form of images of the "rational" mind and the
Copernican universe. As Carolyn Merchant
states in *The Death of Nature:* "Copernicus dis-
placed the female earth from the center and
replaced it with the masculine sun"—a reflection
of the increasingly mechanistic and misogynist
views of the sixteenth and seventeenth centuries.

I altered Leonardo's historic figure to show
it for what I believe it truly embodies: that moment in human history when men consolidated
patriarchal power through force and were able
to represent themselves through art, literature,
and history as the "measure" of all reality.

handle any more emotional drain than the
painting requires. Everyone keeps asking "How is
the project doing?" Fine, I say; it's moving
along—by inches or even millimeters. What can I
say? *Art is slow!*

Santa Fe, NM

November

It's Thanksgiving Day and I suppose I should give
thanks that, after four months, I'm almost done
with the cartoon. I've gotten into the last scene
and just have the scene with the *Sonderkommando*
(the Jewish prisoners who worked in the crematoria) to finish, which I think I can do in three days.
I've completed the section of the people being
shoveled into the ovens, an excruciating image to
paint. I had the most unusual experience during
the days of working on it: I felt convinced I was
bearing witness to the victims' suffering and to
their silent martyrdom, despite the fact that I
wasn't actually there.

I don't exactly know *how* I knew what to paint—
I just knew; and I felt that, if I trusted myself, my
hand would guide me—and it did. But I kept wondering: How did it fall on me to articulate this terrible human reality? And yet I *know* it is what I was
meant to do.

I think the translation of the cartoon into tapestry will be a good step, as it will provide a certain
distance and, at the same time, the warmth of
wool, which will soften the image.

December

I've finished the cartoon—finally. What a relief! It
was painful working on the last scenes; I represented the people as alive, screaming and protesting—
in contrast to the usual Holocaust paintings of
shuffling victims, which always upset me. If one
reads the literature, one discovers that the "victims" did everything that people do: some submit-
ted, others tried to commit sabotage, many actively
resisted; and then, I suppose, there were those who
just tried to survive.

Santa Fe, NM

Anti-Semitism / Antifeminism

One of the discoveries I made during my research on anti-Semitism was the similarities in language between these texts and some of the medieval writings I'd encountered when I was studying women's history, most notably the *Malleus Maleficarum* (*The Hammer of the Witches*), which explained how to identify a witch. I was struck by how similar modern anti-Semitic writings seemed to be to the rantings of these earlier texts.

The specifically antifeminist nature of the witch trials is only now beginning to be acknowledged in Western scholarship, but it was clear to me many years ago, particularly after learning that 85 percent of the witches burned during the Middle Ages were women.

As Carolyn Merchant wrote recently in *The Death of Nature*:

The control and the maintenance of the social order and women's place within it was one of the many complex and varied reasons for the witch trials.

When witch-burnings were commonplace throughout Europe, Jews and witches were often lumped together, both described as "creatures of Satan." The introduction of the Jew badge (upon which Hitler based the yellow star) coincided with medieval accusations of anti-Christian and magical practices and the start of the Inquisition. Allegations of poisoning, desecration of the host, and the consumption and other use of Christian blood and flesh were all leveled against witches and heretics before they were applied to Jews. Moreover, there were frequently iconographic similarities, as Joshua Trachtenberg points out in *The Devil and the Jews*:

It is instructive to compare the graphic representations of the sorcerer and the witch in medieval art, which consistently emphasizes their demonic characteristics—horns, tails, claws, cloven hoof, and the attendant demon or devils—with pictures of the Jew. The devil appeared to his devotees in the shape of an animal; the tomcat . . . became a goat in the later accounts of witchcraft and there are numberless tales and pictures of goats receiving the adulation of witches and sorcerers and serving them on their favorite mount. . . . The same habits were ascribed to the Jewish people as a whole . . . and . . . Jews are occasionally specifically represented as sorcerers and witches, clearly identified by the Jew badge.

Many of the women burned as witches were lay healers, and their deaths wiped out female competition with the new "profession" of medicine, from which women were entirely excluded. The campaign against female lay healers later targeted Jewish doctors. By the sixteenth century no slander was too outrageous to be leveled against Jews practicing medicine, and the goal was the same as in the witch trials: to limit competition by, in this case, restricting the number of Jewish doctors.

Anti-Semitism and antifeminism coincided again in the nineteenth-century eugenic theories that established the "scientific base" for Nazi attitudes. As Robert Proctor writes in *Racial Hygiene*:

In the case of women and Jews, two groups important for Nazi racial science, the results of supposedly objective science were used both to describe their nature (they are irrational or emotional) and to make certain claims about their ability to do science (their irrationality makes them unable to practice good science) and by extension medicine, from which Jews were once again purged.

Interestingly, according to Proctor, the Nuremberg laws, which distinguished between German "citizens" and "residents" ("residents" were excluded from the privileges of citizenry), applied to both Jews and single women. When Hitler took power in 1933, Germany had the largest feminist movement in the world, which the Nazis managed to virtually eliminate.

The historic association between women and Jews, as members of stigmatized groups, is developed in the stream of imagery in the upper-right section of tapestry, which begins with an image of the Egyptian goddess Neith, the goddess of spinning, who is said to have taught the textile arts to women. The takeover of this goddess-given gift is represented in the lower strata in the image of a once-proud woman, now reduced to a wage slave at a totally mechanized job. The spinning jenny (spinning was originally the province of independent "spinsters") was the first machine of the Industrial Revolution. Ironically, it was primarily women who were hired to run them in the early factories.

The burning of witches is linked to the Holocaust through references to such shared symbols as a goat and horns. United by a similar victimization, the woman and the Jew, each depicted with their particular "stigmata," are being burned as part of a ritual sacrifice of those labeled "demonic." Sadly, although the fiery stakes of the Inquisition are quenched and the crematoria of the Holocaust destroyed, woman-hating and anti-Semitism are still with us today.

J.C.

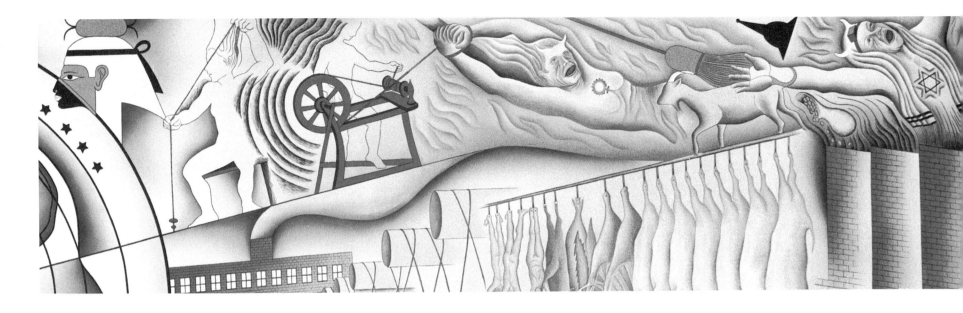

Detail, upper right section of cartoon for *The Fall*

Section of an early seventeenth-century engraving based on a popular medieval anti-Semitic theme.

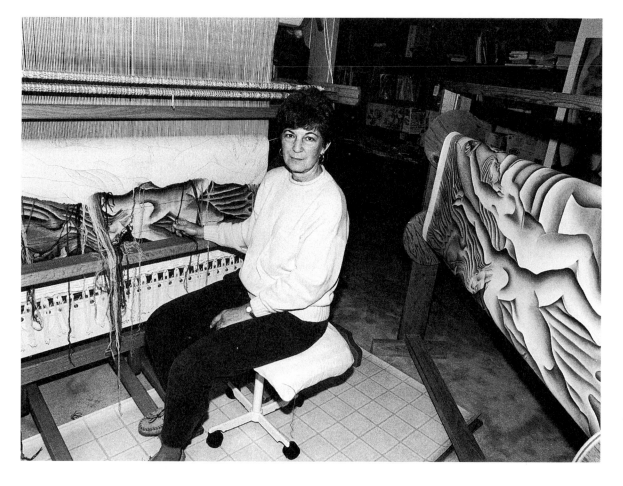

Audrey Cowan at her loom next to the cartoon, which is rolled on a specially constructed frame; Los Angeles, CA, 1989

Tapestry Technique

"I've studied and made art since I was five years old and, in addition to drawing and painting, done much of what is considered traditional women's handwork. However, it wasn't until I discovered weaving that I found the medium I love. Although I had been weaving for a number of years, my first introduction to traditional Aubusson weaving came at the San Francisco Tapestry Workshop, where the entryway banners for *The Dinner Party* were executed. The workshop, established by Jean-Pierre Larochette, taught this technique for the first time in the United States.

"Aubusson tapestry gets its name from Aubusson, France, where it is known to have been practiced as early as the fourteenth century, though its exact origin is unclear. Generations of weavers preserved this craft through many centuries, and recently there has been a revival of both Aubusson and the high-warp Gobelin technique, which was used for such masterworks as the Unicorn and Cluny cycles.

"The principles of high-warp and low-warp weaving are exactly the same; technically speaking, there is no real difference. Generally, high-warp weavers can check their work by means of a mirror set up in front of the loom, as the weaving in both cases is done from the

back. I modified this process in a number of ways. First, I weave from the front so I can see what I'm doing, and second, I work on an upright rather than a horizontal loom, because it allows me a clearer view of the black-and-white outline of the cartoon.

"Over the fifteen years we've been collaborating, Judy and I have developed a unique process involving, first, her creation of a full-scale color cartoon (derived from the Italian word *cartoni*, which means 'paper,' used by the weaver as a guide), then my translation of her design. We often discuss the image as Judy is developing it so I can advise her, though inevitably she gives me some significant technical challenges.

"Tapestry is basically composed of a warp (the vertical skeleton structure, which disappears completely beneath the body of the fabric) and a weft (made up of the different-colored threads forming the decorative scheme, plaited through the warp horizontally). The horizontal-vertical structure of tapestry limits aspects of design, and I try to help Judy accommodate her ideas to these constraints.

"After she completes the cartoon, we do a detailed black-and-white tracing, which I stitch to the warp so that it acts as a linear guide for my work. I have a special frame for the cartoon, which I can move as I roll the tapestry, referring to it for my color decisions. Interpreting Judy's painting using the rich tones of wool provides me with the most satisfying aspect of our collaboration.

"Before I begin weaving Judy and I discuss her overall intentions, and I try to understand what she is trying to express in order to fuse our goals. We select a range of yarn colors to form my 'palette,' and I do small samples as we go along. As the work progresses, we review it

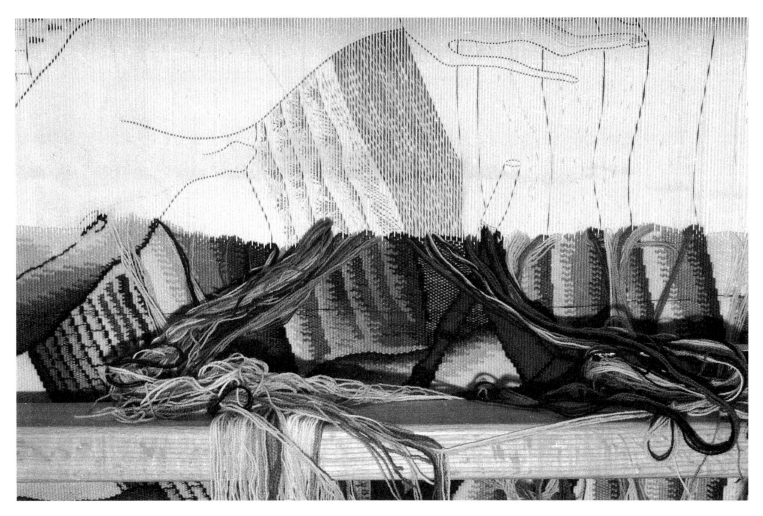

Tapestry on loom,
showing detail of weaving,
warp threads, and
line-drawing guide

and supplement the colors. We generally use Pater-nayan hundred-percent virgin wool crewel yarns, aug-mented by naturally dyed aurora silks in three weights: chenille, plied, and singles.

"The warp is Fiskgarn 12/12 unbleached cotton with ten warps to the inch and I generally use four threads for the weft, which allows me to essentially paint with the thread. Wherever the imagery becomes extremely detailed, however, I decrease my threads, sometimes us-ing only one in a painstakingly slow technique that should properly be called needle-weaving.

"The Dinner Party was my first opportunity to work with Judy; that was the beginning of a partnership that will, I trust, continue throughout our lifetimes. Our col-laboration affords me the chance to work with an artist in a rather unusual way. In most cases, weavers have very little autonomy over how the painted cartoon is translated. I need to be more of a contributor than such a process entails, and with Judy I can be. Because she is committed to an egalitarian collaborative process, I have chosen to work exclusively with her. We both believe that tapestry can reproduce painting while painting can-

not begin to render the special textures, light reflection, mixtures of color, and warmth of material achievable with woven yarn.

"Each of the weavings on which I've worked has a unique message; we are using a very ancient technique to express what we believe are important contempo-rary ideas. When I began this weaving, it was because, as a Jew, I cared deeply about the subject of the Holocaust. Over the years of the work, I felt (sadly) that the subject matter became increasingly relevant to today's world."

—Audrey Cowan

Bones of Treblinka
Treblinka / Genocide

1987

November

I've been gathering and beginning to examine material for the *Treblinka* images; I have one idea that involves flanking photolinen panels, which will present the "vanished" world of eastern European Jewry under the stones of Treblinka. But first I want to alter the photo of the monument so that it is—as it should have been—inscribed with the names of the communities, towns, and cities that were destroyed. I plan to unite the whole image with a sprayed color fade to create an association with flames.

Santa Fe, NM

December

I've been slowly reading material about the Romanies (Gypsies), thousands of whom were murdered by Hitler and the Reich. It's been difficult to gain an understanding of their culture: They apparently came out of India in the Middle Ages and migrated around the Western world; they've been persecuted, enslaved, and, finally, almost annihilated. I wish I could get a better picture of their customs and traditions but, according to my research, they remain quite mysterious to outsiders.

I've also begun reading about other genocides, like that of the Armenians, who are considered the first victims of genocide in the twentieth century. I

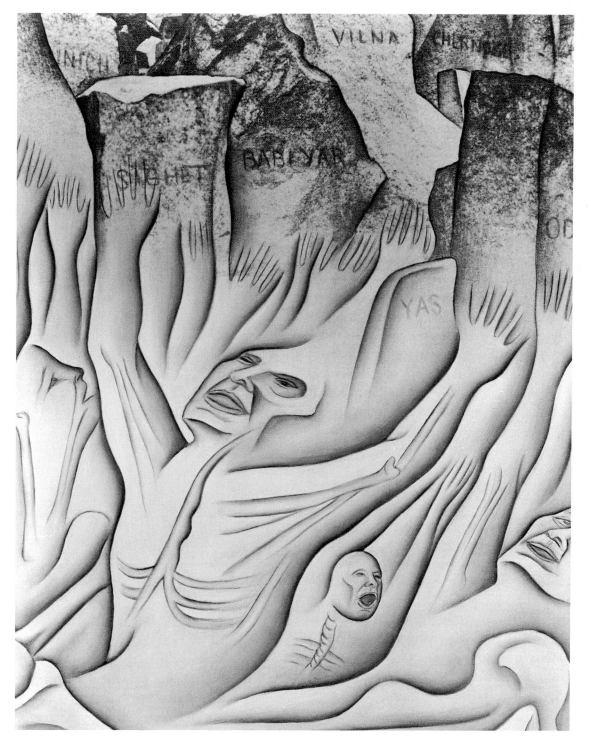

Detail, right panel, *Bones of Treblinka* (see COLOR PLATE 3)

am looking for the link with the Holocaust, I guess, but I don't see it yet.

Santa Fe, NM

1988

January

We're in Australia for *The Dinner Party* exhibition. The other day we visited a small Holocaust museum here in Melbourne, where there is a good-sized community of survivors. It's a survivor-created museum, and an elderly lady (who reminded me of one of my aunts) gave us a tour. Some of the people connected with *The Dinner Party* exhibition were with us, and they were overwhelmed by even this modest exhibition. We often learn quite a lot by going with other people to see Holocaust material. It suggests ways to present our work so that viewers won't be freaked out or turned off.

Being away from home has given me some time to think about whether the Jewish experience can be made to stand for any larger human experience. What is the relationship, for example, between what happened to the Jews and the extermination of the Aborigines in Australia or the Native Americans? What is the difference between the destruction of a people because their land is desired and the Final Solution, and where do you draw the line? From the casual act of plundering someone's territory to the more systematic nature of the Holocaust, there is a profound venality in human beings with which I am only beginning to come to grips.

I'm looking out the window of my hotel. In front of me are the bricks and mortar and totally "unnatural" forms of "modern civilization" that

Detail, micrographic study for *Treblinka / Genocide*

we've imposed upon the land, entirely stripping away the natural landscape. It is very disturbing to realize how much we've destroyed in the process of building civilization and, worse, to understand that most people seem to not even acknowledge or care about what we've done. We've destroyed the landscape, exploited the Earth, wiped out entire species, upset the ecosystem, murdered whole tribes and cultures—why can't we see what we've done and continue to do and stop?

I ran into the writer Germaine Greer here at the hotel. She's very involved with Aborgine rights. She talked about how the Aborigines have gone "mad with grief" at the destruction of their culture, that they are "in mourning" for what they've lost. Something about her description reminded me of Holocaust survivor testimony.

Melbourne, Australia

February

Somewhere in Queensland, Australia, where we were on holiday and I had time and space to reflect, I found the link I've been looking for between the Holocaust and other genocides. I kept thinking about the Aborigines who we saw in all their distress in Alice Springs and how to connect what happened to them and numerous others—the Armenians, Native Americans, et cetera—with what happened to the Jews (though not always in as systematic a way as the extermination of the Jews was enacted).

Recognizing how "modern" civilization is built on top of the destruction of so many other cultures and species resulted in the expansion of the *Treblinka* image in my mind. Now I want the stones of Treblinka to transform into a skyline in the center of the image and to have figures representing vari-

Micrography

In developing my ideas I often did micrographic studies, in which the text communicated the content I was trying to express. Jews generally adapted the visual forms of the countries in which they lived, but micrography was invented by Jews in about the ninth century. It is, of course, usually done in Hebrew, but I used English. The *Treblinka* series includes a number of micrographic works. I incorporated a text I wrote into the rendering of some of the figures; it is based on my research into modern genocide:

In the twentieth century, sixty million women, men, and children from many different races, religious, ethnic groups, nationalities, and social classes, living in many different countries on many of the continents of the world, have died as a result of genocide. This includes the six million Jews, the five hundred thousand European Gypsies, the one and a half million Armenians, the one hundred thousand Brazilian Indians, the one hundred fifty thousand Tibetan Buddhists, the various South American Indian tribes and the one to two million Hindus in East Pakistan and Bangladesh. It does not include the victims of Stalin's death camps which probably numbered in the millions, but nobody knows for sure as the figures have never been released. It also does not count the millions of Cambodians slaughtered by the Khmer Rouge, as that isn't classified as a real genocide, nor is the terrible plight of the Aborigines of Australia, though some would argue that that country, like many others including the United States, is founded on genocide.

These figures also do not include the numbers of creatures and species rendered extinct, nor does it acknowledge the destruction of the rain forests, the depletion of our natural resources, the pollution of our oceans, or the impending loss of the ozone layer. Is it fair to say that the destruction of life on the planet constitutes a form of genocide and that modern civilization is actually built upon many acts of genocide?

—J.C.

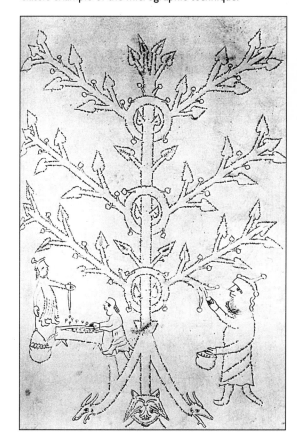

This colophon from a thirteenth-century manuscript is a classic example of the micrographic technique.

ous decimated cultures under the skyline, along with examples of some of the species that have become extinct because of "man's" rapacity.

I've discovered that in the past few hundred years and even today, entire species are being obliterated faster than they can evolve. Between the years 1600 and 1900, species of mammals and birds vanished at the rate of approximately one every four years. In the twentieth century this rate has accelerated to one species every year, and mammals and birds account for only a small percentage of living species. It is estimated that by the end of this century, species will be vanishing at the rate of one hundred per day.

Some people have become offended by the fact that we are suggesting parallels between the destruction of European Jewry and the genocide of other cultures and the mass slaughter of other species. But I believe that it is this larger context of genocide and destruction that created the conditions for the Holocaust and that, in the future, people will look back upon the massacre of other species during the nineteenth and twentieth centuries as being genocidal in nature. But that will become a shared view only when we evolve to the point where we understand that *all* species have the right to coexist on the Earth and that other creatures do not exist merely as means to human ends.

In addition to these images of decimated cultures and extinct species, I intend to place figures on either side of the center panel (under the stones of Treblinka) symbolizing the destruction of eastern European Jewish life. I'm thinking about representing the activities of Jewish men and women on separate panels, like they were/are in Orthodox synagogues.

On the plane home

I've been plowing through books on Jewish history, trying to better understand the nature of the eastern European Jewish experience in preparation for creating the images for the side panels. I must admit that I am having trouble relating to a tradition that excluded women from the most "significant" activity of the culture—that is, Talmudic study. Though women often economically supported the scholarship of their husbands, they were also quite oppressed in the *shtetls*. On the other hand, women enjoyed a level of respect that was greater than that of Gentile women of their same class; it's confusing.

One thing that seems clear is that because Jews suffered discrimination and persecution for centuries, they went through many different political strategies in their efforts to participate fully in societies that often continued to despise them even while interacting with them. A large percentage of the Jews killed during the Holocaust were those who had continued to live traditional Jewish lives, a tradition that was largely destroyed with them, at least in eastern Europe. But how hard it is for me to relate to it: the shaved heads of the women and long sideburns of the men; the dank, dark *yeshivas* where girls weren't allowed; the overlap between religious and secular life. It's all so far away from anything I know.

What about it interests me? It's not a life I'm interested in living, that's for sure; my interest is more theoretical. First, this study is informing me about my roots; second, it's allowing me to explore the whole notion of "differentness" in human society. Clearly, when diversity is denied (as in contemporary Soviet society, where "differentness" has been negated and "sameness" dominates), society becomes stagnant. On the other hand, how much "differentness" can a civilization allow before the structure of the society becomes totally unstable?

And why do people hold on to traditions even when they render them the object of contempt and even destruction?

Frannie Yablonsky (a former *Birth Project* needleworker who, I discovered, has always been extremely interested in the subject of the Holocaust) has done some good research for my image of *shtetl* life, which I'm expanding upon. After I finish my studies, I'll start working on drawings for the side panels of the *Treblinka* triptych. Trying to present female domestic life on one side, male religious life on the other, and, in the center panel, link the destruction of European Jewry with other genocides is an interesting intellectual and visual challenge. I'm eager to get at it.

Santa Fe, NM

I'm reading a book on *shtetl* life called *Life Is with People*, written by a group of anthropologists and sociologists under the direction of Margaret Mead and Ruth Benedict. It's absolutely fascinating—and upsetting. It describes many of the traditions from which I come and explains some of the patterns in my family; it also makes me understand why my father rebelled. It's one thing to study this history from the safe distance I enjoy. It would be quite another to be subject to the practices of traditional Jewish life. My father would have had to study all day long, and I would have had to tend house. There would have been no way for me to be who I am—and not only because I'm a woman; I couldn't even be an artist because of the prohibitions against graven images.

I think I want to use an image of a weeping woman, dressed in traditional black silk and pearls, lighting the Sabbath candles on the women's panel and a man wrapped in a *tallit*, wearing *tefillin* and holding the Torah, for the men's. Beneath them will be scenes from *shtetl* and *cheder* life. I should soon be ready to start working on the drawings; I'm looking forward to it.

Santa Fe, NM

March

After finishing research on eastern European life, I read more on anti-Semitism and plowed through a book called *Why the Jews?*, which portends to answer that question but basically asserts the uniqueness of the Jews as the reason for anti-Semitism. I myself am looking for an answer that gives insight into the larger issues of hatred of the "other."

I just read an astounding book titled *Genocide and the Modern Age*, which really shook me up. According to this book, sixty million people have been the victims of genocide in the twentieth century alone; the twentieth century is, in fact, the *age* of genocide. I can't get that fact out of my mind.

It certainly brings up again the entire argument about whether the Holocaust is unique. Why should the *systematic* slaughter of six million be considered not comparable, worse, or more appalling than the slaughter (deliberate or arbitrary) of fifty-four million others? Is it that those fifty-four million are less important than the six million Jews? Or is it the fact that the *way* they were murdered is different? From whose point of view was the Holocaust unique? Did the fifty-four million other victims of genocide experience their deaths differently from those targeted by the Nazis?

Santa Fe, NM

I did a lot of research and preparatory work this week in the library. I had an idea about which cultures I wanted to include in the center panel but then, as I went along, I changed my mind, primar-

Detail, right panel, *Treblinka/Genocide* (see COLOR PLATE 9)
This *cheder* scene on the bottom of the right panel of the triptych is based on a wood inlay we saw in Kovno.

ily because I didn't like the visual material available about Cambodia. I had been thinking about boat people as an image and then realized they were Vietnamese, not Cambodian, and I really don't want to use an image that raises a red flag immediately, which references to a U.S. "genocide" in Vietnam will certainly do—not that it wasn't genocidal.

I was planning to deal with Native Americans, Aborigines, Africans, Armenians, and Cambodians. Then I started thinking about adding the Romanies to this image, thereby making sure that their particular suffering is acknowledged. It would be difficult to do a separate painting about them, as there is such limited information to draw upon, but they *must* be represented, as they were the only other group specifically targeted for death by Hitler.

By omitting the Cambodians, I can keep the image in the context of Western civilization, which I think is better. I'm all churned up inside and can't think about much else besides this painting.

Santa Fe, NM

I just finished Haing Ngor's book on Cambodia. Somehow, even though I think what happened there was a terrible tragedy, it *was* unlike the Holocaust in that it wasn't motivated by race hatred but, rather, by politics and a struggle for power. In Armenia, however, during the First World War, genocide was clearly the order of the day, and what the Turks did was sickening. The systematic torture and killing of the Jews by the Nazis and the Armenian death marches by the Turks had distinct similarities: Survivor testimonies attest to that. It's just overwhelming to confront the terrible realities of these events. What a scourge the human race can be.

Santa Fe, NM

May

I've worked out the imagery for the two Jewish panels and Donald and I completed the manipulation of the Treblinka photos, adding the names of many of the Jewish communities that were destroyed. Donald will rephotograph them and I'll do some small paintings on photolinen in preparation for the large one. Next I'm going to work on the skyline image.

I've been working on a color study for *Treblinka/ Genocide*, which is what I've decided to call the triptych. Working on the drawing made me realize that I have a definite visual problem: how to go from the black and white of the photos to full color. I haven't resolved it in the drawing—I just adjusted the tones of the drawn stones and skyline to match my color; but when the actual photos are printed on photolinen I won't be able to do that. I need to get onto the fabric to see how to accomplish it. I don't want the color to overwhelm the photo tones, so either the photos will have to be

Combining Painting and Photography

In the *Treblinka* images we established our basic approach to the combining of painting and photography. First, we examined Donald's pictures, choosing those that worked together in terms of alignment, visual rhythm, and overall format. Donald then began manipulating the photos in the darkroom so that the background dropped out and the foreground faded into white. Meanwhile I was developing the skyline profile from photographs of cityscapes.

Donald printed the manipulated photographs of the stones and my line drawing onto matte photo paper, which allows pencil work. I inscribed the names of the towns on the stones, added some shading to enhance the forms, and created a shaded skyline. Donald then rephotographed these and transferred them to the photolinen.

Because these were our first efforts on photolinen, we did many small-scale tests so that Donald could experiment and find the chemicals with which to achieve the proper photo tones. We soon encountered a problem we'd never anticipated: When wet, the photolinen shrinks in one direction and stretches in the other. Since the photos *had* to be printed and stretched wet, Donald spent a considerable amount of time figuring out how to keep the material from distorting the images while also keeping it wrinkle-free.

After many months of trial and error and a number of painted studies aimed at image development, we were ready to try the full-scale work. We received enough donations to build a second, larger darkroom, and Donald mod-

ified one of his enlargers to accommodate what is essentially mural painting. He had special fiberglass tanks built, which required six gallons of photo chemicals per tank. In addition to the printing time, it required two hours to set up and three hours to break down the operation. In order to achieve consistency of both quality and tone, Donald printed all the large prints for each of the images at one time, which often meant he worked for up to eighteen hours at a stretch.

After the *Treblinka* prints were stretched and dried, I sprayed them with an airbrush to create a visual ground for the painted figures, a process I used for most of the later paintings as well. I transferred line drawings of the figures with an opaque projector, then gessoed the areas to be oil painted. Next I began the slow, painstaking task of integrating the painted images with the photographic reality.

As the project developed, we perfected and expanded our process, supplementing it with hand-coloring, silk-screening, and ever-greater manipulation of the photographs. We addressed each image as a new challenge, trying to find the appropriate techniques for expressing that particular subject matter.   —J.C.

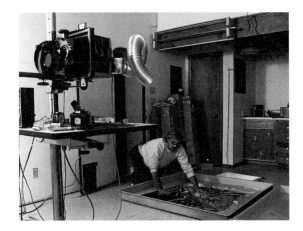

printed quite starkly or I'll have to be really delicate in my paint application. I think spraying will help, as it will allow me to establish a visual space for the figures that relates to the photo tones.

The drawing made me see that I committed one real conceptual error. I wanted all the people and the creatures in the panel to be standing on rivers of blood, but when I did this it didn't work out visually, and besides, I realized that it's corny.

Santa Fe, NM

Donald is preparing some small-scale versions of the *Treblinka* images, which will allow me to work out some of the visual problems. I'm feeling anxious about money (we have almost none) and depressed and discouraged about how slowly the work is going.

Santa Fe, NM

June

Working on this subject is awfully difficult. I begin to get these intense feelings of doubt and despair and also wonder what audience I'm working for. I worry whether anyone will want to see what we're making. Nonetheless, I'm proceeding because *I have to.*

Santa Fe, NM

A number of things have happened. First, while I was working on a small study combining painting and photography, I began to rethink the issue of scale. I began wondering if maybe the images might be better smaller. That thought blew me away, because I've almost always worked large. But the more I thought about it the more I liked the idea—even though we already had eight-foot-high canvases built. If we do work smaller, almost all

The memorial at Treblinka in Poland

Our manipulated photo, with names added to the stones

Manipulated photos on photolinen, ready to be sprayed and oil painted

the paintings can be on photolinen (which only comes forty-eight inches wide). This would definitely be an advantage in terms of visual consistency.

I keep worrying about whether a smaller scale will trivialize the content; however, I'm beginning to think that bigger would *not* be better. In this case it might make the subject matter too overwhelming, which I definitely don't want to do. But working smaller makes me anxious, especially when I think about the monumental canvases of Anselm Kiefer and Robert Morris, which are some of the only significant contemporary

paintings on this subject. Their scale conveys the idea that their content is important, even when the form is abstract and the subject matter not always clear.

Santa Fe, NM

July

Another Independence Day, but this year I had a very difficult time in the studio and ended up frustrated and upset. Donald had prepared all the full-scale *Treblinka* images on photolinen; I sprayed

them last week and did one small painting with images of figures emerging from the tops of the stones. Then I had another idea, which I began today: an image of bones underneath the stones transmuting into people struggling upward. I laid it out in pencil, but when I began to paint I kept feeling inadequate and became consumed with self-doubt.

I was trying to work more directly and intuitively than usual, and I felt like I was all thumbs. I worried that I didn't know what I was doing; that the images were ugly and clumsy. It's probably because

I'm working so differently. First there's the scale—not as large as I'm used to—and second, I really don't have a lot of experience with oil painting.

But that doesn't seem as critical as this terrible lack of confidence. I keep wondering if I'm a good enough artist to deal with this subject matter. My ideas seem beyond my capacity to realize them, which is something I haven't felt for an awfully long time.

Well, tomorrow I'll try again. Maybe I'll find my painting rhythm and it will be okay. Then again, maybe I'm in way over my head.

Santa Fe, NM

Today, while I was working on the *Treblinka/Genocide* triptych, I had the recurring feeling that I'd been chosen to represent those who have had no voices; the images I'm creating are of people who cannot speak for themselves and who could not protect themselves. I haven't had this sense of destiny about my work since *The Dinner Party*, and, interestingly, these images require the same attention to detail.

Santa Fe, NM

August

I'm still working on the *Treblinka* images; they go so slowly. The quality of the photo image requires a corresponding detail in the painting, which necessitates endless hours of painting to achieve. I don't know where the time goes, but I guess if you paint eight hours a day and exercise two, six days a week, then take one needed day off, there's not too muchtime left, especially now that I no longer have the energy (or desire) to work at night. The paint-ing requires intense concentration and is very tiring psychically. As I go along it gets more demanding; I worry about spilling turpentine or dropping the mall stick and thereby damaging or losing months of work.

And then there's the continuing financial anxiety. We're in a period again where we have no money for next month's bills; I have no idea what we'll do. I hate the financial anxiety on top of the difficulty of this work.

Santa Fe, NM

September

I've finished the diptych and triptych at last—almost ten months after beginning the research.

Santa Fe, NM

Pink Triangle/ Torture
Lesbian Triangle
1988

April

When we were in Sachsenhausen, I learned that many homosexuals were imprisoned, tortured, and murdered there and that, ironically, the camp was known for its elaborate flowerbeds, which were tended by the prisoners. I did a sketch at the time for an image combining the pink triangle worn by homosexuals with a field of "pansies." I have always liked turning negative and stereotypical images around (in fact, one could probably say that it's one of the characteristics of my work).

Amazingly, we found a bed of pansies in Melbourne that Donald photographed. I was worried that we'd have to grow them, and that would have taken an awful lot of time, but lo and behold, there was an absolutely spectacular pansy bed at the gardens of the Royal Exhibition Hall.

Santa Fe, NM

May

We're desperately searching for lavender pansies, as the flowers Donald photographed in Australia were petunias (I had them mixed up). They'll be okay for color studies, but for the real thing someone is sure to ask why an image about homosexuals incorporates *petunias* and I can't plead "I meant them to be *pansies*."

Santa Fe, NM

Detail, center panel,
Pink Triangle / Torture
(see COLOR PLATES
11 and 12)

Detail, upper panel,
Lesbian Triangle
(see COLOR PLATE 13)

We sent a color transparency of the petunias to a lab in Dallas as part of our exploration of possible methods for transferring the photo to canvas. Our first test involves pressure-mounting the color photo onto canvas so that the image and surface become bonded; it should arrive any day now. I plan to use this sample (even if it is petunias) to start working out the rest of the image.

After a considerable search we finally found lavender pansies, which Donald will plant; but they'll take a while to grow.

Santa Fe, NM

I've decided to connect the torture of homosexuals during the Holocaust with an examination of torture historically, which means some additional research. I want to construct the image from the information I've uncovered so far and then link it visually with other torture practices.

Santa Fe, NM

June

I did a preliminary drawing for *Pink Triangle*, which is the title I've decided upon, and thought I was moving right along on the image. Then the photo came back from the lab mounted to the *wrong* side of the canvas; but even mounted correctly, the technique won't work. It just looks like a photo glued to the canvas. So we're searching for an alternative, one that transforms the photograph.

I've decided to use a triptych format for the *Pink Triangle* image; I want the image depicting the persecution of homosexuals during the Holocaust to act as a bridge between the images of past and present-day torture, thereby suggesting the idea of the Holocaust as a watershed in history. As Wiesel

Bernard Aloebert, *Gusen II: Block Chief*
These rare drawings document homosexuality in the camps.

Bernard Aloebert, *Gusen II: Death of Joy in Tunnels*

Homosexuals during the Holocaust

"It is often assumed by casual students of Nazism that Hitler and many Nazi leaders were originally quite tolerant of homosexuality.... These assumptions are false.... Most Nazi leaders themselves fought against 'moral degeneracy,' a concept which included homosexual conduct, and, long before their rise to power, actually went on record condemning it....

"[The total number of homosexuals imprisoned] has long been a subject of speculation.... The horror lies not so much in the numbers as in the pattern of persecution which mirrored, in some nightmarish and exaggerated way, the 'normal' harassment homosexuals had suffered before the Nazi regime, and which they still suffer in many countries today.... Homosexuals were usually near the bottom of the prisoner hierarchy; they were often singled out for special tortures and dangerous work, and their mortality rate was very high.... Homosexuals as a group fared very badly.... For historians, the persecution of homosexuals ... [remains] a subject they 'touch with reluctance and despatch with impatience.'"

—Erwin J. Haeberle

once said, the Holocaust made the "unthinkable" possible.

Santa Fe, NM

I spent the day in the library researching torture; seems it started with the Greeks and Romans, was revived during the Renaissance, and was then virtually banned in the West by the eighteenth century. But in the twentieth century, especially after World War II, torture has become almost commonplace, despite all sorts of international bans against it. According to Amnesty International, it's practiced in about 130 countries worldwide, but the Holocaust and Stalin's purges during the 1930s seem to stand out as extreme examples. Both events helped transform torture from its original use in extracting confessions to its contemporary use as a means of forcing people into silence and compliance. Now I'm piled up with research and trying to figure out how to establish the relationship between the central image of homosexuals and torture in general.

Santa Fe, NM

The trip to the photo lab in Dallas was productive; we saw something called a Scanamural, a technique that would allow us to apply the full-color image to canvas. We're doing a test to see whether it works in large scale. In the meantime I've done extensive research for what is now to be called *Pink Triangle/Torture*; I've begun to have a sense of what I want to do, though I haven't completely worked out the image yet.

On the left panel I'm planning to use the figure of a woman being racked, along with other hideous implements of torture used by the Inquisition. On the right I'm struggling to create the image of a woman embracing the shadow of someone who's

"Séance de torture à Buchenwald sous le contrôle du SS Martin Sommer" ("Torture at Buchenwald under the supervision of SS Officer Martin Sommer"); cliché F.N.D.I.R.P. n3219 bis

Homosexual protest at Dachau, May 1987

been "disappeared"—a reference to the way women in South and Central America paint silhouettes of those who've been arrested onto the sidewalks in a kind of public protest art.

Tomorrow I'll see if I can resolve these images and then do a drawing and a small painting using the petunia photos in order to work out the color. If the Scanamural process works, I'll order one from the lab as soon as the pansies we planted are ready to be photographed.

Dallas, TX

I get so psychically tired doing this work—and I also get wacko. It's probably from having to deal with these terrible truths about the ways in which ordinary people can do the most hideous things. I get so deep into my unconscious it's easy to get lost.

Santa Fe, NM

I'm working on the small-scale *Pink Triangle/Torture* painting and it's coming along, but slowly. This project seems to be inching along at a snail's pace, and now we're about to run out of money yet again. I feel scared, anxious, and in a near panic, which makes it go even slower, of course.

My ideas are beginning to outstrip my studio pace, but there's not much I can do but plod on. All of the images will require the work, research, and development of these first few. I don't know what photos will be involved; I do know that each image will take a lot of work, and my financial base is almost completely broken down. I need months and months of uninterrupted work, and I have absolutely no idea where the money will come from.

In the face of the enormity of the project, I feel totally panicked and scared. Where is my courage when I need it most? If only this money terror weren't hanging over our heads—or is it terror at the whole investment this work symbolizes and money only represents? I don't know, but I feel frightened and overwhelmed.

Santa Fe, NM

July

We're still waiting for the pansies to grow; now the grasshoppers are eating them and Donald's organic gardening methods have given way to frantic spraying with pesticide. The humor of this is not lost on us.

I want to do additional research on the torture issue, exploring the use of terror as it developed during the French Revolution. Perhaps I'll alter the first panel—which now deals only with torture during the Inquisition—to include references to the French Revolution, when, I've just learned, terror was used as an instrument of state policy for the first time.

Santa Fe, NM

The pansies are not doing too well, and the Scanamural test is taking longer than we'd planned. Guess I'll try to complete the color studies so I'll be ready when the flowers bloom and the photo tests arrive. I have to adjust the color because the lavender pansies are much more subtle than the garish pink petunias.

Santa Fe, NM

Yesterday Donald announced that John Gurrola, our local florist, had finally found some pansies of the proper color at a nearby nursery. We were despairing of *ever* having any, as our bed was completely devastated by grasshoppers. These pansies turned out to be the perfect color (ours were more blue than pink, but I had planned to fake it). Don-

ald, my assistant Julie, and I went over there. I suggested that perhaps I should take a poster to the woman who owns the nursery (she turned out to be the mother of the owner); Donald said he doubted she knew anything about art.

Well, it turned out that she and her husband are big fans of my work and were thrilled to meet me and be of help. Although these things happen to me all the time, there was something about this situation that really touched me. I don't exactly know why.

Santa Fe, NM

August

The pansy shots didn't come out; the lab screwed up. Donald reshot them yesterday. Hope these work out; we can't keep imposing on the people at the Santa Fe Greenhouses, especially since I decimated the flowers in order to make them visually consistent.

Santa Fe, NM

I'm almost done with the research, and Monday I'll start working on the final drawing for *Pink Triangle/Torture*. I had an instinct about the French Revolution that turned out to be true; if democracy began then, so did terror as an instrument of the state. Now I intend to try and integrate the image of a guillotine and a severed head on the left-hand panel and a hypodermic needle and electronic prod on the right as symbols of the modern counterpart.

As to money, I did a lecture and we've managed to scrounge together another month's worth; I'm trying not to get so panicked. I just keep thinking that if we can hold it together till the end of the year, maybe things will ease up some.

Santa Fe, NM

September

I've been struggling to integrate the guillotine image, which definitely improves the drawing. But the color change from the petunias to the pansies is requiring more adjustments then I'd imagined. While I was making them, I started thinking about how people sometimes consider my color too sweet or somehow inconsistent with my subject matter. I realized that I've used colored pencils for my studies for many years and that their color is very high-key and bright. When I translate the drawings into painting, I often retain a similar kind of color—perhaps that's the problem. I'm going to try and gray these hues some and see what happens. I've already made this image tougher and grittier than it was; perhaps that plus more somber color will seem more in keeping with the subject matter.

Santa Fe, NM

1988

February

We've been working at Unified Arts in Albuquerque on the problem of silk-screening the pansy photo onto the canvas; Scanamural definitely won't work. It looks like we've *finally* got the image solved, though the canvas requires endless coats of gesso and repeated sandings in order to make it smooth enough for the ink to lay flat.

Albuquerque, NM

March

I suddenly realized that if I was going to include male homosexuality in the project, I'd have to in-

Donald at Sante Fe Greenhouses, August 1988

vestigate lesbianism as well. I started by examining feminism in Germany, as I figured that there might have been lesbians in the movement then, as there are now. I already knew from my *Dinner Party* studies that there was an enormous feminist movement in Germany and also a fairly active lesbian scene. But there's incredible silence on the subject in most Holocaust literature, and I have to really dig to find information. I may try to integrate what I find into one of the *Pink Triangle* images, though I'm not at all sure how yet; one idea would be to position a horizontal image under the pink triangle with a scene that refers to the subterranean nature of lesbian life in the early twentieth century. But I'm not sure whether lesbians were arrested under the pink triangle or if they were even persecuted at all.

Santa Fe, NM

April

I am immersed in research on lesbianism in the camps; there seems to have been more than has been acknowledged. Apparently there weren't the same laws against lesbianism in Germany as there were against male homosexuality. But lesbians were generally despised by the Nazis, who referred to them as "Men/Women."

After a lot of searching, I was finally sent some material by the historian Lillian Faderman, including an appalling reprint of an article about lesbians in the Butzow concentration camp. They were put into a completely empty block, and when they arrived, the SS guards announced to the male prisoners, "These women are the worst kind of trash; we wouldn't bang them with the handle of a shovel. We'll give you a bottle of schnapps for fucking each one of them."

Santa Fe, NM

Painting steadily on *Pink Triangle/Torture*. I had a hard day yesterday; couldn't get the paint to do what I wanted it to. Hopefully today it will go better. Sometimes I just *paint*, and other times I struggle and struggle.

Santa Fe, NM

May

I finished *Pink Triangle/Torture* this afternoon and I feel very tired. It came out pretty well, despite a *lot* of technical difficulty, as well as my overwhelming feelings of ineptness. There are moments when I feel completely inadequate, as if I just can't paint at all, and then I get past it and just *paint*. I often feel as if I've never worked as hard as I'm working now. Then I remember some of the days in the *Dinner Party* studio and not being able to even clean my brushes becase I was so wiped out. But still, this work is emotionally so much deeper, and I'm alone a lot—day in and day out, six days a week, six or seven hours a day, with several more years ahead. If Donald weren't working a few hundred yards away I'd never be able to manage.

Santa Fe, NM

I spoke on the phone for a long time last night with a woman from a national group called Jewish Les-

bian Daughters of Survivors. I found their ad in the *Women's Review of Books* and called one of the founders. We made plans to meet when I'm in the East. More about that after I see them; now I have to get going with the paintbrush.

Santa Fe, NM

June

This afternoon I met with two members of Jewish Lesbian Daughters of Survivors. It was terribly painful to hear their stories, which provided me with an entirely new perspective on the effect of the Holocaust upon some survivors and their children. Moreover, their testimony put me in a rage about the mythology that has come to surround the Holocaust experience.

Yesterday I read two articles in the *New York Times*: one by Wiesel proclaiming again how "holy and mysterious" the Holocaust is; the other by a museum director discussing the many "dangers" inherent in trying to represent the Holocaust. Then, today, I listened to stories about survivors who were so damaged that they acted out horribly against their children, especially their daughters. Some fathers even re-enacted the war, casting the girls as Jews and themselves as Nazis. The contrast was quite sharp. It reminded me of the early days of the women's movement, when women first began to speak the truth about their relationships with men: Behind so many myths lay the reality of human pain, ruined families, and failed lives. And the worst suffering often seems to fall on the women and children.

I don't know if I'm being clear here: It's not a matter of sexism (although that's here too) but of *denial*. The idea that the Holocaust is "too holy" to be approached covers a whole range of excruciating

feelings that many Holocaust scholars simply don't seem to want to discuss. Maybe that's what has led to this bizarre isolation of the Holocaust from other historic events, as if the suffering of the Jews is bigger, more important, and more dramatic than any other major historic tragedy, thus elevating Jewish experience to a level above and beyond other human experience and making non-Jews feel that the Holocaust is something they need not concern themselves about.

There has also been significant denial of the fact that Jewish women were the victims of a double jeopardy—as targets of both race and gender policies—and experienced a particularized form of suffering that illuminates the way racism and sexism frequently overlap.

Both of the women talked about the fact that many of their members were rejected by their survivor parents because of their sexual preference. Seems many of the parents had *very* negative feelings about lesbianism because of their memories of some of the female *kapos*. Based on survivor testimony and the information I got from these women, there seems to have been two types of lesbian activity in the camps: one that might be better characterized as female bonding that was nonsexual and another that was coercive and destructive. It is the latter that seems to have shaped the attitudes of many of these womens' parents.

Boston, MA

July

I'm having trouble with the lesbian image. In one drawing I was trying to evoke the dark and smoke-filled atmosphere of the gay bars of the Weimar period and only succeeded in overworking the image. Now I'm trying to create a double image—both the positive and negative sides of lesbianism in the camps—and having trouble. It's upsetting that I can't solve this; I've been working on it conceptually for some time. Maybe I need a break; I'm feeling awfully depressed.

Santa Fe, NM

(It's my fiftieth birthday today.)

I've finished several drawings for the image about lesbianism. I'm doing a layered image. On the top I'll position a triangle, flanked by "pansies" (a reference to the way male homosexuality has subsumed lesbianism historically). Inside the triangle there will be a double image: on the left, women being forced by female SS guards and/or *kapos* to have sex, either through physical coercion or in trade for food—*a dark image*; and on the right, women in the barracks comforting and caring for each other—*a light, warm image.*

The edges of the triangle will be both pink and black in color (pink to symbolize homosexuality, black as a reference to the triangles lesbians wore connoting "asocials"). Below it there will be an image titled *Free to Be Themselves*. This is the drawing I had so much trouble with because I don't exactly know how to draw darkness. I've placed a group of lesbians in a smoke-filled gay bar. Many of them are wearing tuxedos, which they frequently did in the 1920s and 1930s. The figures are fine; it is the darkness I don't quite have yet.

Santa Fe, NM

August

I've done the final study for *Pink and Black Triangle* (I don't like that title but can't decide what else to call it). The good news is that I didn't overwork it; the bad news is that I wasn't able to stay in the

Historic photo of gay bar in Berlin

Lesbianism in the Holocaust

As difficult as it was to obtain information about the treatment of male homosexuals during the Holocaust, it was almost impossible to discover the fate of lesbians. During the Weimar period there was an exuberant and quite open gay scene in Berlin, but that came to an abrupt end with the takeover by the Nazis. Like a number of feminist leaders, many prominent lesbians seem to have left Germany. Others retreated back into the closet or hid in marriage, sometimes with gay men.

The number of male homosexuals murdered in the camps is still unclear, but there seem to be almost no statistics about lesbians. Paragraph 175, the German law against male homosexuality, did not apply to women, as the Nazis could

not conceive of an active female sexual drive. Moreover, the female experience has, as usual, not been considered important enough to study, despite emerging testimony that there were lesbians in most of the camps. They were apparently arrested under the category of "asocials" and wore black triangles, rather then the pink ones connoting homosexuality.

Lesbianism seems to have manifested itself either as a function of the abusive power of female SS guards and *kapos* or, more positively, as a reaching out between women for comfort. Whatever it was, it was in marked contrast to the freedom that lesbians had enjoyed before the war: the freedom to be themselves, even if it was within the dark constraints of smoke-filled bars and private houses.

—J.C.

deeply intuitive place I like to work from, and therefore it's not as refined as I'd hoped.

Anyway, I dramatically altered the painting after realizing that, try as I might, it isn't right to use the pansy photograph for a lesbian image. I started out with that idea because I had extra silk-screened canvases of the pansies, and it took me a long time to realize that it just won't work.

What I've done instead is to use a double photo: on the left, a guard tower and barbed wire; on the right, a barracks. There is a strange outside-inside juxtaposition that's quite visually arresting.

Santa Fe, NM

September

I've been working on *Lesbian Triangle* (the title I finally settled on). Last week I did the airbrush painting, and now I'm laying in the figures and getting ready to start the first coat of oil paint.

Santa Fe, NM

I'm working steadily on the lesbian image, and it's coming along quite well. I really like the way we've integrated the photos so that they both surround and intrude upon the painted images.

Santa Fe, NM

November

I finished *Lesbian Triangle* on Tuesday. I think it looks pretty good.

Santa Fe, NM

Donald's manipulated photo for *Lesbian Triangle*
We combined a photograph of a guard tower from Struthof with one of a barracks from Birkenau to create the photo base.

See No Evil/
Hear No Evil

1988

June

I remember being struck by a quote from Wiesel when I was studying his essays: "Without Auschwitz, there would have been no Hiroshima." It gave me the idea for a work exploring the parallels between the Holocaust and the potential for nuclear holocaust, which I've now begun.

"They went like sheep to the slaughter," many uninformed people still say about the Jews. What they don't or won't understand is that it is more accurate to say that the Jews were *slaughtered like sheep*, as powerless to prevent their destruction in the face of Nazi power as we *all* would be in the face of nuclear disaster. Thus one could say that the Jewish experience of the Holocaust can act as a warning, if we are willing to pay attention to the possibility for omnicide inherent in our global nuclear and weapons programs today.

Santa Fe, NM

Yesterday we went to the museum at Los Alamos as part of our research. I had gone there once before; I'd gotten upset then and I got upset again: all those resources, all that money, all those people working on efforts directed primarily toward death and destruction.

I purchased a book chronicling the many installations around the country that are part of the nuclear industry. I had no idea it was so big and widespread; it made me feel totally overwhelmed

Left three panels, *See No Evil / Hear No Evil* (see COLOR PLATE 21)

and powerless. I woke up this morning with a cold and knew that what I'd once read about getting sick was happening to me. According to this theory, one gets sick when one feels helpless, which is exactly how I felt/feel. It suddenly seemed utterly impossible to alter the self-destructive course human beings seem to be on. I began to feel that I might just as well try to live my life as happily as I could and paint—what? Flowers? Maybe!

I began to understand why some people hate my work: It probably makes them think about things they feel utterly impotent to change, and that makes them existentially sick, just like I feel now.

I've been reading a book by Spencer Weart titled *Nuclear Fear*; it's about how archaic archetypes and stereotypes informed our perceptions of the atom bomb and contributed to the shaping of our nuclear arsenal. It was particularly painful to read about the utopian dream that preceded the reality of the present nuclear nightmare; many scientists, like Oppenheimer, belived atomic energy would lead to peace. He tried to create international controls after the war and to dismantle Los Alamos but failed, of course; in fact, Oppenheimer's career was virtually destroyed as a result.

Santa Fe, NM

July

What an uncanny coincidence! Today there was a "demonstration" to show the supposed safety of the Trupact container in which the Department of Energy (DOE) plans to ship radioactive waste. Westinghouse and Bechtel have been working with the department for years on the Waste Isolation Pilot Project (WIPP) in Carlsbad, New Mexico, where they intend to bury nuclear waste from around the country.

Westinghouse public-relations demonstration of WIPP truck at New Mexico State Capitol building, Sante Fe, 1989
Donald photographed the driver of the truck with his miniature Greyhound. The driver was so considerate of the dog that he left the air conditioning on in the cab during the summer, even when he left the truck.

I really didn't even know what nuclear waste actually was; I somehow imagined it to be piles of dirt. We saw some examples: gloves, objects, and tools for handling radioactive materials. What wasn't included, of course, was the human "waste," and that's what I'm learning about. What, I wondered, have been the human consequences of nuclear energy? What about the Japanese victims of Hiroshima and Nagasaki? What happened to the Native American uranium miners and the residents of Bikini Atoll and other areas where testing was done? It's something I really knew very little about, but I'm beginning to learn—painfully.

After listening to the public-relations people from Westinghouse prattle on about the supposed safety of WIPP and giving out a seemingly endless stream of technical information, which dulled my brain and froze my emotional responses, I suddenly refocused. There was something about their use of language that reminded me of the way the Nazis had used words to obscure, rather than communicate, their real intentions. People weren't about to be murdered when they arrived at the camps, they were told they were "going to the showers." They weren't being transported to their deaths, they were being "relocated." Similarly, in the nuclear industry there's all this technical gobbledygook about high-level, low-level, and transuranic waste and alpha, beta, and gamma rays. By the time they finish it's hard to know what they said or how lethal nuclear material really is—which, I suppose, is the point.

The connections I perceived resulted in my conceiving an image that would juxtapose the transport of the Jews and the transport of "waste"—that is, those who've been "wasted" as a result of nuclear energy. In the center there will be a trainload of Jews going through the forest and, under that, a WIPP truck carrying its cargo. On either side there will be photos of crematoria ovens and atom blasts. Flanking the whole image will be two figures based on historical paintings of Adam and Eve. They will be "seeing no evil and hearing no evil"—a metaphor for the denial that is practiced today, just as it was during the Second World War.

Santa Fe, NM

I'm on my way to the library to expand my knowledge about the human and ecological consequences of the nuclear energy/weapons industry.

Santa Fe, NM

September

I'm still doing research for *See No Evil/Hear No Evil.* How am I ever going to convey the horror of nuclear power? Reading about the people who've worked in the nuclear industry and become ill and about those who were devastated by the bomb blasts in Japan is almost like starting this journey all over again; the pain is like the pain I felt when I first began studying the Holocaust. I now refer to Donald and me as Mr. Doom and Ms. Gloom: We're such a drag to be around!

Santa Fe, NM

"The majority of TRU waste is categorized as contact-handled (CH) TRU. This category of waste has a minimal gamma radiation level and is handled directly (without shielding). The container package itself provides sufficient shielding so that no extra shielding is required. A small volume of TRU wastes emit significant gamma radiation. Gamma radiation is high penetrating and must be heavily shielded for safe handling and storage. This waste is referred to as remote-handled (RH) TRU waste; RH TRU is distinguished from CH TRU on the basis of the higher level of gamma radiation RH TRU emits."

—Department of Energy

• • •

"Entering the world of defense intellectuals was a bizarre experience—bizarre because it is a world where men (and indeed, they are virtually all men) spend their days calmly and matter-of-factly discussing nuclear weapons, nuclear strategy, and nuclear war. The discussions are carefully and intricately reasoned . . . without any sense of horror, urgency, or moral outrage—in fact, there seems to be no graphic reality behind the words. . . .

"What is striking about the men themselves is not . . . their cold-bloodedness. Rather, it is that they are a group of men unusually endowed with charm, and decency. . . . The attempt to understand how such men could contribute to an endeavor that I see as so fundamentally destructive became a continuing obsession for me. . . . What hit me first was the elaborate use of abstraction and euphemism, of words so bland that they never forced the speaker or enabled the listener to touch the realities of nuclear holocaust that lay behind the words."

—Carol Cohn

• • •

"Nazi and nuclear ideologies have in common an impulse to slaughter human beings in numbers that can only be termed infinite, and to do so in the name of preserving one's own group. . . . In the case of nuclearism, that translation of security into absolute power can seem relatively innocent; there is no overt intent to victimize a particular people. Yet the potential consequences—and it must be noted that they are still just potential—could be absolute for the world at large."

—Robert J. Lifton and Eric Markusen

• • •

"I'm sitting in my tractor, and reality is sinking in—As 'downwinders,' born and raised downwind of the Hanford Nuclear reservation in Washington, we learned several years ago that the Government decided—with cold deliberation . . . to use us as guinea pigs by releasing radioactivity into our food, water, milk and air. . . .

"Now we've learned that we can expect continuing cancer cases from our exposure in their 'experiment.' . . .

"I was born a year after my stillborn brother. I struggled to breathe through underdeveloped lungs, and suffered to overcome numerous birth defects. I underwent multiple surgeries, endured paralysis, endured thyroid medication, a stint in an iron lung, loss of hair, sores all over my body, fevers, dizziness, poor hearing, asthma, teeth rotting out, and at age eighteen, a diagnosis of sterility. . . .

"Are we just so much nuclear waste?"

—Tom Bailie

I'm reading about Hiroshima; it's terribly sad—not just the horror of the bomb blast itself but the years of suffering endured by those who were radiated. They survived with the ongoing shadow of the bomb on their lives and with the unknown consequences on their physical health and progeny. I don't care how many rationalizations there have been about how the atom bomb saved Allied lives during the Second World War; it should *never have been dropped*, and we should stop all nuclear work and end its use on the planet. There's absolutely no way to contain radiation; it's lethal and it's *terrifying!*

Santa Fe, NM

I did a drawing titled *Nuclear Waste(d)*, dealing with the human consequences of the bomb: a disfigured Japanese woman, a Native American uranium miner with lung cancer, and a grief-stricken mother with a mutated child—a *very* sad, *very* true drawing. I plan to place some of these figures inside the image of the WIPP truck in order to demonstrate what "waste" really means.

Donald and I spent two days hand-coloring the photos of the trucks and trains for some small studies. This is a complicated image, requiring extensive tests, drawings, and studies. We're going to silk-screen the oven and bomb images at Unified Arts, the silk-screen shop where we did the pansies and where I've worked for so many years.

Santa Fe, NM

I've been researching and working on the nuclear transport and train images. On Saturday we're going to the Trinity site (where the Manhattan Project realized its goal)—they open it twice a year—and to Grants, New Mexico, in search of the piles of uranium tailings left over from mining.

I'm making progress on uniting the photography

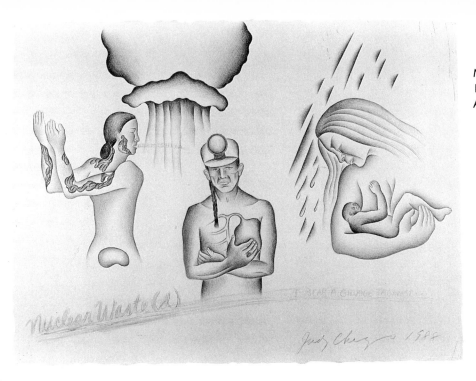

Nuclear Waste/d, 1989; prismacolor on Arches, 23" x 29"

"I am the daughter of a U.S. Air Force colonel. Several decades ago, he observed nuclear weapons tests. ...My father died five years ago from leukemia. ...Three years later I became academic and scientific chairperson of Atomic Veterans. ...[Many of] the servicemen who worked in the contaminated cities of Hiroshima and Nagasaki ...have developed cancer and other debilitating diseases. ... Fifty percent of second-generation children have suffered genetic damage or other serious health problems."

—Sandra Marlow

• • •

"I was a uranium miner for twenty-seven years. ... We were never told of any radiation effects. ... I think we actually breathed a lot more uranium dust than any person on earth. ..."

Uranium Miner Ken Begay

• • •

"They all had skin blackened by burns. ... Their hair was burned, and at a glance you couldn't tell whether you were looking at them from the front or in back. ... They held their arms bent ... and their skin ... not only on their hands but on their faces and bodies too—hung down. ... I can still picture them in my mind—like walking ghosts."

—Hiroshima survivor

• • •

"There are only 90,000 people out there [Bikini Atoll]. Who gives a damn?"

—Henry Kissinger

and painting, though I keep overworking the color and obscuring the photographs—which contradicts my intention. Lighten up there, girl!

Santa Fe, NM

October

We've just returned from our field trip to Grants and the Trinity site. In Grants there are signs welcoming visitors to "Uranium Country" and large piles of tailing sitting around right next to the highways, fenced off with only meager fences or wire and occasional signs bearing the radioactive symbol. For years Indian children played in the tailings, which were described as being perfectly safe.

One city, Grand Junction, Colorado, even hired a contractor who used some of the tailings as aggregate in the sidewalks and foundations for public buildings and schools. The consequence was a significant increase in leukemia among the population.

The Trinity site was very disquieting; there were a lot of visitors motivated by who knows what? I listened to some interviews (there was a considerable amount of media). Most of the people tried to rationalize the "inevitability" of the bomb. Maybe it *was* inevitable, given the development of science and weapons systems, but it was a tragedy, a terrible human tragedy.

There was a lot of documentation, all presented from the point of view of the "victors"—those who developed the bomb. No mention of the victims; of the uranium miners dying of lung cancer; the sheep who bore mutated lambs, lost their wool, and keeled over and died; the children who developed leukemia as a result of exposure to radiation fallout from testing; the Japanese fishermen in the Pacific who died of radiation poisoning; the peoples of Bikini Atoll and the Marshall Islands who were irradiated and relocated and whose culture was destroyed; much less any mention of the civilian populations of Hiroshima and Nagasaki. They all crowded into my head while we were out there, leaving me with a heavy heart.

Santa Fe, NM

December

A nice quiet week in the studio hand-coloring and working on the images for the train and truck: developing them, then doing the line drawings, which I'll transfer to the canvases. I read a book on nuclear waste and discovered that after their "lifetimes" of thirty or forty years, nuclear plants will also become "waste." Of course, the nuclear enthusiasts have no idea what to do with the gloves, lab coats, and tools, much less the huge power plants themselves.

Santa Fe, NM

1989

April

We went to Carlsbad yesterday to tour the WIPP plant. After months of effort we finally got in, thanks to a guy from Jal, New Mexico (a small town of two thousand near the site), who owns an alternative paper. He's been a lone, dissenting voice down there, trying to fight the inevitable opening of the plant, which is desired by many people in southern New Mexico because it brings jobs and money; they simply don't deal with all the ills it will bring as well.

One thing I didn't really understand about the WIPP plant was its vital importance to the nuclear industry. At the moment the nuclear industry is in great trouble: The waste, which no one knows what to do with, is piling up in horrendous quantities and many of the nuclear plants are shut down— the result of DOE mismanagement and/or popular opposition to nuclear power plants and waste sites. Solving the waste problem is an essential step if the nuclear industry is to start up again, which Westinghouse—with help from the Bechtel Corporation (a private corporation deeply involved in the military-industrial complex)—is trying to accomplish. They are taking over some of the plants and seem determined to demonstrate that "nuclear energy can be safe" and the problems of transport and storage can be solved.

They've invested millions of dollars, enormous amounts of technology, and years of problem-solving, plus an extensive public-relations campaign, to tout the wonders of WIPP, a technological nightmare that sits on top of miles of tunneled earth. They've dug myriad chambers into the salt beds under the soil and are planning to stuff them chock full of radioactive material, counting on the salt beds to close around the material once it oozes out of the metal containers and, as they say, "contain" it. What they don't count on, of course, is the inevitable reaction of the Earth to pockets of radioactivity implanted in her body. Unfortunately, most nuclear scientists don't seem to view the planet as a living substance but something to be "mastered" or dominated as they wish, without thought of the ecological effects. And the nuclear industry is so big and seemingly unstoppable.

I came away from there profoundly depressed. I am a positive, optimistic person who believes that I have some amount of power to affect the world; but now I feel humble and as if all efforts are futile.

Our only possible hope is that eventually human beings will evolve to the point where enough of us see what is happening and stop it—hopefully before it is too late.

However, power on the planet is being accumulated by fewer and fewer people, most of whom seem to have little regard for the future, nor any ethical framework that requires them to face the ultimate consequences of their actions. Some of the same forces that produced the Holocaust are still alive and well.

Santa Fe, NM

June

I'm on the last section of *See No Evil/Hear No Evil*, which, like all the paintings, seems to be taking forever to finish. It took two hours yesterday just to paint the fuel rods, which totally wiped me out. It must have been the tiny detail; it was exhausting.

Santa Fe, NM

July

I'm about to finish *See No Evil/Hear No Evil*, trying not to overwork it but, rather, just let it be what it is and trust myself. It's hard for me; I feel overcome with anxiety about the work and afraid that I'll ruin the painting. You'd think I'd be over all that by now, but I'm not.

Santa Fe, NM

I finished *See No Evil/Hear No Evil*—or, rather, I stopped working on it, even though to my mind it isn't perfect. But I just can't do anymore.

Santa Fe, NM

Working on *See No Evil / Hear No Evil*

"Once upon a time it happened to my people, and now it happens to all people. And suddenly, I said to myself, maybe the whole world, strangely, has turned Jewish. Everybody lives now facing the unknown. We are all, in a way, helpless." —Elie Wiesel

See No Evil/Hear No Evil

I didn't know what was going on
I didn't see what was happening
I was only doing my job
I need(ed) the work
I need(ed) the money
They said it was safe
That there was no significant risk
They said there was no radioactivity
*   in Hiroshima or Nagasaki (after they*
*   dropped the bomb)*
They said that they were being relocated
They said they were only going to the showers
*   (after their long and dusty ride)*
They said that every truck would meet safety
*   regulations*
They said they do an excellent job handling wastes
*   (but they didn't say how many people had*
*   been wasted)*
They said that work makes you free
*   (what they didn't say was that work made*
*   you dead)*
They said things that weren't true
And millions of people died
They say things that aren't true
and thousands of people suffer and die
But we hear no evil
See no evil
Why?

—J. C

Wall of Indifference

1989

January

'm doing research for the next image, to be called *Wall of Indifference*. It will deal with the world's indifference to the plight of the Jews, symbolized by figures representing the Allies, the Vatican, and the International Red Cross, all resolutely turning their backs on a transport.

While researching, I stumbled on the fact that, as a result of the Enlightenment and the liberalization of laws restricting Jewish economic activity, Jews played a major role in financing the development of the European railroad industry—ironically, the very transportation system that afforded the Nazis such an efficient network.

Santa Fe, NM

February

This image developed very quickly, and now Donald and I are working together on hand-coloring, which, in large scale, is much more difficult than the small studies we worked on before. Donald has been doing most of the large areas, while I've been laying in the detail with oil pencils, but we've had to undo areas and also work back and forth a lot. We have certainly evolved in our working relationship; it's actually become quite pleasurable. We can spend days working together without any struggle. It's a real achievement.

Santa Fe, NM

We finished the hand-coloring, and I've begun the painting of the people in the train, which is *very*

Detail, *Wall of Indifference* (see COLOR PLATES 5 and 6)

painful. On Wednesday I painted a long time and became entirely lost in the work. I was a basket case afterward and just stared at the TV until I slowly came back to life. While I'm painting I *feel* so much grief and anguish. I try to imagine what the people being transported must have experienced and then just allow myself to express the feelings as directly as possible.

Santa Fe, NM

I painted really hard last week, wrestling with the details of the landscape; I just couldn't seem to make it work, but finally it came together.

Santa Fe, NM

March

I struggled all day Tuesday with the image of a woman trying to save her child by throwing her

"Accusations have been leveled against the . . . Western Allies and the Soviet Union, against the Vatican and the Red Cross and almost everyone else for having betrayed the Jews. . . . For all these countries and organizations the Jewish catastrophe was a marginal issue. . . . Their paramount aim was to win the war against Hitler. . . .

When all allowances have been made, when all mitigating circumstances have been accorded . . . few come out of the story unblemished. It was a story of failure to comprehend . . . [and of many people] who did not care."
—Walter Laqueur

Train in forest, Frankfurt, Germany, 1987

Manipulated photograph base for transport images

Donald first printed a black-and-white photo of a train in the forest in Frankfurt, after which I whited out the areas where the painting was to go. Donald rephotographed the image, enlarging the center and fading the bottom and sides.

He then transferred it to the photolinen, and after it was stretched, I spray-painted a ground color for the figures and walls, adding a green fade on the bottom, top, and sides of the landscape. This prepared the surface for the way we wanted the painted and photographic elements integrated, which our hand-coloring also helped to achieve. We then spent many weeks hand-coloring the image, after which I oil painted it. Our goal was to create an image in which the photographic and painted realities were entirely fused.

—J.C.

from the train. It took me ten hours, and I pushed myself too far emotionally and went to pieces Wednesday morning, feeling as if I were the mother and had thrown/given everything away and had nothing left.

Amazingly, after I had finished the mother and child (which took several days), I read a story in the *Jerusalem Post* about a Polish woman who had visited Yad Vashem in search of information about her parents. As a child she had been thrown over the wall of the Warsaw ghetto by her mother and saved by a Polish couple who had raised her as their own.

I *must* pace myself better; the work pushes me into terrible, anguished places. In order to execute these images I have to find the emotional place inside me and *feel* the truth of these experiences—and it's very dangerous psychologically.

Santa Fe, NM

I finished *Wall of Indifference* yesterday after a lot of struggling: struggling with the image, struggling with the paint, struggling with the despair brought on by the subject matter. When I finished I no longer knew if what I'd painted was any good. An artist friend asked me if I had the stamina to sustain this work for so many years. I said yes, but I'm beginning to wonder.

Santa Fe, NM

Study for *Transports,* 1988; prismacolor on Arches, 22" x 30"

"I saw the trainloads of Jews arrive, the transports of Jews evacuated from the Polish camps. There were almost two hundred padlocked in each boxcar. . . . I hadn't tried to picture what it could be like to be two hundred in a boxcar. . . . Later, yes, when I saw trainloads of Jews from Poland, I did try to picture it. And that winter of the following year had been a harsh one. The Jews from Poland traveled six, eight, ten days in the cold of that harsh winter. With nothing to eat, of course, and nothing to drink. When they arrived, when they pulled back the sliding doors, nobody moved. They had to pry loose the frozen mass of corpses, the Polish Jews dead, standing up and frozen standing up—they fell like tenpins onto the station platform of the camp."

—Jorge Semprun

Banality of Evil/ Struthof Banality of Evil/ Then and Now

1989

July

'**ve** had an idea for some images to be titled *Banality of Evil*. The first image will deal with the inn at Struthof outside Natzweiler. Ever since we saw it, I haven't been able to erase the memory of the gas chamber that faced the patio. I want to "paint in" what happened there. The other will be a then-and-now picture, making a parallel between an SS officer coming home from a "hard day at the crematoria"—patting his dog, playing with his kids, and kissing his wife—and a nuclear scientist at one of the labs in New Mexico doing a modern version of the same thing.

I had this then-and-now idea after learning that inside the verdant hills of the Manzano Mountains in Albuquerque (not far from where we live and which we pass every time we drive to the airport), the largest nuclear arsenal in America is housed.

My research on nuclear waste and our proximity to the Los Alamos and Sandia labs, along with all those bombs in our own backyard, made me think about the phrase coined by Hannah Arendt.

I plan to paint the images almost entirely in black and white—all grays, in fact, just like the moral quandaries involved. We photographed the Manzanos a few weeks ago; it was odd. There is an

Detail, *Banality of Evil / Then* (see COLOR PLATE 15)

This image of a Nazi youth playing with war toys suggests the dangers inherent in the ever-increasing array of toy guns and weapons offered to children.

upper-middle-class housing development right outside the fence to the Air Force base. You can look in and see the bunkers in the sides of the mountains; I had never noticed them before.

I'm planning to do a Grant Wood–type family scene in front of one of the houses in the tract: Daddy barbecuing, kids playing—all in front of the nuclear weapons that are safely out of view. In the "then" image I'll position the family scene in a typical German town, with the chimney of the fiery crematorium in the background.

Santa Fe, NM

September

I'm working on painted studies for the *Banality of Evil* (Then and Now); they are interesting. I'm *inserting* the figures into the photo landscape; there's something quite surreal about it.

Santa Fe, NM

October

For some reason the photolinen is being difficult, and Donald is having a lot of trouble getting it flat. If he ever gets the panels stretched, I will underpaint the figures with white oil so as not to get any water on the surface, which would make the photolinen shrink or stretch all over again.

Santa Fe, NM

I've laid out all the *Banality of Evil* images. It was really difficult to get the gesso on the figures, and I struggled with it for the last two days. Now that it's applied and drying, you'd never know how hard a time I had.

Santa Fe, NM

November

It's interesting painting only in grays: There are really lots of "colors" inside the tones of "gray."

Santa Fe, NM

I've completed all the base painting on the *Banality of Evil* images. I've painted *every day*, despite having a bad case of bronchitis.

Santa Fe, NM

December

I *love* to paint, which is a good thing, as I have so many days of painting ahead of me before I finish. I'm pushing forward on the *Banality of Evil* images.

Santa Fe, NM

I've finished the *Banality of Evil* images, which brings us to the halfway point in the project. I feel a certain sense of accomplishment, even though I know I have more years of painting ahead. Nonetheless, this feels like a milestone of sorts.

Santa Fe, NM

TOP: Study for *Banality of Evil/Then,* 1989; ink on Polaroid, 4" x 5"

CENTER: Study for *Banality of Evil/Now,* 1989; ink on Polaroid, 4" x 5"

BOTTOM: Study for *Banality of Evil/Struthof,* 1989; ink on paper, 3" x 5"

One of the interesting visual challenges in these images was to match the grays of the painted figures to the photographs. I decided to vary the tones only for emphasis or meaning; for example, in the Struthof image, I made the SS officer's uniform a cold gray as a metaphor for his dehumanized behavior, while keeping the figures entering the bathhouse/gas chamber all in warm tones to emphasize their vulnerability.

After completing *Banality of Evil/Then and Now*, I realized that I had made the father the central figure in both images and that, in fact, all the characters—though separated by time and geography—are essentially the same types of people.

—J.C.

Stairway to Death, 1989; mixed media on Arches, 23" x 29"

"When I speak of the banality of evil, I do so only on the strictly factual level, pointing to a phenomena which stared one in the face at [Eichmann's] trial. . . . He was not stupid. It was sheer thoughtlessness—something by no means identical with stupidity—that predisposed him to becoming one of the greatest criminals of that period. . . . That such remoteness from reality and such thoughtlessness can wreak more havoc than all the evil instincts taken together . . . that was, in fact, the lesson one could learn in Jerusalem."

—Hannah Arendt

Double Jeopardy

1987

September

’m beginning to realize that the experience of women has been omitted from most of the exhibitions on the Holocaust that we've seen. I've asked Frannie Yablonsky to begin researching some of the many women's memoirs there turn out to be. The investigation I've done so far suggests that women were doubly victimized—as women *and* as Jews—but I want to discover if there were particular ways in which women suffered differently.

Recently I made contact with Dr. Joan Ringelheim, who's doing research and writing on women and the Holocaust. I'm really looking forward to meeting with her next week when I'm in New York. I'm determined to do one work that focuses entirely on women and am thinking about a large installation combining painting, photography, and needlework.

When we were in Ravensbruck we saw a number of small, embroidered objects that the prisoners had created for their children. I've also been quite surprised by the many drawings we've seen showing women sewing in the camps. Somehow I had never imagined people doing "normal" activities, but the numerous images we viewed of inmates mending, playing cards, and socializing attest to these human activities.

Santa Fe, NM

Detail, Panel 1, *Sewing Circle* from *Double Jeopardy* (see COLOR PLATES 7 and 8)

Excerpts from Round-Robin Dialogue

"I have done a close study of a non labor camp called Gurs in the Pyrenees, where the difference between men's and women's lives is marked. It's important to say that the men who were fathers in Gurs suffered a lot from separation from their children; but the women with responsibility for children had a wretched time. Partly because of the children's presence, the women were what informants call 'hysterical all the time.' There was a great deal of screaming and complaining among the women—much more than men ever report. But the men had to make formal institutions to guarantee sharing; otherwise, they assumed, everyone would cheat. The women assumed just the opposite and were shocked and disgusted by selfishness. They used family metaphors to describe their camp community. They portrayed sharing in their art; the men portrayed alienation. The men depended on the discipline and values of Communism; the women depended on a kind of inexplicit morality which constantly broke down in practice but was not seriously questioned.

"However, for so many women, the issue of being a woman just did not surface in their consciousness as primary. Their daily conditions and the issue of their race swallowed up everything else."

—Mary Felstiner, Ph.D

• • •

"In their descriptions of the tragedy of Jews during the Holocaust, the women I interviewed discussed women's particular victimization. They spoke of their sexual vulnerability: sexual humiliation, rape, sexual exchange, pregnancy, abortion, and vulnerability through their children—concerns that men either described in different ways or, more often, did not describe at all. Almost every woman referred to the humiliating feelings and experiences surrounding her entrance to the camp (for my interviewees this was Auschwitz): being nude, shaved in a sexual stance, straddling two stools; being observed by men, both fellow prisoners and SS guards. Their stories demonstrate shared fears about the experiences of sexual vulnerability as women, not only mortal danger as Jews.

"Although there are many stories about sexual abuse, they are not easy to come by. Some think it inappropriate to talk about these matters; discussions about sexuality desecrate the memories of the dead, or the living, or the Holocaust itself. For others it is simply too difficult and painful. Still others think it may be a trivial issue. One survivor told me that she had been sexually abused by a number of Gentile men while she was in hiding when she was about eleven years old. Her comment about this was that it 'was not important . . . except to me.' She meant that it had no significance within the larger picture of the Holocaust. But why should ideas about the Holocaust exclude these women's experiences—exclude what is important to women—and thus make the judgment that women's experiences as women are trivial?"

—Joan Ringelheim, Ph.D.

• • •

"One story from my own experience haunts me when I think about the issue of women's experience in the Holocaust. A friend's mother, when the Russians were close to Budapest and there was no food to be had for the last six weeks before liberation, had hidden in the ghetto. She was able to hide her children, too, but then it became clear that they had to get out of Budapest in order to obtain some food.

"There she was—alone, her husband dead. She escaped on a hundred-mile walk with her children and the oldest female member of her family, an eighty-year-old aunt, whom she pushed in a wheelbarrow while her children walked beside her. All of them, weakened from hunger and hiding, reached the second-largest town in Hungary, where there was still some food available. There she met the wife of a friend and they looked at each other and said, "Why us, why are we alive? We're not so important as our husbands, why are we alive?" But at the same time that she could say that and mourn the loss of her much beloved husband, there was no question in her mind, not for a moment, that she would rebuild her life and that of her children, as well as the eighty-year-old aunt whom she pushed so far.

"This story illustrates the complexity of women's experiences: On the one hand, women had/have a sense of marginal and diminished importance in relationship to men, but at the same time, they evidenced incredible strength.

"I asked this woman what gave her this strength. Where did she get it? She said the source was the Jewish family. 'The family is what makes us survive. As long as there was one member of my family alive, I could go on.' Michael Lerner wrote in one of his early editorials in *Tikkun*: 'Human beings are fundamentally in relationships; they are part of a family and part of a people.' Although I am reluctant to make great generalizations about women during the Holocaust—as I am fearful that it will be one more 'universal' that will be turned against us—nonetheless, I believe that it is the rootedness in community that is ontologically fundamental to Jewish culture, and it is the effort to maintain community that can be specifically seen in the female Holocaust experience."

—Vera John-Steiner, Ph.D.

1988

October

Frannie has been sending material, which I've been slowly studying and thinking about. Today I had a long and stimulating meeting with Dr. Vera John-Steiner, a psycholinguist, a survivor, and one of our advisors. As a result of our discussion, I decided to establish a round-robin dialogue with a number of writers and scholars on the Holocaust in order to expand my perspective.

Vera agreed to help me formulate some questions. I'm interested in knowing how best to arrive at an understanding of women's relationship to the Holocaust and whether the prevailing male bias in Holocaust history and literature distorts our understanding of the female experience. In addition I want to know if women experienced the Holocaust differently from men and, if so, what factors (class, education, geography, et cetera) shaped their experiences.

Because the investigation of this information is so new and the material, though abundant, still lacking analysis, I think that it is important to involve a number of women in thinking about these issues. I want the image to be grounded in as solid a historic foundation as is the rest of the *Holocaust Project*, which is harder to achieve because feminist scholarship is so recent and, to some Jewish scholars, still questionable.

I chose a round-robin letter format because the participants are geographically scattered and because it allows an open, egalitarian dialogue, which is a form with which women generally feel comfortable. In addition to Vera, I will seek responses from Frannie Yablonsky, Joan Ringelheim, Konnilyn Feig, Mary Felstiner (a scholar, philosopher, and author), Ruth Linden (a sociologist), Aviva Cantor (a journalist, Jewish activist, and co-founder of *Lilith* magazine), and Nan Fink (a writer and co-founder of *Tikkun* magazine).

I'm already beginning to formulate a concept for the image, even though I'm a long way from the specifics. I discussed my idea with Vera, something I rarely do when my thinking is at an early stage, but I wanted to try it out on her. I told her I was contemplating a series of panels in which women's experiences were painted and juxtaposed against black-and-white photographs of male experiences. The men's activities would thereby provide the *historic context* for the women's. This would be a metaphor for the fact that women are generally *impacted* by the historic events that men *orchestrate*. Vera loved it.

Santa Fe, NM

1989

March

The answers have been slowly coming in to the questionnaire; some of them are fascinating, while others are awfully timid. Perhaps people will go further in their thinking in round two.

Santa Fe, NM

June

Isaiah was here to see the project; the Spertus has hired him as a consultant. After a long discussion about how the point of view of Donald and myself differs from the ways in which the Holocaust is usually presented, we spent time examining standard texts and talking about the way the "Holocaust story" is usually told in America. By the time he'd left, my idea for the women's image was dramatically expanded.

I plan to tell "the story of the Holocaust" as it's generally told, using standard photographs to illustrate the "orthodox" themes: Humiliation, Ghettoization, Concentration Camps, Mass Killings, Resistance, Liberation. Then I want to "paint in" the untold story of women's experiences of those same events. The images will also explore the ways historic events impact on women in general; thus there will be a dual level of meaning.

Santa Fe, NM

1990

January

We did a slide presentation at the Judah Magnes Museum in Berkeley. While we were at the museum I ran into Helen Eisenberg, a former *Birth Project* needleworker and, at one time, a docent at the museum. We discussed the *Holocaust Project* and my interest in incorporating needlework into the women's image. She offered to head up a team of stitchers.

Now that she's made this commitment, I'm going to get started on a pattern for the needlework. I want to silk-screen a field of Jewish stars onto fabric in shades of gray to match the photo tones, then print a series of female symbols on top of that in graduated shades, which can act as a guide for the stitchers. The women's symbol will be embroidered in muted colors similar to those I'll use in the paintings. The black and white in both the photos and stitched panels will thus provide the *ground* or historic background against which women's experiences will be presented.

My sense is that there should be six painted

panels (42" x 36") interspersed with the stitched ones, which would be long and thin (maybe 42" x 6"). That would make the whole image over twenty feet long, a scale commensurate with the subject matter, which is complex.

In order to arrive at the images I want to paint, I must plunge into all the research material I've been accumulating and move the round-robin along. But first I need to work with Helen on needlework tests, select the appropriate fabric, and find stitchers to do the work. They can get started even if I haven't resolved the painted images.

Berkeley, CA

I have been working on the women's image, which I plan to call *Double Jeopardy*, to reflect the ways in which women were victimized in terms of both race and gender. After reviewing a considerable amount of material, I've concluded that there are a number of basic areas in which women's experience of the Holocaust differed from men's, and I'm working on clarifying these.

Donald and I have selected a number of "familiar" photos from the Holocaust that could form the backgrounds for the painted tableaux; I'm slowly working on ideas for the foreground images. I'm pretty sure I want to use the figure of a woman having a child pulled from her arms and another of female prisoners being raped by the liberating soldiers, something that seems to have occurred rather often. Surprisingly, there is actually a considerable amount of source information about sexual abuse. It's amazing that so little attention has been paid to it by the historians; and the questions asked of survivors in the oral history projects scarcely mention it.

I definitely want to include an image of women sewing Jewish stars onto their family's clothing,

Study for *Maternal Woe,* 1989; prismacolor on Arches, 23" x 29"

Panel 4 from *Double Jeopardy* (in progress)

maybe in a little quilting-bee format. Everyone has seen photos of Jews wearing stars, but little consideration has been given to those who sewed them on—another example of how women's experience has remained invisible.

I'm researching the resistance movement now. Of course, resistance is usually defined as *armed* resistance, but I'm looking for a more meaningful way to define resistance generally. I keep thinking about Congresswoman Jeanette Rankin standing up to a whole nation committed to the Second World War or Virginia Woolf drowning herself to get away from "masculinity gone mad" in the fascist march across Europe. How much courage it takes to "resist" all the patriotism and violence associated with a war effort—and war inevitably takes its worst toll on women and children.

I'm corresponding with various needleworkers; Helen and I are lining up a team. The next step is to work out the pattern for the overlap between the Jewish stars and female symbols, then decide on the fabric and get the frames made. Our graphics designer, Ginna Sloane, is working on the design for the needleworked panels. In February I'll work at the silk-screen shop transferring the pattern to fabric.

Santa Fe, NM

Between my research and the material from the round-robin, I've pretty well worked out the concept for the overall piece, though I still need to do the drawings and select the background photos. Next week we're going to the Simon Wiesenthal Center to try and find historic photographs. The librarian there, Adair Klein, has been very helpful to us.

Santa Fe, NM

Paula Strongheart Garfield and her children modeling for one of the Resistance images.

"Armed resistance was, I would say, the last ring in the long chain of resistance that Jews put up through the Nazi occupation. . . . We had our spiritual resistance,

Detail, study for *Resistance*; prismacolor on Arches, 29" x 23"

ethical resistance, cultural resistance, and in all those cases, women played a significant role."
—Survivor Vladka Meed

Paula Strongheart Garfield and her daughter Lake —and sometimes her other children and even her husband, J. D. Garfield—worked with us extensively to create the poses, emotional tones, and human interactions for the *Double Jeopardy* images. This involved a series of intense photo sessions, which provided the pictures from which I worked.

After the sessions I made drawings, then line drawings, which I transferred to the manipulated spray-painted canvases. Each of the six photo images was altered to create the basis for a metaphor representing one of the various ways in which women related to the Holocaust and, by implication, to historic events generally.

In the first panel we cut the photo with a pinking shears to show the way history can be *cut away* to reveal women's experience. The other five images involved placing an image *behind* the historic picture of men building the Warsaw ghetto; *juxtaposing* male and female reality to reflect the similar types of victimization they experienced in concentration camps; positioning a woman's particular suffering in relation to her children *against* the male experience of mass killings; placing women's resistance activities around the *perimeter* of male armed resistance; and *peeling back* an experience that was entirely positive for men to reveal a more complex liberation experience for women.
—J. C.

March

I met Helen Eisenberg while we were in New York. Choosing fabric that can be both printed and embroidered has proven to be more difficult than either of us ever imagined. After months of searching, we finally found some *very* expensive linen. She's testing it now for stitching ease, while I'm doing paint tests.

Santa Fe, NM

I've been working on Image #1 of *Double Jeopardy*: three women—a mother, daughter, and a grandmother—sewing yellow stars on the family clothing. It took a week just to do the drawings: one afternoon photographing the models, then all week to do the drawings. I did four, one of each of the figures, then another combining them. I had much more energy at the beginning of the week, and the drawings reflect it—at least to me. I wanted an air of sadness, which the single figures have, but by the end of the week I was tired and it was harder to maintain the emotion.

I've been struggling to solve a spatial problem: how to establish a visual place for the figures that relates to the photo reality. I've decided to spray a ground in grays, like the photo, then paint the figures against that in the same grayed tones as the thread colors.

Santa Fe, NM

April

I'm doing better. After much effort I managed to resolve the second image for *Double Jeopardy*, and I am preparing to work tomorrow with the Stronghearts and another of Paula's daughters for Image #3. I've been very focused, trying to evolve a way to work that is not so emotionally exhausting that I give out, as I did after the first image. Doing four drawings was just too many. By the time I got to the last one I didn't have enough stamina to express my intentions properly. So I've decided to conceptualize the image, then work with the model. Donald is going to photograph (we tried my doing it, but I was hopeless) and then I'll do the drawings. I plan to transfer the line drawings directly to the canvases and paint—no small-scale models. I don't have the energy that I had at the beginning of the project, so I want to save all the emotion for the real paintings, as the feeling is what carries them.

Santa Fe, NM

I'm exhausted and stressed out. I've been working on Image #3 and have three drawings laid out; they're titled *Behind the Ghetto Wall* and deal with food. There are many references to food in women's memoirs: hoarding or sharing it, discussing meals or exchanging recipes in order to stave off hunger pangs. One of the images comes directly from a survivor's testimony, who said "I never cooked as good as I did in the camps with my mouth."

We worked again last Sunday with the Stronghearts; they were great. We're supposed to work with them again next Saturday, along with more of the kids and Paula's husband. What we've been doing is getting the models in the poses I want for the images. Donald photographs them and then I draw from the pictures. It works out very well.

Santa Fe, NM

I spent Thursday and Friday at Unified Arts, printing the stitching panels; they're all ready and are going out to the needleworkers next week. We've decided to do a half-scale mockup after all; Donald needs it to adjust the photo tones, so we printed a set of panels in small scale. Then Donald had to go back to the Wiesenthal, as almost half the photos didn't come out in the processing. I'm pretty far along in the drawings: only two more images to go. Today we do our last model sessions, and if all goes well I'll have the drawings done soon.

Santa Fe, NM

August

I'm working on the scale model for *Double Jeopardy*, which, even though I didn't want to do it, proved to be essential, as we really needed to work out some visual problems: i.e., the overall scale, as well as the dark and light relationships from panel to panel. Had we gone directly to large scale, we would have had a disaster.

I've done all the black-and-white sprayed painting, which established an overall unity of tone; now I'm intent on finishing the scale model quickly, as I want to save my energy for the large paintings. I'm going to try and finish one of these each day—not labor them, just lay in the color simply and directly in order to see how it will work with the black-and-white photos.

Santa Fe, NM

I've painted every day this week, including Sunday, which I usually take off. I've been trying to get the color laid in on the scale model, which is taking more time than I'd planned. So what else is new?

Santa Fe, NM

September

I've been working *very* hard, and on Thursday I finished the scale model. I used my personal fear of rape in the last image; it was very hard to be in there with those feelings.

Santa Fe, NM

Donald has finished all the final photos for the full-scale *Double Jeopardy* panels, and next week I plan to begin work on them. I learned a lot from the half-scale version: like the necessity for graying the colors more and doing more preliminary spraying so as to integrate the painted and photo grounds better.

Santa Fe, NM

I worked all week transferring and modifying images and laying down the acrylic gesso grounds; to-morrow I start taping and spraying the figures.

Santa Fe, NM

October

I've been painting all day every day; I'm laying in the flesh areas, and it's going very slowly. I thought it would take a week, but it's already taken two, with no days off. The rest of the painting will probably take six to eight weeks. My goal is to finish by the end of the year.

Santa Fe, NM

"While Men Marched, Women Mended . . ."

The stitched panels in *Double Jeopardy* are meant to honor Judaic needlework and the effort by women during the Holocaust to retain their dignity and sense of worth in the face of heinous actions against them and their families.

All of the stitchers were former *Birth Project* needleworkers whose skills were excellent and who were also familiar with the problems of translating my painted, blended colors into thread. In addition to Helen Eisenberg, who coordinated and supervised the work (pictured on the following page in her Berkeley, California, studio), other stitchers included Joyce Gilbert and Jane Thompson from Houston, Texas, and Candis Duncan Pomykala of Belvidere, Illinois.

Helen and Jane relied on stem-stitching and Joyce used cross-stitching with a stem-stitch outline. Candis has developed an extraordinary method of using French knots, which would, Helen and I agreed, be impossible to match; so we asked her to execute two panels. All the embroidery is done on a counted-thread linen with DMC floss and includes stitches traditionally used in domestic Judaic needlework, which tends to be modest in both scale and imagery.

—J. C.

Women sewing Nazi flags

"While men marched, women mended," commented Claudia Koontz in *Mothers in the Fatherland*. Women have used their needleworking skills historically in a variety of ways: to further male ideologies; to express resistance; to create art; and to produce clothing, comforters, and objects of pleasure for their families.

Jozef Kowner, drawing of women sewing
Sketches like this affected me deeply and made me want to honor the ways in which women attempted to retain a measure of human dignity in the ghettos and camps.

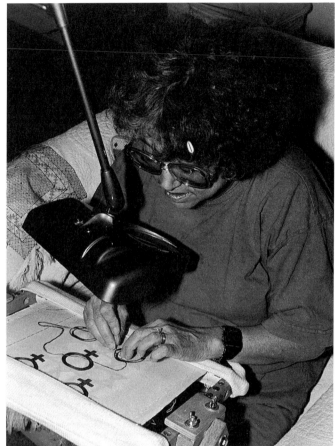

Helen Eisenberg at work in her studio, Berkeley, CA, 1989

"Whose memory will be respected? Whose memory will be hidden or undermined? What will be considered the truth? Who will decide? Who controls the identity of the past? In other words, since decisions are always being made about what will be emphasized in history . . . we must always ask: 'Was that all there was?'"

—Dr. Joan Ringelheim

November

I painted fourteen days straight and finally finished the base coat on all the flesh areas. I painted too many hours and was overcome by the feelings I was expressing with my brush. Oddly enough, if I am measured in the number of hours I paint, I can maintain some distance from the pain. It seems to pass through my arm and out my fingers without my consciously registering the nature of what I'm representing. But if I work too many hours I become overwhelmed by the feelings, and only intense exercise brings me back to a place where I can bear to be with the images again the next day.

Santa Fe, NM

We saw Helen Eisenberg's stitching—it's great! I'm trying to get her to complete it so I can have it while I'm finishing the painting in order to match the stitched tones.

Berkeley, CA

December

I painted steadily all week on the first image in *Double Jeopardy.* I can't do much else except paint and exercise. I have my painting rhythm now and I just want to work steadily till I'm done—five more weeks, I think.

Santa Fe, NM

I finished painting #2 of *Double Jeopardy* and started #3. I'm hoping to get a little ahead and be able to take some time off. But I don't know if I'll make it; the last two paintings look like they could be slow.

Santa Fe, NM

I'm working on painting #4 of *Double Jeopardy*; it is the hardest work I've *ever* done. I end up exhausted every day; sometimes I go to bed at six in the evening and sleep a black sleep until the morning. Nothing else seems real except the struggle to finish. I seem to have a well of pain and sorrow to draw from; when I paint these tortured women, it's my own torment I'm expressing. And even though I know that events like the Nazi enactment of the "dark forces" must, as Dylan Thomas said, be countered by "railing, railing against the dying of the light," the light of truth has been diminished so many times in human history. I am exhausting myself and depleting all my life's energy in fighting for the truth to be seen and heard.

Santa Fe, NM

This morning when I woke up I was wiped out: I painted a long time yesterday and didn't (couldn't) exercise and so was left with all the tension in my body. I worked out this morning for two hours and slowly brought myself back.

I need to rest before I begin the rape image. Not only is it an intense, painful image, but it makes me very anxious. I keep thinking: Am I going to get raped after I do this image? What is it? I'm afraid that painting a rape image is bad karma? Maybe.

But of course, I have no choice—so I'll just have to hope that art won't translate into life.

Santa Fe, NM

Two more painting days and I should be done with *Double Jeopardy.* I'm on the final details. What a struggle!

Santa Fe, NM

1991

January

After years of research and preparation and ten solid months of painting, *Double Jeopardy* is finally done.

Santa Fe, NM

Im / Balance of Power

1990

June

I've begun research on the next image, which will deal with children. I keep looking at the famous photograph of the Nazis pointing their guns at the small boy in the Warsaw ghetto and wondering: How can grown men point guns at children?

I've read a fascinating book by Alice Miller titled *For Your Own Good*, in which she argues that many of the world's problems are a result of our unexamined child-rearing methods—methods that generally oppress rather than nurture children. She goes on to decry the fact that we spend billions of dollars on weapons and sophisticated technologies and appallingly little on the real human challenge: raising healthy, independent, self-sufficient children. She is convinced that much of the terror, violence, and greed of the world can be traced back to abusive childhoods.

Santa Fe, NM

September

I'm slowly working on the children's image, trying to construct a global picture of how we treat children so that what happened to Jewish and Romany children during the Holocaust can be seen in a larger context.

Santa Fe, NM

Detail, center panel, *Im / Balance of Power* (see COLOR PLATES 16 and 17)

November

I'm plugging away on the children's image—mostly reading and thinking. I'm looking for the connections between the brutality toward and murder of children during the Holocaust and that evidenced in their worldwide treatment today: abuse, neglect, malnutrition, and disease. It's not clear to me yet, but I know there's something that links all these, partly the distorted priorities of our world.

Santa Fe, NM

December

It's terribly painful to confront the conditions of many of the world's children. They are so utterly powerless. I'm trying to find a way to suggest (gently) that, even though the murder of one and a half

"The men and women who carried out the 'Final Solution' did not let their feelings stand in their way for the simple reason that they had been raised from infancy not to have any feelings of their own.... The citizens of the Third Reich were offered an object to serve as the bearer of all those qualities that were abhorred because they had been forbidden and dangerous in their childhood—this object was the Jewish people.... The cruelty inflicted on them, the psychic murder of the child they once were, had to be passed on in the same way; each time they sent another Jewish child to the gas ovens, they were in essence murdering the child within themselves."

—Alice Miller

RIGHT: Waldemar Nowakowski, *Nazi and Child*, 1943; 125cm x 19cm

"Many SS men committed suicide and there was a major danger that many could not take the strain of killing children. To combat this danger, SS documents taught . . . the Jewish child is a cultural time bomb."

BELOW: *Grown Men Pointing Guns at Children*, 1991; mixed media on rag paper, 30" x 40"

"At times, my life seemed to be not my own. Hundreds of people lived through me, lives that had been cut short in the war. They saw in my life the years they had lost in the war and the years they had lost emigrating to America. My life was not just another life, it was an assignation. 'Every one of you is a miracle,' my mother would say about children of the people she had known in the camps. 'None of you was supposed to have been born.'"

—Helen Epstein

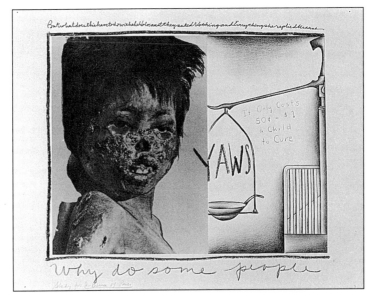 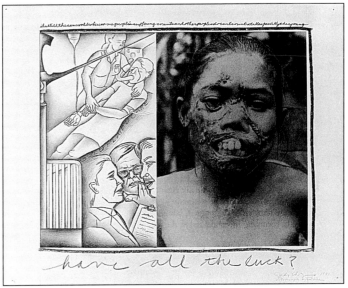

Why do some people have all the luck? 1991; mixed media on rag paper, 23" x 58"

"Our sensitization to the cruelty with which children are treated, until now commonly denied, and to the consequences of such treatment will as a matter of course bring to an end the perpetuation of violence from generation to generation."

—Alice Miller

million Jewish children was a terrible tragedy, we should also think about children today and how they're suffering and dying by the millions all over the globe.

Santa Fe, NM

1991

February

I've decided to title the children's image *Im/Balance of Power*, as I've discovered the connection I've been seeking. What links the treatment of children during the Holocaust with conditions today is exactly what the title implies: their powerlessness. As I read somewhere, "Those who have the least to say about the course of events are apt to suffer most gravely from the consequences."

At the moment I'm sifting through photos, try-ing to find images that will work with the Warsaw ghetto picture. Many of the pictures of children I've seen are either romantic, arty, or too formal. This points out how subject children are to adult versions of their realities.

In all the earlier images I was able to draw on personal testimony. There is a lot of material by Holocaust child survivors, but there are mostly sta-tistics documenting the experiences of the millions of contemporary starving, diseased, homeless, illit-erate, and abused kids—and numbers are difficult to translate into meaningful images.

We're going to Los Angeles to spend a few days in the UCLA library in search of visual material.

Santa Fe, NM

March

I've been working on drawings for *Im/Balance of Power*. I decided to start with some of the pho-tographs we found that I don't think are usable in the final image because they're just too horrific. I want to see what the aesthetic limits are in terms of what I can and cannot transform. Both Donald and I had a difficult time even *looking* at some of these, much less figuring out how to incorporate them, particularly some hideous pictures of chil-dren with a disease called yaws, from which thou-sands of children suffer.

The contrast between what we spend on war and defense and what we allocate for human needs is appalling. Three-quarters of the world's children grow up in countries where poverty and depriva-tion are the rule rather than the exception. Poverty, hunger, and malnutrition claim the lives of four-teen million people each year; seventy percent are children under five. But it's one thing to read these facts; it's totally overwhelming to express them visually.

For example, a soldier's equipment in the recent

Gulf War cost $1500 per person, while disfiguring diseases like yaws could be cured with one injection at a cost between fifty cents and one dollar per child. But we can't find the money for that, nor for food or education, health or housing—except for the privileged few.

It's really difficult to deal with this subject matter because it brings one face to face with the world's real priorities—and they aren't children. How we treat them is an international disgrace.

I'm trying to figure out how to convey all this information through the art. It's a particularly difficult problem because rage is in order here. But the excruciating nature of most of the photographs we chose require strict emotional and formal visual control in order to make them work with the drawn (or painted) images, so I have to channel my anger.

The first drawings were very direct and crude; I just let my feelings get away from me. I always feel uncomfortable when I create images like that—as if they're terribly ugly. I then went through an agonizing struggle to try and grab hold of the subject matter; I hope I finally made some progress.

The last drawing (which I just laid out) places the image in the highly rigorous visual format of a set of scales, which I've decided to use to represent the terrible imbalance of priorities in the world's treatment of children.

I'm trying not to work too many hours a day on this particular image, as facing the way we treat children makes me both wretched and infuriated.

Santa Fe, NM

April

After much anguish I finished the final study for *Im/Balance of Power* on Saturday. But on Friday I just lost it. Donald has been working at construc-

tion to make money and has not been around much. Even though we absolutely need the money, it's been very hard on me to be so alone with the work, standing in my studio day after day. On Friday I just couldn't do it anymore. I called him crying, and Donald came home early and just sat with me; it helped a lot. I was shocked and so was he, I think, to realize how much I need him nearby in order to handle this work.

Santa Fe, NM

May

I've been working very hard the last two weeks—about ten concentrated hours a day—on *Im/Balance of Power*, which I finished spraying yesterday. I used airbrushing more than I usually do in order to integrate the painting more fully with the pho-

tographs. As the painted images came to life, the work became increasingly painful to look at. The sections painted in color represent people whose lives are privileged or who are members of an "important" country or class. The children imaged in the black-and-white photographs are the victims of our "imbalanced" priorities. Their suffering is in the background, just as it is in real life. Our global treatment of children thus becomes *very* visible and very tragic.

Santa Fe, NM

July

I finished *Im/Balance of Power* today after weeks of struggling to stay in the studio because the images unnerved me so.

Santa Fe, NM

From a United Nations Report on Children

Two-thirds of the world's peoples live in countries that have not yet reached a level of economic and industrial development sufficient to ensure their inhabitants even a minimum measure of "freedom from want."

There is an *increasing* disparity between living standards in the low-income and high-income countries, but people in economically advanced countries generally have great difficulty conceiving of the extreme poverty that dominates life in the "developing" countries. With poverty comes many ills, the consequences of which fall most heavily on children. Their general condition is so grim that efforts to alleviate their plight on any significant scale can appear hopeless. Moreover, female children suffer even more than male; they receive less food, health care, and education.

The proportion of international resources devoted to children is minute: 3 percent of national income goes to education, 1 percent to health care, and 1 percent to social services.

—*J. C.*

Logo
Rainbow Shabbat

1989

August

Some time ago, at a fundraising talk we gave in New Haven, Connecticut, I was approached by Michael Caudle, a stained glass artisan. He suggested that the logo I'd designed for the project would lend itself beautifully to glass and volunteered to work on it. Although I've often used multiple types of media, I've never worked in stained glass and I became intrigued by the idea.

The logo combines the different-colored triangles worn by inmates in the concentration camps with references to barbed wire and flames. I used the color yellow twice to emphasize the particular suffering of the Jews and as a metaphor for the idea that the Holocaust "began with the Jews, but it did not end with them." I intended the design as a memorial to all those persecuted by Hitler and as a symbol of courage and survival. It occurred to me that the quality of stained glass might perfectly express transcendence and decided that it could also provide a perfect technique for the last image in the exhibition—which I want to be one of hope, optimism, and transformation.

Santa Fe, NM

September

Michael and I are going forward with plans for the logo; he's going to start with a scale model of the design. Seeing my drawn logo translated into glass

Detail, upper right section, center panel *Rainbow Shabbat* (see COLOR PLATES 27 through 31)

will give me some sense about the potential of this medium.

Santa Fe, NM

October

I went up to New Haven to work with Michael. I sent him a drawing and pattern and now want to start choosing the glass. Before visiting him I went to a stained glass supply house in New York. It was a lot like the china-painting shops I used to visit when I was working on *The Dinner Party*: full of patterns and how-to books. The once glorious techniques used in medieval cathedrals and by such masters as William Morris and Tiffany are now degraded into hobby-shop, lamp-shade directions. Except for the Matisse chapel and the Chagall windows, most contemporary stained glass seems extremely decorative. Moreover, everyone was mysterious at the suppliers, as if they were guarding the Queen's jewels. It was comical, but frustrating, because I need to start learning about the different types of glass. But trying to buy sample boxes was like pulling teeth.

Santa Fe, NM

November

The model for the logo is progressing more slowly than Michael and I had planned. Apparently it is more complicated than either of us realized.

Santa Fe, NM

December

I'm going to do research on the traditional rituals associated with Shabbat and then do some draw-

Michael Caudle working on *Logo* in Santa Fe, NM, 1992

ings for the stained glass installation I'm envisioning for the end of the exhibition.

Santa Fe, NM

1990

January

I've decided to incorporate multiple panels into the *Shabbat* image. In addition to a central window, based on the *Shabbat* service, there will be two side panels incorporating a prayer for a more peaceful world, one based on equal rights for all peoples and species. These panels will be rainbow windows, at the center of which will be placed yellow stars. The despised badge Hitler forced Jews to wear as a symbol of our humiliation will become glorious testaments to that which allows us as human beings to prevail over despair. The prayer will be inscribed on the stars.

When I was in the Bay Area I prayed for the first time in my life, and after that experience I realized that the *Holocaust Project* is like an invocation: a prayer for human awakening and a global transformation. So it seems appropriate to end the exhibition that way.

I think I'll ask Rabbi Lynn to help me; perhaps there's a traditional prayer that I can use.

Santa Fe, NM

Bob Gomez and I consulting with Rabbi Lynn Gottleib in Santa Fe, NM, 1990

I'm working on drawings and plans for the *Shabbat* windows. Last night I spoke to Rabbi Lynn, who agreed to do some research into prayers that express the meaning I wish to convey in the side panels. We decided that one window should be in English, the other in Yiddish: Yiddish because it comes closest to being an international language, at least for many Jews in the past.

Santa Fe, NM

February

I've been working steadily on the stained glass image, to be called *Rainbow Shabbat*. I've decided that I want the heads of everyone turned toward the woman—as they would be during her blessing over the candles—while her husband raises his *kiddush* cup (a special vessel used for the traditional blessing over the wine or bread) and sings his wife's praises. (This compresses the actual sequence of *Shabbat* events but is true to its spirit.) Thus the windows will celebrate both the Jewish and the female experience and suggest that both offer the potential for human transformation.

Santa Fe, NM

Rabbi Lynn suggested a poem by a survivor from Theresienstadt, which we rephrased to read:

Heal those broken souls
who have no peace
and lead us all
from darkness into light

Shabbat **prayer, in which the man sings his wife's blessings:**

A woman of valor, who can find?
She is more precious than rubies.
The heart of her husband trusts in her,
And he has no lack of gain.
She does him good and not harm
All the days of her life.
She seeks out wool and flax
And works it up as her hands will.
She is like the ships of merchants,
From afar she brings her food.
She arises while it is yet night,
And gives food to her household,
And a portion to her maidens.
She examines a field and buys it,
With the fruit of her hands she plants a
*   vineyard.*
She girds herself with strength,
And braces her arms for work.
She perceives that her profit is good;
Her lamp does not go out at night.
She lays her hands on the distaff,
Her palms grasp the spindle.
She opens her hands to the needy.
She does not fear snow for her household,
For all her household are clad in warm
*   garments.*

(Proverbs 31: 10–31)

Twentieth-century Jew badge

I was horrified when I first saw a yellow star, at the Anne Frank house in 1972. It gave me great satisfaction to transform this hideous symbol into an image of survival and hope in the side panels of *Rainbow Shabbat*.

Now we're having it translated into Yiddish and then I'll have the lettering for the yellow stars in the side panels laid out. The same symbol that degraded Jews will thus become an image of triumph and hope.

Santa Fe, NM

March

I finished the final studies for *Rainbow Shabbat* before we left for the East, where we visited Michael in New Haven. I've been waiting for more glass samples in order to finalize the color, but I'm still having trouble obtaining them.

In Chicago we met another stained glass artisan, Bob Gomez (who lives in California), who is very interested in fabricating *Rainbow Shabbat*. I explained that we had very limited funds and that he, like us, would have to work for nothing. But I of-

fered to pay him if we ever sell the finished work, and he agreed. He's planning to pay us a visit this summer to discuss translating the painted cartoon into the three windows, which will fill a small room.

Santa Fe, NM

April

After *finally* obtaining the rest of the glass samples, I'm pretty close to arriving at the final colors for the scale model of the logo. I then have to color-code the pattern and send it off to Michael so he can get going (at last).

Bob is planning to visit us in June.

Santa Fe, NM

June

Bob arrived last Sunday and we spent several days working on *Rainbow Shabbat*. We decided to start by doing a mockup of a section of one of the side panels in order to work out the colors. That means getting even more sample boxes, so I'll have a wide range of hues and types of glass from which to choose.

Once I select the colors, he'll fabricate the sample section, which I'll review in California in November. By then I hope to have samples of the lettering in both silk-screening and sand-blasting to see which I prefer.

In discussing my cartoon for the center panel, Bob pointed out a significant technical problem in the leading of the faces and hands; it seems all the detail would be lost. When I asked him for a solution, he suggested painting them instead. As a fabricator, he knows very little about painting on glass, so I guess I'm on my own. When I was studying china-painting, I remember glass-painting seminars. Perhaps I can enroll in one.

Santa Fe, NM

July

I'm trying to resolve the color for the mockup of the rainbow section of *Rainbow Shabbat*; sample boxes keep arriving by UPS. The array of colors is glorious. Also, I found a stained glass shop in Albuquerque where I can take a three-day painting class in September.

Santa Fe, NM

August

It's the anniversary of Hiroshima. It's somehow fitting that Michael has finished the scale model for this symbol of triumph over victimization. We've decided on the glass colors; now he'll cut out all the sections and I'll go to New Haven to review the work before he begins to solder the pieces together. He has some technical problems to solve, like the way the lead lines come together and how to join the flames so the joints are delicate and graceful.

Santa Fe, NM

September

I've been in Albuquerque at a glass-painting seminar with a woman named Dorothy Maddy, who has proven to be remarkably knowledgeable. In three days I learned about the ways in which much of the medieval glass-painting was done and the differences between the approaches of William Morris, who loved painting, and Tiffany, who loathed it. I've decided I'd like to combine some of the decorative types of glass Tiffany employed with the traditional type of painting done in medieval church windows and, more recently, in the nineteenth-century Arts and Crafts movement.

I asked Dorothy if she'd help me do an analysis of my painted cartoon in terms of translating it into glass. We made plans for me to visit her in Scottsdale. Her class certainly made me realize how much I have to learn about painting; applying glass paints requires enormous skill.

Albuquerque, NM

Yesterday Donald and I went to Scottsdale. He accompanied me in order to photograph Dorothy and me working together, but as it turned out his architectural background came in very handy in dealing with some of the structural problems of fabricating the windows. The technical challenge is apparently formidable. We asked Dorothy to come to Santa Fe in January when Bob visits in order to help conceptualize the design and arrive at appropriate fabrication techniques.

She *hated* the yellow glass I'd chosen for the stars and suggested a translucent, hand-blown glass instead. We agreed that sand-blasting was much more beautiful than silk-screening.

Santa Fe, NM

October

We're buying a traveling light box to send to Bob and to Michael for use whenever I go to review the

ABOVE, RIGHT: Glass-painting seminar with Dorothy Maddy at Stained Glass Designs, Albuquerque, NM, 1990

BELOW, RIGHT: Working with Bob in San Rafael, CA, November 1990

works in progress. It will have a light quality similar to the one we plan to incorporate in the final installation.

Santa Fe, NM

November

Donald and I saw the mockup for the side panels of *Rainbow Shabbat*; it looks great. Bob's a fine craftsman, and the way he fabricated the section allowed us to make choices about which weights and types of leading to use. It was wonderful to see my painted cartoon translated into the rich rainbow hues of translucent glass. The next step is to solve the sand-blasting problem for the lettering. We visited a place that makes engraved monuments and gravestones in Albuquerque. The owner, Bill Worthen, was formerly a sculptor and was quite interested in our project. He thought the same technique he uses on marble and granite could be applied to glass.

San Rafael, CA

December

Ginna is preparing the lettering for the sandblaster. Neither of us speak Hebrew (Yiddish is written with Hebrew letters), so she's been consulting with Isaiah to make sure the lettering is right; Hebrew letters keep going back and forth on the fax machine.

Then Isaiah decided he didn't like the Yiddish

translation and changed it. Somehow his mother got hold of it and added her two cents. Finally we arrived at a translation everyone liked. Now the problem is finding a Hebrew type face that matches the English one we chose. There is a limited range in America, so it looks like we'll have to go to Tel Aviv, which means more faxing of Hebrew characters across the phone lines.

Santa Fe, NM

1991

January

Last week Dorothy, Bob, and I spent long hours working on *Rainbow Shabbat*. We designed the cutting pattern for the center panel, modifying the design to accommodate the structural limits of glass. We also spent a lot of time discussing the way the panels would be constructed, concluding that the rainbow stripes and side panels would need to be drafted so that Bob would have an accurate guide. Donald's going to do that and also draft a corrected pattern for the logo, which, fortunately, Michael hasn't started yet.

Dorothy and I spent several days choosing glass from my many sample boxes, and she began doing painting tests. Our plan is for her to continue over the next few months and then, in the fall, come to Santa Fe for a few weeks and help me paint. We've agreed that, in addition to the heads and hands, the clothing and tablecloth will have to be painted, which makes this a *big* job.

After they had left I called Bendheim, our glass supplier. I was sitting on the floor with boxes of glass and my light box and the salesman was doing the same thing in New Jersey. Turns out that they

Choosing glass colors with Dorothy in Santa Fe, NM, January 1991

don't have a lot of the colors we chose, so I have to start all over again with about a third of the design.

Santa Fe, NM

It's a good thing I came to see the logo before Michael began to solder it. There are problems with some of the colors in the bands, and the flames are a long way from being right. Michael and I spent hours recutting them, working with the glass to create a gradual fade from yellow to red.

Santa Fe, NM

February

Dorothy suggested that I do a full-scale, shaded drawing of the center panel from which she can begin to do paint tests. She thinks that the best approach would be for her to lay down the base painting, then finish it with me in the fall, as some of the glass pieces will require as many as three firings of the paint.

When I finish the drawing, I plan to take it to Scottsdale and discuss ways of translating my shading into paint on glass.

Santa Fe, NM

March

What has happened is quite hard to believe: I went to Scottsdale yesterday, where I was met at the airport by Dorothy and her husband, Ken. They seemed strained but didn't say anything. We went to their house, and Dorothy and I started working. After a while she stopped and said she had to speak to me. That very morning she'd been diagnosed with cancer and, it seemed, might only have a short time to live.

I couldn't believe she hadn't canceled our meeting, but she said she wanted to work. I didn't exactly know what to do but decided honesty was the best policy, so I told her how impressed Donald and I had been with her knowledge, talent, and skill. Perhaps, I suggested, if it would give her a sense of satisfaction, she could use *Rainbow Shabbat* as a vehicle to demonstrate her abilities. I knew that she'd never before had an opportunity to work on something of this scale, which so many people would see.

Her first priority, of course, has to be her health, and she has further tests, then treatment. I left in a

Working on shaded pattern for *Rainbow Shabbat*
in Santa Fe, NM, March 1991

to Dorothy. She's found a former student to help her, and even though I've invested thousands of dollars in a kiln and painting supplies, it's clear that the work is way beyond my ability to do alone. Only someone with a lot of painting experience could hope to translate the very detailed drawing that Dorothy encouraged me to do.

Santa Fe, NM

I just returned from a *very* intense work session in San Rafael with Bob: long days in the dark, hunched over the light table, cutting glass and choosing matching pieces.

I brought the sand-blasted center sections with me, carefully packed in foam. When I got to the airplane gate I begged the flight attendant to let me board early, but he said I didn't really qualify. He did, however, stow the glass in a safe compartment—under the peanuts. I was very nervous because, with all the breakage from cutting and the sand-blasting tests, these pieces ended up costing several thousand dollars—and they're just the centers of the two yellow stars.

Santa Fe, NM

state of shock but with the hope that things would work out both for her and the stained glass.

When I got home I called Bob, who agreed to fully cooperate so that, if Dorothy decided that she wanted to paint, he'd provide her with all the cut glass as quickly as possible.

I feel that this drama, as painful as it is, somehow seems consistent with the whole human story the *Holocaust Project* tells.

Santa Fe, NM

April

Dorothy's decided that she wants to go ahead with the work, but we agreed that I'd better go to San Rafael to help Bob with the cutting of the glass. We noticed that in some of the samples he'd sent the color and pattern didn't match—for example, the head, body, and tail of the dog. It's a visual problem, which fabricators often overlook. They tend to try to be cost-effective and don't necessarily notice visual discrepancies. So I'm going to California again to make sure that the decorative glass gets cut so that it all has continuity; then Bob will pack it and send it

May

I went to Scottsdale yesterday to see how the painting was coming along. Dorothy wanted me to look at tests for the tablecloth, place settings, and fabrics and also review the portraits she'd done. She and her husband are going to Colorado for the summer, and her plan is to finish all the heads and hands before she leaves, then have her assistant

ABOVE: Dorothy painting in her studio in Scottsdale, AZ, Spring 1991

LEFT: Sand-blasting at Worthen Memorial in Albuquerque, NM, 1991

finish the rest. Her courage is quite admirable—as remarkable as the painting, which looked fantastic.

Santa Fe, NM

June

I hadn't heard from Dorothy for a while and didn't want to pester her, as I knew she was having a difficult time with chemotherapy. Then she called and asked me to come to Scottsdale. I didn't really want to break my painting rhythm but I had promised her I'd come whenever she asked. Donald went with me to photograph the work in progress.

She'd been sort of mysterious on the phone and I was feeling out of sorts, hassled by Scottsdale's traffic and horrendous summer heat. But all that simply vanished when we walked into her studio and saw all the work Dorothy had done. She'd painted nearly all of the pieces with a level of skill and attention to detail that overwhelmed us both. I couldn't have asked for a more exquisite rendition of my design, and I certainly couldn't have achieved it on my own.

Santa Fe, NM

July

Buoyed, I think, by our reaction and a sudden burst of energy, Dorothy finished all the painting and Donald flew to Scottsdale, rented a truck, and, after he and Dorothy carefully packed all the hun-

dreds of painted pieces, drove to Santa Fe. I hope Dorothy feels a satisfying sense of achievement and closure. I just hope she lives long enough to attend the exhibition opening.

We are trying to get Bob to come here to fabricate the center panel. There will be many decisions to make as he goes along, and we just can't spend weeks in San Rafael. In the mean time, he's working on the side panels, which he plans to finish by the end of the summer.

Santa Fe, NM

October

We rented a U-Haul truck for Bob; he packed up the finished side panels and all his tools and drove to Los Angeles, where he picked up the specially fabricated frames and crates for the three sections of *Rainbow Shabbat*. Now he's somewhere between Needles, Arizona, and Santa Fe; we expect him to roll in some time tomorrow.

Santa Fe, NM

November

Bob will probably finish *Rainbow Shabbat* some time next week. It's a good thing he agreed to come here to work, as the piece requires constant consultations among the three of us and a lot of Donald's time.

Santa Fe, NM

Donald decided to build a special frame and set up the center panels of *Rainbow Shabbat* so we could see it and also show it to some people here. We invited Bill Worthen, the sand-blaster from Albuquerque, along with friends and members of the art community. By this time I'd worked on it for so long that I couldn't evaluate it at all. It definitely doesn't look like any other stained glass work I've ever seen.

So far everyone who has viewed it has reacted *very* positively. Bob just sat and stared at it for several hours. I called Dorothy to tell her it was done and she said she was determined to come to the museum opening. We drank champagne with Bob, who really did a terrific job on the fabricating.

Santa Fe, NM

1992

May

We visited Michael Caudle in New Haven to view the finished logo. I had last seen it before it was put together. Somehow, in the process, some of the glass was discolored; the copper foiling on the flames is very inconsistent and the overall effect disappointing. It's much to Michael's credit that he accepted that the piece was not up to my aesthetic standards, and we made plans for him to spend a week in early July reworking it under our direction in Santa Fe.

We called Bob and asked him if he could come too. He is such an expert fabricator that we thought the piece would benefit from his craftsmanship. As long as we're redoing it, I've decided to reconceive it, as I know so much more about stained glass now than when I began.

There's a local artisan named Flo Perkins whom I met recently. I visited her show of blown glass objects and thought she might be able to make a contribution to the reworking of the logo. She agreed to help and made some very good suggestions, which I've incorporated; she volunteered to work with Michael and Bob.

Santa Fe, NM

Working with Bob Gomez and Flo Perkins to complete the *Logo* in Sante Fe, NM, Summer 1992

July

In addition to reworking the original logo we decided to make a new one in case the first one couldn't be resolved. Now it looks like both of them will be interesting; perhaps one can be used if there's a traveling drawing show. Michael has to leave at the end of the week, but Bob and Flo are going to hang in until the work is done. Donald's going to help them, as his many skills include soldering.

Santa Fe, NM

The glass team has been working long hours, but it's worth it: The new logo looks spectacular, and Michael's original piece has also turned out quite well. My decision to use hand-blown glass for all the stripes was a good one, as it's given the pieces an incredible beauty. I had mentioned to Flo that I'd intended the image to suggest barbed wire but that somehow this reference had gotten lost. She suggested incorporating real barbed wire. We ended up taking the barbs off the irregular wire, putting them on straight rods, and soldering them in position. The effect was amazing: It immediately altered the decorative quality of the glass and made the pieces work exactly as I had hoped they would.

The evening before Bob left, we drank champagne and toasted the way art allows us to express our hopes for a better world. The ways in which people came forward to do the stained glass work is indicative of the support that has helped to sustain me for all these years. I guess it's the sense of working for a larger vision that captures us all.

Santa Fe, NM

Four Questions

1991

April

I'm about to start the research for the next image. I had originally planned to deal with the ethical issues involved in scientific and medical experiments—those performed on human beings during the Holocaust and those done on animals. I thought I had a clear idea of what I wanted to do, which was to juxtapose images of animal experiments with the high-altitude experiments from Dachau. Then I decided I wanted to look at human and animal experimentation generally. I wondered whether there had ever been human experiments other than those conducted by the Nazis.

Ironically, the Nazis seem to have stopped most animal experimentation when they banned vivisection. In 1933 they passed legislation explicitly stating that it was designed to prevent cruelty and indifference toward animals and, bizarrely enough, aimed at developing sympathy for animals as one of the "highest moral values of a people."

I'm really petrified to deal with this material, because I'll have to look human sadism right in the face. As for experiments, all I have to do is think about my kitties and what medical researchers do to cats and I get weak in the knees and sick to my stomach.

Donald and I have been discussing the difficulty of presenting these horrific images and wondering if there's a way to transform them visually so that they can even be looked at. Moreover, as I told him, our method of combining painting and photography could become predictable and, hence, ineffective,

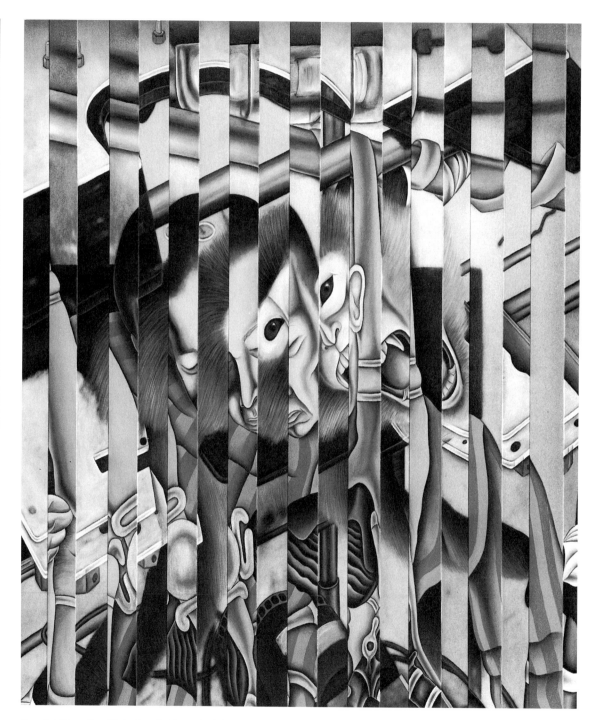

Detail, *Where Should the Line Be Drawn?* 1991 (see COLOR PLATES 22 through 24)

unless we introduce some dramatic visual surprises. Perhaps we can come up with a new format.

I happened to hear a radio play about the relationship between genetic engineering, animal "management," and female reproduction, which I found quite intriguing. Then I thought about the exhibition on racial hygiene theories and eugenics (organized by Michael Nutkiewicz) that we saw at the Martyrs Memorial and Museum of the Holocaust. It raised a number of contemporary ethical issues that I want to explore.

I know this research is going to tear me apart, but I have to see where it will take me. I certainly expanded my ideas for the children's image after I got into the material.

Santa Fe, NM

June

I'm doing research on the "management" of animal reproduction, animal and human genetic engineering, and looking again at Nazi eugenics policies, which determined who should have children and who should be sterilized.

I've also been studying modern farming techniques and the processes by which living creatures are turned into packaged meats. The same psychic mechanisms of distancing, so well described by Robert Lifton in *Nazi Doctors*, are employed by those engaged in factory farming, animal management, slaughterhouse work, and even we who are the consumers of the end products.

Santa Fe, NM

The subjects I'm investigating are causing me to reflect upon our lack of ethical development as a human species. In the concentration camps the Nazis implemented programs made possible by modern

High-altitude experiment at Dachau

"Nazi racial science is probably most often associated with the medical experiments performed on so-called lower races. Testimony presented at the Nuremberg and Buchenwald trials documented the involvement of German physicians in a series of brutal and often 'terminal' experiments, where prisoners in concentration camps were forced to submit to bone grafts or limb transplants, or were exposed over long periods to severe cold or low pressure, or were forced to drink seawater. . . . Evidence presented in the trials revealed the involvement of doctors in a massive program for the extermination of 'lives not worth living,' including, first, infants with heritable defects, and later, handicapped children and patients of psychiatric institutions, and finally, entire populations of 'unwanted races.'"

—Robert Proctor

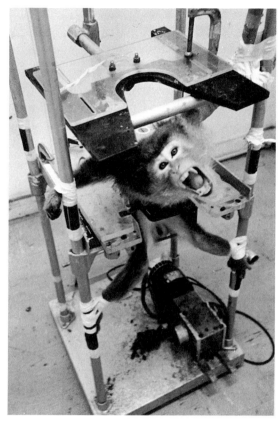

Experiment at Silver Spring, MD

"When local police raided an animal research laboratory run by the Institute for Behavioral Research in 1981, they not only opened the door to a shocking case of animal abuse, they also opened a floodgate of outrage and determination aimed at ending laboratory animal abuse. . . . The Silver Spring monkeys were locked away in a shoddy laboratory in barren wire cages less than eighteen inches wide. . . . The stress and pain the monkeys endured caused them to become neurotic, chewing off their own fingers and toes, mutilating their own wounds, and displaying other abnormal behavior." [The researcher's grant was eventually terminated and the lab closed.]

—From a PETA casework report

technology. For example, farms began to be "industrialized" shortly before the Second World War, when factory farming techniques were introduced. The Nazis used these same methods in the "processing" centers and incorporated a kind of early genetic engineering when they attempted to control reproduction and "engineer" which babies would be born. Had they been as ethically developed as they were technologically, they would have questioned whether these scientific "advances" should have been employed in these ways. Similarly, we would all be able to understand that the horrid ways in which we treat animals today—even when they produce scientific benefits—are often ethically dubious. Moreover, we would discuss the moral implications of genetic engineering before scientists made decisions of such great consequence for us. But because many people don't yet share these perceptions, I want to create an image that educates as well as protests.

Santa Fe, NM

I'm beginning to worry about whether I have the stamina to finish; this has been such a long haul and the end is not in sight. I'm so exhausted that I cry at the drop of a hat. Also, we're running out of money again. All these wealthy people come to see the project, tell us how moved they are and how they want to attend the opening, then leave without buying a drawing or making a contribution. It's very demoralizing.

Santa Fe, NM

August

I just read *The Death of Nature*, by Carolyn Merchant, which examines the historic change from an "organic" to a "mechanistic" worldview of nature.

It's a provocative book that made me question the philosophical tenets put forth by Descartes, which I had studied as an undergraduate without really understanding.

For centuries, scientists experimented on animals (without the benefit of anesthesia) with impunity and without many moral qualms. They accepted Descartes's mechanistic ideas that animals were entirely inanimate—like clocks—and that they therefore did not experience pain. If one can so contradict the evidence of common sense and deny the suffering of sensate creatures, how large a step is it to apply the same denial to the pain inflicted on people defined as "unfit to live," "vermin," or "inessential" to the Reich?

When this psychic distancing is linked to advanced technology, events like the Holocaust become not only inevitable but predictable. In fact, it seems to me that one of the important lessons of the Holocaust is what can happen in a society that possesses advanced technology but lacks a humane ethical framework.

Santa Fe, NM

I'm reading a book by Linda Hunt titled *Secret Agenda*. It's about Operation Paperclip, the project that brought Nazi scientists and their research into the United States. It's quite appalling. It makes it clear that Oliver North's activities were nothing out of the ordinary. It was just "business as usual" for what some people have described as a "shadow" government, which seems to operate as it wishes by bending or ignoring the laws.

Santa Fe, NM

We're planning a few days of research at the UCLA biomedical library. When we return we're going to explore a new Polaroid photo process Donald learned, which allows the transferring of color photographs to paper. We plan to use this technique to work with the photos of Nazi and an-

Eugenics

The term *eugenics* is derived from the Greek term for "well-born." It was coined in the late nineteenth century by Francis Galton, an English mathematician. He was looking for a word to express the "science of improving the stock" so that the "most suitable races" would stand a "better chance of prevailing, especially over the less suitable."

In Nazi Germany the movement for eugenics or racial hygiene led to the sterilization and, later, the killing of people with particular mental or physical disabilities. But the German eugenics policies were not the creation of evil or uneducated politicians. They were constructed and implemented by professionals: professors at major universities, department heads, distinguished textbook writers, and heads of research institutes, as well as legal experts. Nor was Germany the only country in which there was an interest in eugenics. In America early in the twentieth century the eugenics movement resulted in compulsory sterilization laws in many states. In fact, the Nazi sterilization law was modeled on American policies.

—J.C.

imal experiments that I've been accumulating. Then I'll supplement the images with drawings.

Reading *Secret Agenda* triggered a number of ideas. I'm thinking of a second image that deals with the Nazi underpinnings of our space program. It turns out the Nazis *weren't* the only people to do human experiments. A series of tests were performed on people at the Edgemont Arsenal outside of Baltimore as part of the research that produced the Apollo space launch and the manned landing on the moon. A number of Nazi scientists were involved, but there were Americans as well.

Santa Fe, NM

We're back from L.A. and I'm ready to move ahead. I did some fairly extensive research and want to start making images to see if I can get a handle on such complex material as this is turning out to be. Donald and I are going to start transferring the photos to see if the Polaroid technique could be of use in developing the ideas.

I'm still rummaging around in books and making links between racial hygiene theories, eugenics, reproductive technology, genetic engineering, Nazi and other human experiments, animal research, factory farming, ecofeminism, and ethics. It's a gigantic area intellectually, and the gap between our technological capacity (which is huge) and our ethical development (which is minimal) was further illuminated when I went to the UCLA medical school's bookstore looking for books on medical ethics. There were none, which seems to demonstrate a glaring omission when one thinks about the number of moral decisions with which doctors are confronted every day.

We had a very interesting evening with Michael and Abby Nutkiewicz. I wanted to discuss my thinking about these different subjects, and I

"Documents provided by the Department of Energy reveal the frequent and systematic use of human subjects as guinea pigs for radiation experiments. Some experiments were conducted in the 1940s at the dawn of the nuclear age and might be attributed to an ignorance of the long-term effects of radiation exposure.... But other experiments were conducted during the supposedly more enlightened 1960s and 1970s....

"Literally hundreds of individuals were exposed to radiation in experiments. ... In some cases the human subjects were captive audiences or populations that experimenters might frighteningly have considered 'expendable.'"

—*American Nuclear Guinea Pigs*

• • •

"It has been nearly sixty years since 412 poor black sharecroppers suffering from syphilis were rounded up in Tuskegee, Alabama, for what would become the most notorious example of human experimentation in this country.

"For forty years, the men were never told what had stricken them, while doctors observed the ravages of the disease, from blindness and paralysis to dementia and early death....

"The horrors of medical research in both Nazi Germany and rural Alabama have raised troubling questions about the humanity and propriety of such research. 'When and under what conditions, if ever, can human beings be used for purposes of acquisition of knowledge?' asked Jay Katz, professor of law, medicine, and psychiatry at Yale University. 'In most cases,' he said, 'the despised, the disadvantaged, the disempowered, will become the first cannon fodder for research. They may be blacks, Jews, the mentally handicapped, women or children—all those with whom it is difficult to identify.'"

—*Isabel Wilkerson*

thought that the work Michael had done for his exhibit might have prompted him to consider some of the same questions I'm pondering, which it had. We had a very free-ranging conversation, which helped me clarify some of my thoughts; but still, the more I read, the more cloudy some of these ethical issues seem.

Santa Fe, NM

September

I've been absorbed in the process of trying to work out the next image—or, rather, we've both been preoccupied. We're planning to employ photography much more extensively than in anything we've tried before and also to blur the line between

the painted and photo realities as a metaphor for how unclear some of these issues are.

For example, I keep asking: Where should the line be drawn between human experiments (which are generally unacceptable to most people) and animal experiments (which usually inflict intense suffering on the subjects but which most people accept, particularly if they "save human lives")? We're posing this question in the form of a juxtaposition of photographs: one, the high-altitude experiments at Dachau; the other, a monkey in a restraining device used at a research lab in Silver Spring, Maryland. The lab contended that its work benefitted medical research, but this has been challenged by many people, animal rights activists as well as many scientists. What is incontestable was the hideous way the primates were treated and the ghastly pain they were forced to endure.

The second image we've been working on will be titled *When Do Ends Justify the Means?* We're exploring the moral quandaries surrounding the fact that our space program was built on secrets garnered from the Nazi's V-2 rocket program and their slave-labor system, as well as with the help of the Nazi scientists employed by the U.S. Army. We're working with photos of Dora, one of the slave-labor camps where the rockets were built. At liberation 20,000 bodies were found, the remains of those who'd worked in tunnels like the ones we saw at Ebensee. While U.S. soldiers were liberating the camp, intelligence officers were looking for scientific information and commandeering the scientists who had engineered the rockets, which were more advanced than the weapons of the Allies.

For this image we intend to create a cleverly manipulated photo using a picture of a V-2 rocket, one of the barren tunnels of Ebensee (which was also used for armaments work), and a painting of a pile of bodies. This will be contrasted with a painted image of the "triumphant" moon walk. We're going to mix the photographic and painted realities in an entirely unique way.

I've decided to do four of these juxtapositions and to title them *Four Questions*, after the traditional ritual of asking a series of questions at every Passover Seder. Originally, these were significant moral queries, but their relevance has been somewhat blunted by repetition.

I will have to create the third and fourth images entirely from written information, as there aren't *any* photographs of the subjects I wish to address. In the third image, I plan to inquire *What Determines a Quality Life?* by comparing the Nazi T-4 euthanasia program (in which sick, disabled, and

Liberated slave laborers and a V-2 rocket, Nordhausen, Germany, April 12, 1945

"Today in many minds, there is a reluctance to accept the facts of history. This inclination or attitude is in some way similar to the fantasies which permeated the Third Reich. It will be fatal for us to lose touch with the truth of what happened then. We must struggle to seek out the truth of that era rather than search for improved defenses to hide us from this truth."

—Alexander and Margarete Mitscherlich

The famous photograph of the first man on the moon, which served as inspiration for a section of the painting *When Do Ends Justify the Means?*

mentally handicapped people were put to death) with the "privilege" of those people who enjoy advanced medical care and are kept alive by extraordinary technology.

In the last piece I plan to ask *Who Controls Our Human Destiny?* by representing Hitler's sterilization program (of "racially impure" women) and juxtaposing it with an image dealing with surrogate motherhood and the use of minority or Third World women to provide middle-class white couples with babies.

These four questions will, I hope, stimulate dialogue about the moral lessons of the Holocaust, which, to me, are some of the least addressed but the most crucial of the issues raised by this historic event.

Donald has come up with a format for these images that employs a technique most often associated with the Israeli artist Agam. He uses an optical system of slats that depicts one image when looked at from one side and a different image when looked at from the other. When one gazes at our panels from the front, the questions we're raising will be clearly visible in lettering. But the paintings themselves will appear as visual jumbles, as jumbled as the ethical questions.

When one views the paintings from the left, one will see only images associated with the Holocaust. The perspective from the right side will present more contemporary issues. Together they will suggest that the ethical questions raised by the Holocaust remain unanswered today, their implications growing more threatening the longer we avoid confronting them.

This work is a big undertaking, but I think it will be extremely provocative. It will probably be the last piece we finish, however, as it presents some daunting technical challenges.

Santa Fe, NM

Hartheim hospital in Austria, one of the six official centers for the enactment of the T-4 euthanasia program

"The Nazis did not direct their physicians to kill but instead lifted the sanctions against such behavior—and they did so in the name of science. The physician in the service of science and the new order could act out his inner hostility, could eliminate his frustrations—his patient. *This authorization of license in the service of science proved irresistible.* [author's emphasis]"

—Hugh Gregory Gallagher

Painted and collaged image for *What Determines a Quality Life?*, 24" x 18"

"When Hitler gave the German doctors license to deal with handicapped people, free from the restraints of law or ethics, when he allowed the doctors to proceed in secret away from the cleansing force of public awareness, the members of the medical establishment were free to act upon their most base and primitive feelings concerning the handicapped. There is a term used by psychiatrists which is relevant here—detoxification. This describes the process by which the unacceptable, the taboo practice, is rendered somehow acceptable by clothing it in a new name.... [When] they said 'euthanasia' ... they meant murder."

—Hugh Gregory Gallagher

LEFT: Painted image #1 for *Who Controls Our Human Destiny?*; sprayed acrylic and oil on canvas board, 24" x 18"

"In the winter of 1942 . . . a professor . . . established an experimental X-ray station at the women's camp . . . at Birkenau. His work was to sterilize young women by the use of powerful X-rays. For this purpose the camp authorities supplied him with as many Jewish prisoners as he asked for. . . . The professors and scientists who carried out these experiments made no secret of the fact that their purpose was to prepare for the sterilization of the European nations after the war."
—Ota Kraus and Erich Kulka

RIGHT: Painted image #2 for *Who Controls Our Human Destiny?*; sprayed acrylic and oil on canvas board, 24" x 18"

FACING PAGE: Working together on *Four Questions* in Santa Fe, NM, Fall 1992

Donald worked with Steven Prins, a conservator who assisted us with a number of technical problems, and devised an ingenious design for *Four Questions*. After photographing my painted images, he collaged some of them with photos, then sprayed all of the eight pieces to create visual continuity between the painted and photographed sections. Donald then photographed these, stripped them apart, and reassembled them in overlapping strips. He rephotographed them, printing them full scale on photolinen, and he and Steven wrapped the linen around aluminum tubes. Each of the four sections is composed of sixteen linen-wrapped tubes, which we placed side by side for hand-coloring and painting, turning them in order to work on the opposing images. When they were complete, the sections were bolted together to create the optical effects.

"The Reproduction Revolution we are in the midst of brings to us and to all future generations changes more profound than those brought by the Industrial Revolution. We need, each of us, to reflect on these technologies. . . .

"1. Throughout the industrialized world, human embryos are now being created in laboratories where they are accessible for genetic engineering, and this engineering can exert some control over human evolution.

"2. In-vitro fertilization clinics in a number of countries are freezing human embryos.

"3. A pioneer in in-vitro fertilization has announced plans to work on the division of human embryos.

"4. Commercial firms in the United States are offering the rental of surrogate mothers (breeders) to paying customers, some of whom are infertile couples, others single men.

"5. Physicians have artificially inseminated women, flushed embryos out of them, and transferred those embryos to other women, and a commercial firm plans to set up a network of clinics around the United States offering this 'service.'

"6. Sex-predetermination clinics are providing services to couples who want boy babies."
—Gena Corea

Arbeit Macht Frei / Work Makes Who Free?

1991

June

I've had an idea for the slave-labor image, which I'm planning to call *Arbeit Macht Frei*. I'm thinking of using a gate structure based on the one at Auschwitz and positioning images within it. These will include photographs representing the slave-labor aspect of the Holocaust. I may add painted inserts of scenes showing those who benefited from the prisoners' work. Jews and non-Jews were enslaved, but as part of the Final Solution Jews were to be murdered or "used up" (*verbraucht* in German) through heavy manual labor.

Santa Fe, NM

November

Because I've been so engrossed in *Four Questions*, I haven't had time to do any significant research for *Arbeit Macht Frei*. I have, however, been slowly gathering materials. I've decided to go to Los Angeles and work at the library at UCLA in order to have some uninterrupted time and also access to a good library.

Santa Fe, NM

The research I did in L.A. resulted in my broadening the concept dramatically. I now plan to juxtapose a photograph of slave labor during the Holocaust with an image of American slavery. I'll

Detail, Panel 2 right, *Arbeit Macht Frei / Work Makes Who Free?* (see COLOR PLATES 18 through 20)

Panel 2 left, *Arbeit Macht Frei / Work Makes Who Free?*

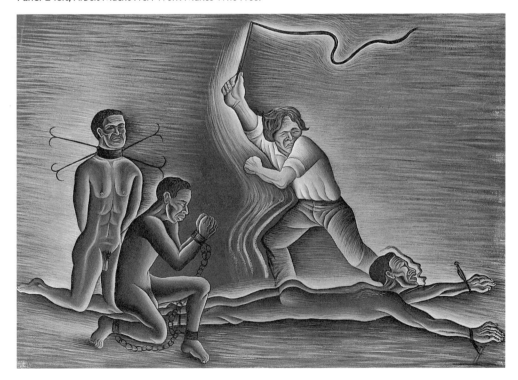

use a historic photo of the quarry at Mauthausen and try to find a comparable picture from a Southern plantation. My idea is rather complex, although the presentation will appear simple.

I want to have a metal sign fabricated that will read: *Arbeit Macht Frei/Work Makes Who Free?* It will be supported by two wooden forms: on the left (with the photo of American slavery) a plantation column, and on the right (next to the picture of the quarry) a column painted like the one at the Auschwitz gate.

The images themselves will be layered. The slavery and quarry pictures will be at the bottom of a pyramid form. Above them will be positioned small paintings: Above the slavery picture there will be a picture of a Southern cotillion and above the quarry a scene of tourists eating pastries in a Viennese cafe with a cobblestone patio (Vienna is quite close to Mauthausen). Flanking these images, outside the pyramid shape, will be ghost images of the "enforcers" of these unjust systems: the Ku Klux Klan and Nazi stormtroopers.

On either side of this fabricated gate structure, I want to place a series of small canvases that, on the left, will depict the treatment of African-American slaves and, on the right, the prisoners in the camps. I intend to "appropriate" images for these, using engravings and drawings of the barbaric practices to which slaves were subjected (these were extremely hard to find—another example of significant omissions in iconography) and some of the prisoner/survivor drawings we've compiled.

I envision the overall painting in black, white, and blood-red, except for the sections on the "benefiters," which will be painted as small, full-color inserts in the stark field of the realities the other images depict.

Now that I've begun to do research on slavery,

Gate at Auschwitz

"The American plantation was not even in the metaphorical sense a 'concentration camp,' nor was it even 'like' a concentration camp, to the extent that any standards comparable to those governing the camps might be imputed to any sector of American society, at any time; but it should at least be permissible to turn the thing around—to speak of the concentration camp as a *special and highly perverted instance of human slavery.*" [author's emphasis]   —Stanley Elkins

I'm embarrassed to admit how little time I've spent studying this shameful part of American history. And when people protest—and many do—that as wretched as slavery was, African-Americans weren't "exterminated" in a systematic program, I now realize that although that's true, there are many parallels between the Nazi slave-labor campaign and how African-Americans were treated here and throughout Latin America.

I've also been reading about the Soviet system of slave-labor camps. Almost ten million people were imprisoned there, partly for political reasons (eliminating dissidents) but also because of the enormous need for labor in the rapidly industrializing countries. I had absolutely no idea that forced labor was so prevalent in modern times (it's still practiced in a number of places around the world and includes a significant amount of sex slavery). According to a recent article in the *Albuquerque Journal*, each year an estimated one million or more Asian women and children are sold, auctioned, or lured into slavery.

I then became curious about slavery historically. It turns out that ancient slavery was not at all the same as the more modern forms, and many commonly held notions—for example, that the pyramids were built by slave labor—turn out to be partial truths or myths. The pyramids were actually built by a kind of peasant class. The Borowski quote from *This Way for the Gas* I referred to previously is really an overlay of contemporary ideas onto the past, but his comments do hold true for industrialized societies. The wealth of the few is built on the labor (mostly underpaid, alienated, or forced) of the many.

Another fiction concerns the supposed "golden age" of Athenian democracy; Greece was actually a slave society. Most of the "enlightened" philosophers accepted slavery (as well as severe limits on women's freedom). They argued that slavery was essential in order for the "higher" persons to be free to pursue philosophy and politics; it seems a form of "selection" was implemented even then.

However, slavery in Greece and Rome was a more mutable state than the chattel slavery of the American South and also, it was not intertwined with racism. In the latter days of the Roman empire, when expanded conquests produced many slaves and the great estates required a cheap labor force, slavery both increased and became more dehumanized. The development of feudalism replaced slave labor with serfdom. Slavery declined until European expansionism into the New World, which was accompanied by greed, exploitation, and racism.

This analysis applies primarily to the West; Eastern traditions are different. But the *Holocaust Project* focuses on Western civilization, as the Holocaust occurred at its very center.

Santa Fe, NM

December

I've been working on a series of slavery drawings, both American and Holocaust. I had plenty of

"The institution of slavery was universal throughout much of history. It was a tradition everyone grew up with. It seemed essential to the social and economic life of the community, and man's conscience was seldom troubled by it. Both master and slave looked upon it as inevitable.

"How much slavery was taken for granted can be judged from the absence of discussion in ancient literature. Slavery existed in every society as a vital part of economic life. Yet most ancient authors did not write about it as a problem. They may have conjectured about its origin or detailed the slave's life, but few imagined it was possible to abolish it. . . .

"In contrast to Mideastern countries where societies developed on a foundation of slavery, Egyptian civilization flourished without reliance on a slave system. . . . Near the bottom of society was the great mass of peasants. They were technically free, but lived almost like serfs who traditionally are bound to the land. . . . Worked harshly, they produced a surplus that supported the large numbers of nobles, priests and officials. . . . They were drafted between labor seasons to build the modern pyramids.

"Men, women, and children from all parts of the ancient world were enslaved. They came from all the continents surrounding the Mediterranean—Europe, Asia, and Africa. A slave might be of any color—white, black, brown, yellow. The physical differences did not matter. Warriors, pirates, and slave dealers were not concerned with the color of a man's skin or the shape of his nose. Among the Greeks there seems to have been no connection between race and slavery. Captured blacks and captured whites were enslaved, and no one debated whether the one or the other was better suited to this condition."

—Milton Meltzer

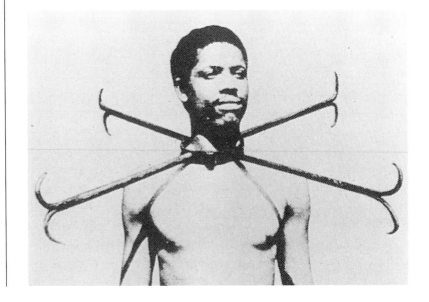

Historic photo of slave collar
Runaway slaves were often forced to wear a barbarous iron collar like this one, intended to deter escape.

prisoner and concentration-camp art to draw on, but, as I mentioned, art depicting American slavery was hard to come by. I had to basically invent the drawings myself from old engravings, some abolitionist images, cartoons (oddly enough), and the historic information I was able to put together. I've decided to position these images on splashed fields of red as a sort of obvious metaphor.

Working on the drawings has made me profoundly conscious of contemporary class and racial injustice. For example, when we go out to dinner, I notice how many people work at the restaurant who can't afford to eat there, and I am constantly aware that whatever ease and comfort I enjoy is built on the suffering and/or deprivation of others.

Santa Fe, NM

1992

January

I'm still working on the slavery drawings for *Arbeit Macht Frei/Work Makes Who Free?* They will probably take another few weeks.

Santa Fe, NM

It required another research trip to L.A. to find the rest of the photographs for the slavery images. Now I think we finally have all the component parts.

Santa Fe, NM

March

I've begun the final study for *Arbeit Macht Frei/Work Makes Who Free?*, in which I will assemble all the drawings and photos and position them within a drawn gate framework to make sure the disparate parts work together. The image is so pow-

Mieczyslaw Koscieniak, prisoner drawing

"It was forced labor that marked the day in the concentration camp. Its stamp was deeply imprinted on camp life. . . . Some of the work in camp was useful but some of it was utterly senseless, intended only as a form of torture."

—Eugene Kogan

erful that I kept running into the house (my studio is separate) on one pretext or another. If I work too many hours I get depressed, but if I don't push myself the project will never get done.

Santa Fe, NM

The drawing came together perfectly. Now we're having our carpenter, Russell Elliott, create the columns and build the stretcher frames. Donald will begin preparing the photolinen panels, and by summer I should be able to start on the large-scale images.

Santa Fe, NM

May

I've been spraying *Arbeit Macht Frei*, laying in the red fields and transferring the line drawings. I want to get going on the oil painting, but I can't begin until the columns are finished and the sign welded because I need to see their visual weights. Michele Maier, the former *Birth Project* photographer turned welder, paid us a visit recently and volunteered to fabricate the sign. She'll bring it in July. After that it won't be too many months before the project is done.

Santa Fe, NM

"No one is innocent of the Holocaust; everyone participates in maintaining the hard-hearted objectivity; the self-deceived concept and practice of rationality that eventuated not only in the Holocaust but also in the Russian mass murders of the 1920s and 1930s, or in Vietnam or Cambodia. For we live and participate in a world which believes, mistakenly, that it is rational to define oneself against one's feelings and thus to be inured against the pain of others. In that world, the suffering we witness or know about does not move us to act. That objectivity makes us into guilty bystanders to past and future holocausts. It may well be the death of us all."

—Richard Smith

Detail of photograph of Nazi rally used in *Arbeit Macht Frei / Work Makes Who Free?* (Nuremberg, Germany, 1930s)

Photograph of Klan rally used in *Arbeit Macht Frei / Work Makes Who Free?* (Birmingham, AL, 1960s)

Legacy

1991

May

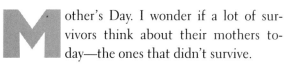other's Day. I wonder if a lot of survivors think about their mothers today—the ones that didn't survive.

Santa Fe, NM

1992

January

I've started the research for the last work in the series on survivors. I've seen and read a lot of survivor testimony over these years, both about the Holocaust and other intensely traumatic events. I first thought about doing an image of a Holocaust survivor reaching out to others who've suffered comparable traumas. The various figures would be painted on top of photos of that which they had survived: war, torture, sexual abuse, et cetera.

However, when I looked up "survivor" in the subject listings at the library, I discovered that the term applies only to survivors of the Holocaust. This means (in addition to the fact that only surviving the Holocaust qualifies as a classification) that it would be difficult to find photo images; I would have to search category by category. Then I considered how far we've broadened our view of the Holocaust in some of the images and decided that I wanted to focus specifically on the Jewish survivor experience.

I plan to position this work before *Rainbow Shabbat* in the exhibition in order to suggest that surviving the worst human beings can do to each

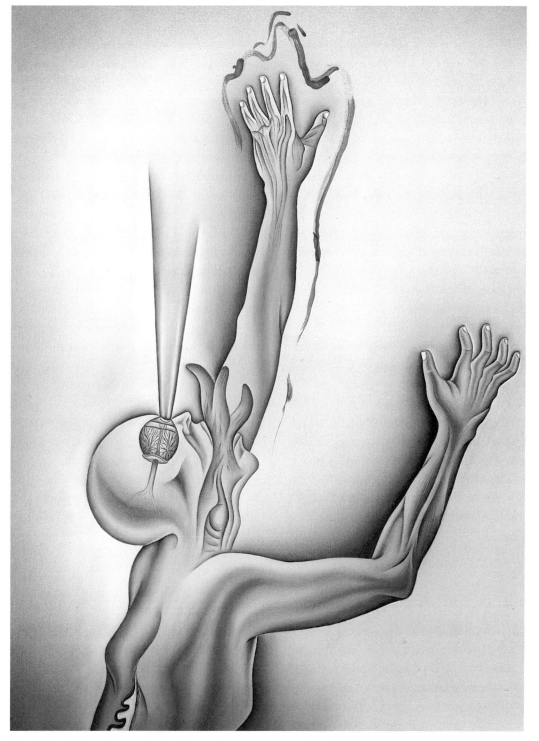

Detail, Panel 3 from *Legacy: Bearing Witness* (see COLOR PLATES 25 and 26)

other can lead, as it has done for some survivors, to an enlarged human and global perspective. Moreover, I decided that, if *Four Questions* depends heavily on photography, perhaps this image should rely more on painting.

I'm contemplating three panels: in the center, an image of two survivors—a male and a female, hands joined—positioned so that they appear to be emerging from a photo of one of the bombed-out crematoria of Birkenau. The side panels will be entirely painted: One will deal with the creation of the state of Israel—one of the triumphant achievements of Holocaust survivors—and the other with their efforts to create a new life and rebuild the personal family structures that were shattered.

For a number of years I've been accumulating material on the history of Zionism, on the creation of the state of Israel, and on the psychology of survivors. Some time ago, my therapist told me that I had a number of traits that were similar to Holocaust survivors and that, in many ways, my life has been more like theirs than most "normal" people's. I didn't understand what he meant, except insofar as the number of deaths, tragedies, and struggles I've experienced. Perhaps my research will make his insight clear.

Santa Fe, NM

February

I've been immersed in the research for *Legacy*, which is what I've decided to call the survivor image. I've been thinking about creating a painting of Israel as it was envisioned in the early Zionist ideal: as a democratic, egalitarian state. But then I began to question the entire notion of any abstract "ideal." Some of the greatest evils ever perpetrated have been done in the name of utopian visions, most notably the Soviet system, where Marx's dream became a totalitarian nightmare.

Other political revolutions have been shaped by abstract ideals and they have often failed, partly because their leaders didn't take basic human needs into consideration: needs for family, intimacy, and emotional connection. The *kibbutz* system illustrates this problem: As soon as Israel began to be made habitable, human needs reasserted themselves and people were no longer willing to sacrifice individual freedoms and satisfactions in favor of group or collective needs.

I've been reading about the early Zionists, many of whom were truly wise. They anticipated a number of the problems Israel has been struggling with, and some contemporary Israeli writers like Amos Oz are articulating many of the same thoughts I've had. In *The Land of Israel*, Oz writes:

Perhaps it was a lunatic promise: to turn, in the space of two or three generations, masses of Jews, persecuted, frightened—into a nation that would be an example . . . a model of salvation for the entire world. Perhaps we bit off too much. . . . Perhaps we should have aimed for less. Perhaps there was a wild pretension here, beyond our capabilities—beyond human capabilities.

I started out with the notion of making an image of the ideal because I longed for Israel to *be* that ideal, but now I'm thinking about just trying to create an image of Israel in all its *real* contradictions. "Ideal" or not, Israel has a right to exist; and the fact that survivors—with all that they endured—have had the strength to forge a state that can be a haven for all Jews is a remarkable feat.

Santa Fe, NM

I am deep into the research for *Legacy*, looking at the personality traits common to many survivors and beginning to understand Dr. Fineberg's comment that I exhibit many of these same characteristics. I have not included much information about my personal life because I felt as if my experiences paled in the face of the overwhelming losses that Holocaust survivors suffered. But I can't continue to do that, because by the time the *Holocaust Project* exhibition opens almost all my immediate family will be dead, and my grief is intruding into the process of creating this image.

My father died when I was thirteen, and from the time I was nine until I was seventeen, numerous family members and friends either died or were killed. My first husband was killed in an automobile accident when I was twenty-three, and my trust in life was shattered early.

I've been acutely aware of both my vulnerability and my mortality for a long time. I've learned that fear has permeated the lives of many survivors, and fear has often gripped me. It took me many years to build the confidence to believe that life could go on without being constantly interrupted by death or loss. Since our marriage Donald and I have seen both his father and my mother develop cancer, and I had a serious accident plus several operations. Then the day after my fiftieth birthday, I received a phone call from Ben, my younger brother (and only sibling). He'd been diagnosed with ALS (Lou Gehrig's disease) and had been told he had only a few years to live. Since that fateful day in 1989, Donald and I have lived with the shadow of his progressively paralyzing disease. In our daily struggle with the material about the Holocaust, my grief for my brother and his family (he has two young sons) has suffused the subject matter with a profoundly subjective meaning.

Today I received a phone call from Ben's friend (my brother lives in Japan, where he has been a potter for more than a decade). He had suffered cardiac arrest and was taken to the hospital. He is expected to die within twenty-four hours. Donald and I are preparing to go to Los Angeles to tell my mother, whose cancer is now widespread and whose grief will certainly be intense. Ben and I had hoped that she would die before him, but it's not to be. I feel so badly for her, and so helpless. I keep remembering a phrase in the early survivor testimony we viewed: "I feel like my heart is a stone."

Santa Fe, NM

In the face of intense personal pain I'm forcing myself to do what I've always done: continue working. I've just read *The Survivor*, by Terence Des Pres, which I found absolutely riveting. He argues that one of the reasons the subject of the Holocaust is so compelling is that it was the actual enactment of human fantasies—and artistic images—of Hell. We who deal with the Holocaust must face what survivors experienced: the reality of evil.

Reading Des Pres gave me the notion of transforming the central panel into an image that suggests otherworldliness, and I've begun looking at artists' conceptions of Hell.

Telling my mother about my brother was my own version of Hell: She experienced the reality of his death like a body blow. I could see her crumple.

Los Angeles, CA

March

I've been reading more survivor testimony, various analyses of that testimony, material on children of survivors (and the often unconscious process of "transmission" of the Holocaust experience from parent to child), and some writings on the aftereffects of massive psychic trauma generally. The scholarship on the relationship between the effects of the Holocaust and other traumatic events is still at an early stage. I'm glad, therefore, I decided not to try to deal with more than the Holocaust experience. I've also been learning about the salutary effects of survivors who settled in Israel and helped build the state.

After a lot of soul-searching, I've concluded that I do not personally understand the experience of the children of survivors, except intellectually, and that's not enough to make authentic images. What I *do* understand is the struggle to survive the trauma of loss, death, threat to the ego and sense of self, and destruction of one's family.

Therefore I've decided to make one of the paintings focus on the struggle to recover. I'm using a lot of my own experiences and personal pain in the formation of the images. I intend to have three figures or scenes. The first will represent bearing witness, which was a very profound impulse for many survivors and has also been what I've tried to do through my art and writing for many years: for example, "bearing witness" to women's suffering and oppression. The second figure will be a man fighting a Nazi death's head. This will act as a metaphor for the unending struggle waged by many survivors and some Jewish organizations to prosecute Nazi war criminals and to alert the world to outbreaks of anti-Semitism.

The last tableau will be of a mother and a child; the mother will be passing a "burnt offering" (the translation of the Greek term from which the word Holocaust is derived); she will be "transmitting" the legacy of her experience to her child. Many of the people active in Holocaust institutions are children of survivors, and the recent literature on this subject attests to the complexity of feelings that many second-generation people experience.

Both this image and the one on Israel will be placed on fields of color that change from the murky hues I plan for the center panel to rainbow tones that suggest integration, a psychological state that survivors sometimes achieve and toward which I am also working.

It's only now that I have been immersed in research about the survivor experience that I have come to understand one of the reasons I was so drawn to this subject. My personal experiences of loss did in fact leave me with many of the characteristics of a Holocaust survivor. Now I must do what the most courageous of them have done and reach a place of empathy and compassion for other people and the human condition.

Bringing the art in this project to completion requires of me, as it did of survivors, both courage and forgiveness but, most important, the ability to move beyond a sense of myself as a victim. I know I can bring the work to an end, but not without another deep plunge into human pain—my own as well as that experienced by those I'm struggling to represent in my art.

Santa Fe, NM

March

I'm wrestling with the image representing Israel. I've decided to use a Jewish flag as a symbol of the "ingathering" of Jews from around the world. I want to include Jews of many persuasions within the embrace of the flag, but I also want it to be ripping apart to reflect the way Israel is being torn asunder by the Occupation and the antiquated attitudes and influence of the religious right.

I just read a memoir titled *Exile in the Promised Land*, by Marcia Freedman, who made *aliyah* in

Theodor Herzl, more than any other person, is identified with the emergence of political Zionism. His vision for Israel was influenced by nineteenth-century utopian ideals in that he envisioned the country as becoming a model of social justice. Moreover, at a time when no European country had yet granted the franchise to women, Herzl postulated universal suffrage and women's full participation in the political life of the community.   —J.C

"We are told that when we become the majority we shall then show how just and generous a people in power can be. That is like the man who says that he will do anything and everything to get rich, so that he will do anything with the money thus accumulated. Sometimes he never grows rich—he fails. And if he does grow rich under those circumstances his power of doing good has been atrophied from long lack of use. In other words, it is not only the end which for Israel must be desirable, but what is of equal importance, the means must be conceived and brought forth in cleanliness. If as a minority we insist upon keeping the other man from achieving just aims, and if we keep him from this with the aid of bayonets, we must not be surprised if we are attacked and, what is worse, if moral degeneration sets in among us."   —Judah Magnes

the late 1960s and then became the first feminist member of the Knesset. Her book dramatically documents the enormous gap between the egalitarian ideals of early Zionism and the reality of Israel today. Freedman's experiences paralleled others I'd read about and highlighted the tension of my dual loyalties. As a Jew I support Israel's right to exist, but as a woman and a feminist, I deplore what it does in the name of "security." But how can there be freedom without *bitachon*, which is the Hebrew word for "security"?

Dealing with Israel presents a thicket of problems. I don't want to be critical, but I also have to express what I believe. I'm trying to wind my way through this thicket and create a simple image that is not entirely time-bound by this particular historic moment. It is a big challenge, but one I cannot avoid, because Israel is certainly part of the legacy of the Holocaust.

Santa Fe, NM

April

I'm working on the drawings for *Legacy*. I know exactly what I want to express, but I feel anxious about doing so, as if I'll do harm to the survivors, who have already suffered enough. I want to honor them and their achievements without denying the human price they and, unfortunately, those close to them have frequently paid. It's a daunting task, and I've been deeply engrossed in it.

Santa Fe, NM

I've struggled all week with the drawings and think I've finally made some progress. I'm almost ready to do the final study, which will be a big relief because, at last, all the remaining images will be conceptualized.

Studying various artists' interpretations of Dante's *Inferno* and visual renditions of Hell led me to change the central image. Instead of holding hands, the female figure will be helping the male figure out of the "inferno" of the ruined crematorium. Though more weakened than the woman by his ordeal, the man's arm will be upraised in a gesture of defiance and triumph.

Both of the other panels have evolved as well. In the left panel (without realizing it) I positioned three male figures on the right side of the torn flag: a member of *Gush Emunim* (the new Zionist group that has been settling the Occupied Territories and believes in the concept of a greater Israel); an Orthodox rabbi dispensing his version of the law; and a soldier dressed in riot-control gear. These figures could be said to embody Israel's right wing.

On the left side of the flag is a woman in black (representing the peace group in Israel), wearing an Arab headdress to symbolize her commitment to Palestinian self-rule. She is holding a Torah to signify her love of the commandment instructing Jews not to inflict pain. Next to her is another soldier, but this one is part of the military airlift of Ethiopian Jews, one of whom he is embracing. This expresses the "miracle" of that effort and the positive aspect of possessing a military, as the airlift would have been impossible without one. The last member of this group is a Holocaust survivor who, like many of the early *kibbutzniks*, worked the earth with a hoe, which he is depicted as raising aloft.

Despite their political differences, however, all of the figures are being embraced by the flag of Israel, an image of the capability of Jewish culture to tolerate diverse points of view. Our differences may threaten, but ultimately cannot tear apart, the larger historic continuity of Judaism.

"It is often difficult to listen to the message of the survivors, but they have experienced the hell of loneliness and are simply trying to predict something of the future based upon the past."

—Florabel Kinsler

• • •

"I have exposed myself to you, so that you may understand how it feels to be a concentration camp survivor.

"A survivor wears nice clothes with a matching smile, trying to recapture the forgotten pleasures of life, but is unable to fully enjoy anything. A survivor will go on vacation and, while watching a show, will picture her mother, holding her grandson in her arms, gasping for breath.

"A survivor will read about a fire and desperately hope that her brother had died from the fumes before the flames reached him.

"A survivor will think of her sister with her three dead children and inhale the gas to feel the gasping agony of their deaths.

"A survivor will go to a party and feel alone.

"A survivor appears quiet but is screaming within.

"A survivor will make large weddings, with many guests, but the ones she wants most will never arrive.

"A survivor will go to a funeral and cry, not for the deceased but for the ones never buried.

"A survivor will reach out to you but not let you get close, for you remind her of what she could have been, but will never be.

"A survivor is at ease only with other survivors.

"A survivor is broken in spirit, but pretends to be like you.

"A survivor is a wife, mother, friend, neighbor, yet nobody really knows her.

"A survivor is a restless tortured person; she can only enjoy her children. Yet it is not easy to be the children of a survivor, for she expects the impossible of them—to be constantly happy, to do and learn all the things denied to her.

"A survivor will awaken in a sweat from her nightmares, unable to sleep again. In vain does she chase the ghosts from her bedside, but they remain her guests for the remainder of the night.

"A survivor has no fear of death, for peace is its reward."

—Cecilie Klein

I was entirely freaked out by the images I drew for the right panel; they are so powerful and painful that I was afraid they were grotesque. There is almost no effective painting about the survivor experience; most of it is either abstract, unclear, or too horrific to view. There is a considerable amount of literature, but words are more distant from feelings than art, which is therefore more potent, or can be.

Dr. Fineberg helped me understand that I will have to traverse the terror that these images induce, a terror that arises from the interaction between the subject matter of the Holocaust and my own personal pain.

Santa Fe, NM

I've finished the final study for *Legacy*. I don't know if it's any good, but I am convinced that I cannot do better. Now I want to use large scale, expansive color, and thin oil painting to transform these images of intense human struggle into a visual atmosphere of hope and integration.

Santa Fe, NM

June

I've finished the spraying, and there's no question that the large scale of the paintings makes a considerable difference in the effectiveness of the images. I still have to do the oil painting, and I know I'll have to hold myself back from overworking the figures. I've decided to add some encaustic (a wax process), which my assistant Jessica Buege will help me with. I'm very timid about this technique, but she's been employing it in her own painting and is more direct in her application of it than I could be. By mid-August I hope that *Legacy* will be done.

Santa Fe, NM

If All Else Fails, One Must Scream, 1992; sprayed acrylic, oil, and photography on photolinen mounted on rag paper, 30" x 22"

"Confronting radical evil, men and women instinctively feel the desire to call, to warn, to communicate their shock. Terror dissolves the self into silence, but its aftermath, the spectacle of human mutilation, gives birth to a different reaction. Horror arises and in its presence men and women are seized by an involuntary outburst of feeling which is very much like a scream . . . and in this crude cry the will to bear witness is born." —Terence Des Pres

"One man who had spent five years in a ghetto and a concentration camp encountered a German *kibbutz* volunteer in the fields. Rage welled up in him, but he mastered it and presented the grapes he had cultivated, saying 'Your father gave my father Cyclon B. I am giving you the fruit of the land of Israel.' They both cried and were then able to see each other as individuals rather than stereotypes."

—Martin S. Bergman and Milton E. Jucovy

If nothing else is left, one must SCREAM. Silence is the real crime against Humanity. SCREAM

Conclusion

It is the summer of 1992; we still have six months of artmaking ahead of us, but the conceptual work is finished and the various parts of the project are beginning to come together. The last of the needleworks for *Double Jeopardy* have just arrived; the logo has been remade and put into its crate. As the opening date draws nearer, I become increasingly anxious about whether we will achieve the goals we've been working toward since 1985.

We began so naively: wanting to learn about our Jewish heritage and the Holocaust; then desiring to honor the memory of the Jewish victims so that their experiences would not be forgotten. When our rather dramatic education led us to a greatly expanded view of the Holocaust, we became committed to contributing to an enlarged dialogue— one that would include the experiences of women, homosexuals, and, in fact, all of Hitler's victims.

The connections we made between the sufferers of the Holocaust and other victim experiences altered our perspective and broadened our aspirations. We became dedicated to the hope that our art could provide a passageway to examining the Holocaust in a new way, one that could demonstrate how much the Jewish experience of the Holocaust could teach us all.

In 1991 we viewed the *Degenerate Art* exhibition organized by Stephanie Barron at the Los Angeles County Museum of Art. The show documented an exhibit mounted by the Nazis in 1937 in Munich, which was aimed at proving that modern art was nothing but "modern horrors." This exhibition was one of the most virulent attacks ever mounted against art and, in an odd way, demonstrated how potentially threatening visual images can seem.

At the time we visited the exhibition, the right-wing assault on the arts was in full swing in America. My own work, *The Dinner Party*, had been "debated" for over one hour on the floor of the House of Representatives and lambasted in language as vile as anything the Nazis had ever used. *The Dinner Party*'s planned permanent housing was blocked and its imagery assaulted and trivialized. The chilling fact that we were working on a project about a time in history when the state had turned upon its own citizens was not lost on me during this debacle. The question "Can we learn from history or must we repeat its mistakes and tragedies?" became increasingly pressing.

I wondered again whether art could really help in confronting the Holocaust so that its lessons could be applied. Perhaps the Nazis were afraid of modern art for a good reason: Visual art has the power to provide us with a way of facing aspects of reality that are too painful to approach except through the oblique path that art allows. Donald and I hope that we have succeeded in creating a body of work that can help accomplish this goal and that our work will stimulate people to think about and grapple with some of the issues that we've raised.

Elie Wiesel once remarked that facing the Holocaust "requires an attitude of total honesty." We have tried to be faithful to that stance, however demanding it became intellectually and/or emotionally. Donald and I are fortunate that we had each other on this dark journey; now we face the challenge of bringing the exhibition, the book, and our ideas into the world. We have never experienced married life when we weren't working on the project, and we're both somewhat apprehensive about what it will be like.

Creating this body of art has deepened our commitment to each other, helped us clarify our worldview, and reinforced our deeply held mutual values. When I first came upon Tadeus Borowski's assessment that the world was run not by justice or morality but by power, I was both unconvinced and shocked. Now both Donald and I concur with his assessment, a conclusion Borowski reached as a result of his Holocaust experience and which our work has also brought us to. But we also insist on the importance of hope and the possibility for transformation. We believe that someday, human beings everywhere will be linked by a shared ethical system that will make the recurrence of another event like the Holocaust an impossibility.

People frequently ask me about the connection between my previous art and the *Holocaust Project*, usually implying that somehow I've swerved into surprising terrain. To me my interest in the Holocaust seems, as I've tried to point out, both logical and inevitable. But I never anticipated the many ways in which this project would affect me, nor did I understand that it would lead me to such an enlarged human and global perspective. I learned so much more than I'd ever imagined; one of the most crucial lessons is the importance of humility. The men who engineered the Final Solution or any of the wars or genocides that afflict us today seem to operate out of a sense of entitlement: that they are "entitled" to squander the world's resources for their personal priorities. The consequences of their actions are with us everywhere on the planet in the form of gross injustice and extreme human suffering.

Our deepest aspiration is that our art will lead our viewers and readers to a renewed empathy with those whose experiences we have tried to represent. I now invite you to peruse the reproductions in the final section of the book and, if you can, see the exhibition.

PART FOUR

Reflections

Bones of Treblinka

PLATE 3: *Bones of Treblinka*; sprayed acrylic, oil paint and photography on photolinen, 48½" x 50½"

Banality of Evil / Struthof

PLATE 4: *Banality of Evil / Struthof*; sprayed acrylic, oil paint and photography on photolinen, 30¼" x 43¼"

Wall of Indifference

PLATE 5: *Wall of Indifference*; sprayed acrylic, oil paint, Marshall photo oils and photography on photolinen, 43 ¼" x 8' 1 ¼"

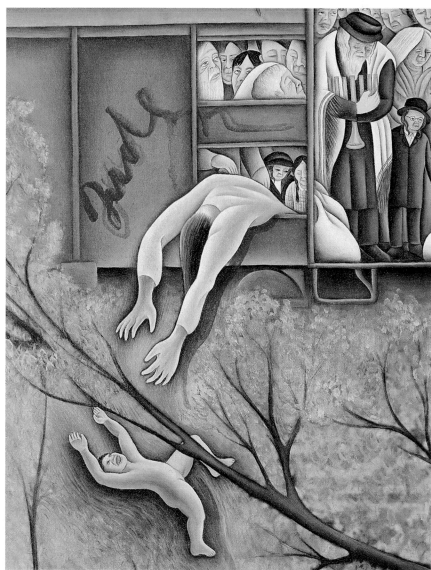

PLATE 6: Detail, *Wall of Indifference*

Double Jeopardy

PLATE 7: *Double Jeopardy*; sprayed acrylic, oil paint and photography on photolinen, silkscreen and embroidery on linen, 43 ¼" x 22' 5¾": Needlework by Helen Eisenberg, Candis Duncan Pomykala, Joyce Gilbert, and Jane Gaddie Thompson

(overleaf) PLATE 8: Detail, needlework panel 5 executed by Helen Eisenberg

Treblinka / Genocide

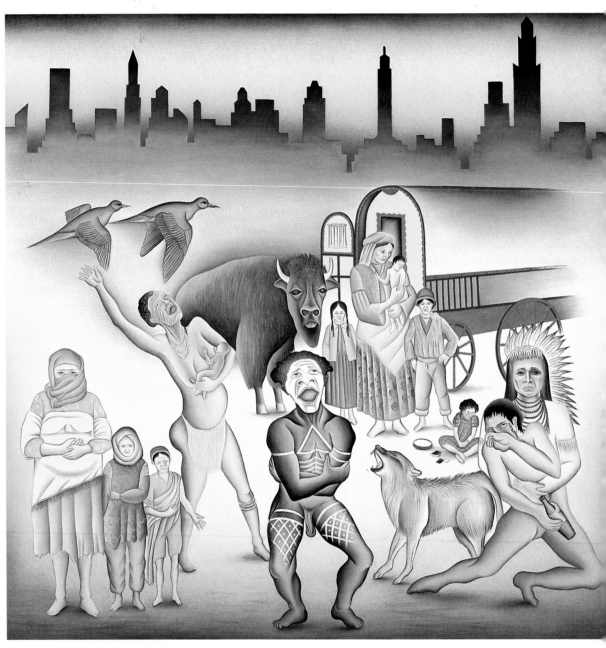

PLATE 9: *Treblinka / Genocide*; sprayed acrylic, oil paint and photography on photolinen, 48 ½" x 7'10 ½"

PLATE 10: Detail, center panel, *Treblinka / Genocide*

Pink Triangle / Torture

PLATE 11: *Pink Triangle / Torture*; sprayed acrylic, oil paint and photo silkscreen on canvas, 48 ½" x 8'10 ½"

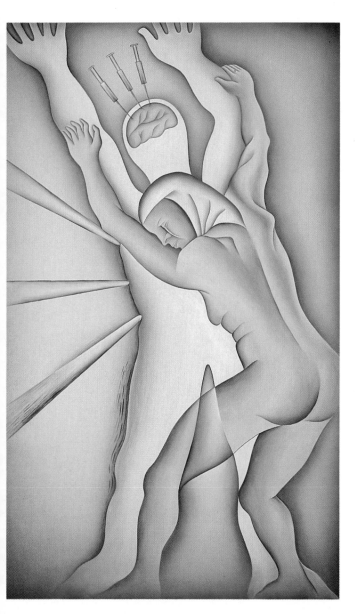

PLATE 12: Detail, center panel, *Pink Triangle / Torture*

Lesbian Triangle

PLATE 13: *Lesbian Triangle*; sprayed acrylic, oil paint and
photography on photolinen and canvas, 5' 8 ½" x 48 ½"

Banality of Evil / Then and Now

PLATE 15: *Banality of Evil / Then and Now*; sprayed acrylic, oil paint and photography on photolinen, 43 ¼" x 12' 3 ¼"

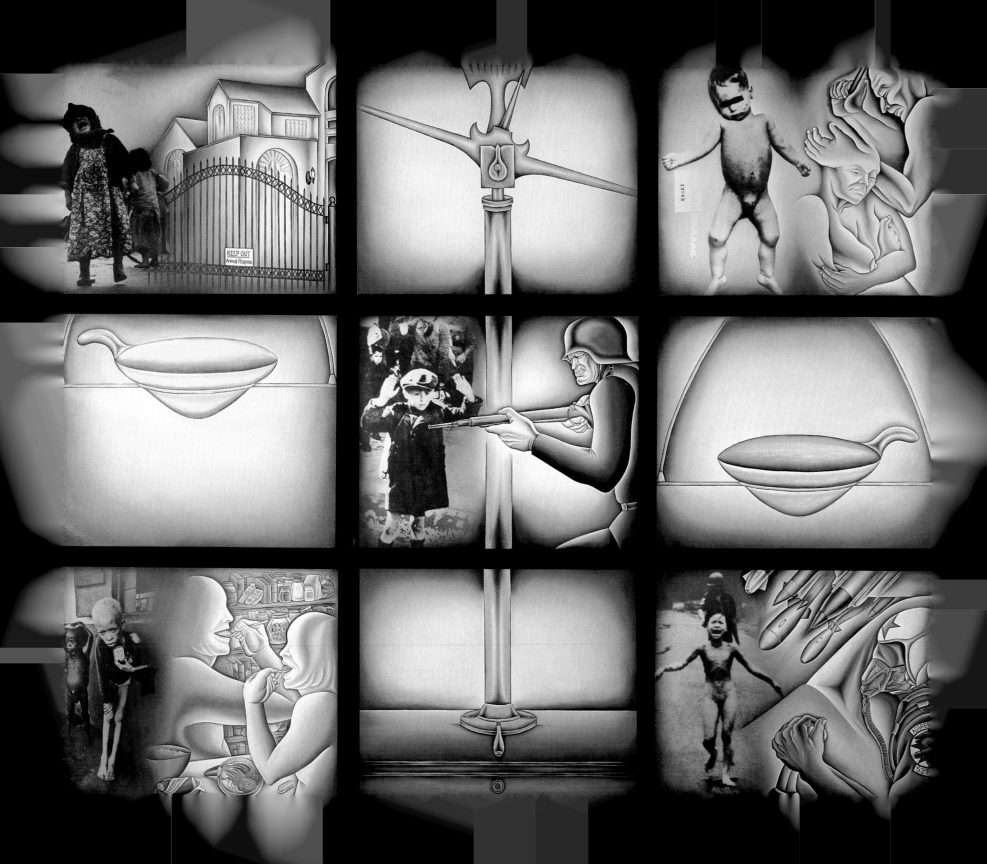

Im / Balance of Power

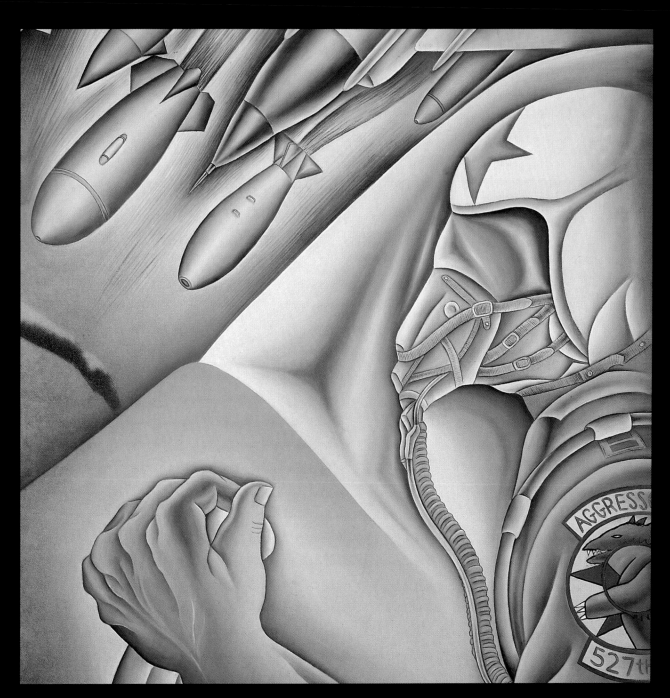

(facing page) PLATE 16: *Im / Balance of Power*; sprayed acrylic, oil paint and photography on photolinen, 6' 5¼" x 7' 11¼"

(left) PLATE 17: Detail, bottom right panel, *Im / Balance of Power*

Arbeit Macht Frei / Work Makes Who Free?

PLATE 18: Detail, center panel, *Arbeit Macht Frei / Work Makes Who Free?*

See No Evil / Hear No Evil

PLATE 21: *See No Evil / Hear No Evil*; sprayed acrylic, oil paint, Marshall photo oils, photography and photo silkscreen on photolinen and canvas, 45 ¼" x 14' 8 ¼"

Four Questions

Where Should the Line Be Drawn?

When Do Ends Justify the Means?

PLATE 22: Front view, *Four Questions*; sprayed acrylic, oil paint, Marshall photo oils, and photography on photolinen, mounted on aluminum, 42" x 16' 6" x 4"

What Determines a Quality Life?

Who Controls Our Human Destiny?

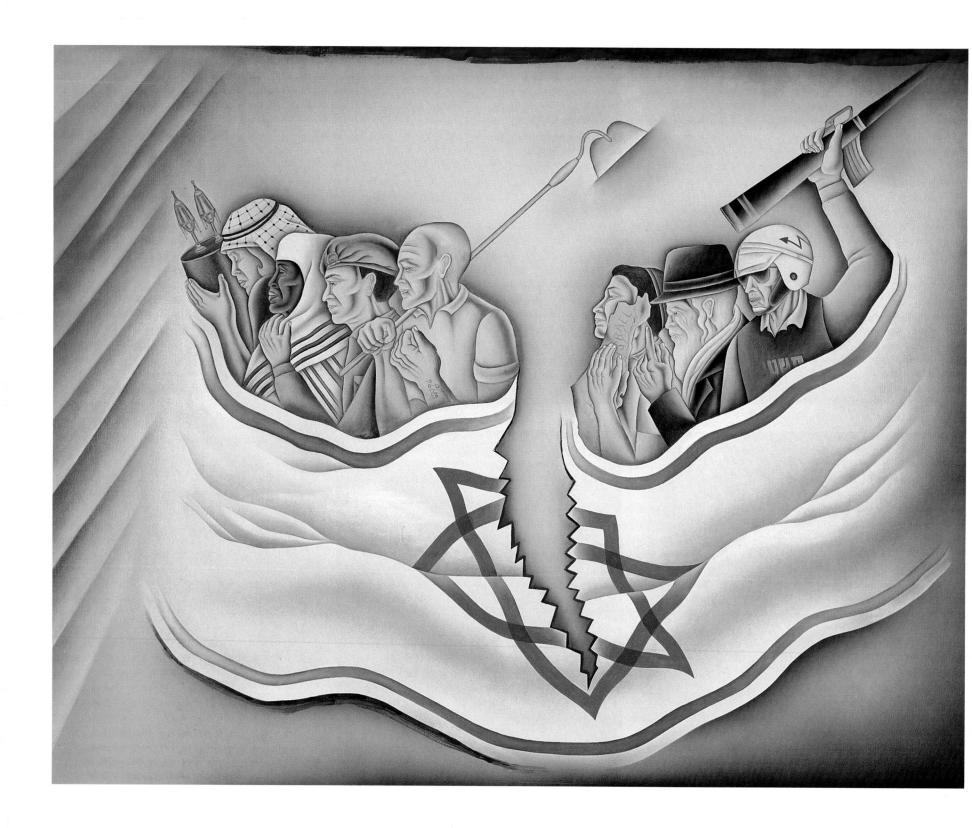

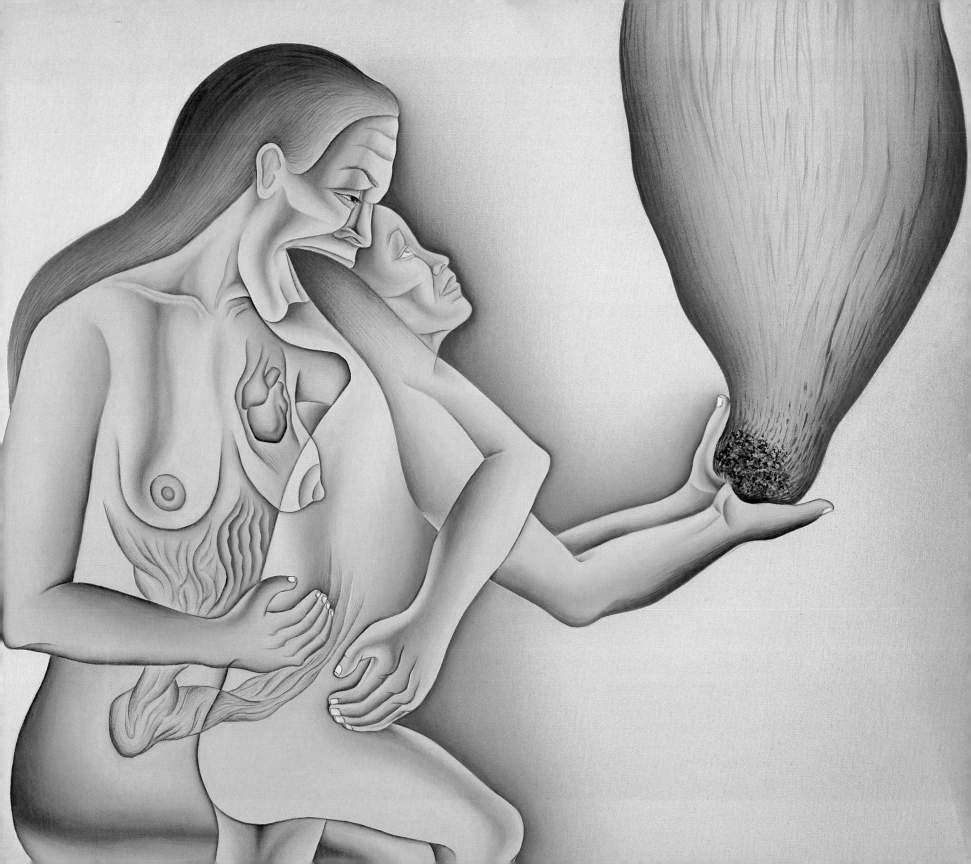

Rainbow Shabbat

PLATE 27: *Rainbow Shabbat*; stained glass, 54" x 16'; hand-painted by Dorothy Maddy from cartoon by Judy Chicago; fabricated by Bob Gomez

Heal
those broken
souls who have
no peace and lead
us all from
darkness into
light

PLATE 29: Detail, center panel, *Rainbow Shabbat*

PLATE 30: Detail, center panel, *Rainbow Shabbat*

(left) PLATE 28: Detail, center panel, *Rainbow Shabbat*

Heal
those broken
souls who have
no peace and lead
us all from
darkness into
light

: Detail, right panel
Shabbat

Appendix

This selected bibliography and filmography does not represent all the books, films, and videos that I and/or Donald reviewed, nor the ones I always thought the best. Rather, I've included those that (1) provide a sense of the range of my or our research; (2) indicate the works that were most valuable in the development of our ideas; and (3) demonstrate the way I read across subjects, often looking at the same issue from differing perspectives.

My research was aimed at first learning about the Holocaust, then expanding the context for understanding this historic event. My goal was always to be able to translate what I learned into visual images. Not all historic information lends itself to this process, nor was I interested in the kind of detail that historians ponder. Rather, Donald and I tried to achieve artistic truth that is grounded in historic reality.

Selected Bibliography

Indicates books I found particularly illuminating

ANTI-SEMITISM

Katz, Jacob. *From Prejudice to Destruction: Anti-Semitism 1700–1933.* Cambridge, Mass.: Harvard University Press, 1980.

Prager, Dennis, and Joseph Telushkin. *Why the Jews? The Reason for Anti-Semitism.* New York: Simon and Schuster, 1985.

*Trachtenberg, Joshua. *The Devil and the Jews: The Medieval Conception of the Jew and Its Relation to Modern Anti-Semitism.* Philadelphia: The Jewish Publication Society of America, 1983

ART AND PHOTOGRAPHY

Altshuler, David, ed. *The Precious Legacy: Judaic Treasures from the Czechoslovak State Collections.* New York: Summit Books, 1983.

*Beller, Ilex. *Life in the Shtetl: Scenes and Recollections.* New York: Holmes and Meier, 1986.

Blatter, Janet, and Sybil Milton. *Art of the Holocaust.* New York: The Rutledge Press, 1981.

Costanza, Mary S. *The Living Witness: Art in the Concentration Camps and Ghettos.* New York: The Free Press/A Division of MacMillan, 1982.

Czarnecki, Joseph P. *Last Traces: The Lost Art of Auschwitz.* New York: Atheneum, 1989.

Dobroszycki, Lucjan, and Barbara Kirshenblatt-Gimblett. *Image Before My Eyes: A Photographic History of Jewish Life in Poland, 1864–1939.* New York: Schocken Books (in Cooperation withYIVO), 1977.

Grossman, Mendel. *With a Camera in the Ghetto.* New York: Schocken Books, 1977.

Hellman, Peter. *The Auschwitz Album: A Book Based upon an Album Discovered by a Concentration Camp Survivor, Lili Meier.* New York: Random House, 1981.

*Hinz, Berthold. *Art in the Third Reich.* New York: Pantheon Books, 1979.

Kampf, Avram. *Jewish Experience in the Art of the Twentieth Century.* South Hadley, Mass.: The Jewish Publication Society of America, Bergin and Garvey Publishers, Inc., 1984.

Kantor, Alfred. *The Book of Alfred Kantor: An Artist's Journal of the Holocaust.* New York: Schocken Books, 1987.

Kleeblatt, Norman L., and Gerard C. Wertkin. *The Jewish Heritage in American Folk Art.* Catalog for Exhibition Organized by the Jewish Museum and the Museum of American Folk Art. New York: Universe Books, 1984.

Krajewska, Monika. *Times of Stones.* Warsaw: Interpress, 1983.

Niezabitowska, Malgorzata. Photographs by Tomasz Tomaszewski. *Remnants: The Last Jews in Poland.* New York: Friendly Press, 1986.

*Novitch, Miriam, Lucy Dawidowicz, and Tom L. Freudenheim. *Spiritual Resistance: Art from the Concentration Camps 1940–45.* Philadelphia: The Jewish Publication Society of America, 1981.

Salomon, Charlotte. *Charlotte: Life or Theatre?* New York: Viking Press, 1981.

*Spiegelman, Art. *Maus: A Survivor's Tale.* New York: Pantheon Books, 1986.

*—. *Maus II: And Here My Troubles Began.* New York: Pantheon Books, 1991.

Toll, Nelly. *Without Surrender: Art of the Holocaust.* Philadelphia: Running Press, 1978.

Ungerleider-Mayerson, Joy. *Jewish Folk Art: From Biblical Days to Modern Times.* New York: Summit Books, 1986.

Vishniac, Roman. *A Vanished World.* New York: Farrar, Straus and Giroux, 1975.

*Wigoder, Geoffrey, ed. *Jewish Art and Civilization.* Secaucus, N.J.: Chartwell Books, 1972.

CAMPS AND SITES

Adelson, Alan, and Robert Lapides. *Lodz Ghetto: Inside a Community under Siege.* New York: Viking, 1989.

Abzug, Robert H. *Inside the Vicious Heart: Americans and the Liberation of Nazi Concentration Camps.* New York: Oxford University Press, 1985.

*Arad, Yitzhak. *Belzec, Sobibor, Treblinka: The Operation Reinhard Death Camps.* Bloomington: Indiana University Press, 1987.

Donat, Alexander, ed. *The Death Camp Treblinka.* New York: Holocaust Library, 1979.

Gilbert, Martin. *Auschwitz and the Allies*. New York: Holt, Reinhart and Winston, 1981.

Kaplan, Chaim A. *Scroll of Agony: The Warsaw Diary of Chaim A. Kaplan*. Translated and edited by Abraham I. Katsh. New York: Collier Books, 1973.

Sloan, Jacob, ed. *Notes from the Warsaw Ghetto: The Journal of Emmanuel Ringelblum*. New York: Schocken Books, 1974.

Steiner, Jean-Francois. *Treblinka*. New York: Simon and Schuster, 1967.

*Stroop, Jurgen. *Stroop Report*. Translated and annotated by Sybil Milton. New York: Pantheon Books, 1980.

CHILDREN

Aries, Philippe. *Centuries of Childhood: A Social History of Family Life*. New York: Alfred A. Knopf, 1962.

*Bar-on, Dan. *Legacy of Silence: Encounters with Children of the Third Reich*. Cambridge: Harvard University Press, 1989.

Boswell, John. *The Kindness of Strangers: The Abandonment of Children in Western Europe from Late Antiquity to the Renaissance*. New York: Pantheon Books, 1988.

Breiner, Sander J. *Slaughter of the Innocents: Child Abuse Through the Ages and Today*. London: Plenum Press, 1990.

Brown, Roy E. *Starving Children: The Tyranny of Hunger*. New York: Springer Publishing Co., 1977.

Crewdson, John. *By Silence Betrayed: Sexual Abuse of Children in America*. New York: Harper and Row, 1988.

*de Mause, Lloyd, ed. *The History of Childhood: The Untold Story of Child Abuse*. New York: Peter Bedrich Books, 1988.

*Epstein, Helen. *Children of the Holocaust*. New York: Bantam Books, 1980.

Korbin, Jill E., ed. *Child Abuse and Neglect: Cross-Cultural Perspectives*. Berkeley: University of California Press, 1981.

*Miller, Alice. *For Your Own Good: Hidden Cruelty in Childrearing and the Roots of Violence*. New York: Farrar, Straus, Giroux, 1983.

UNICEF. *Children of Developing Countries*. London: Thomas Nelson and Sons Ltd., 1964.

United Nations. *Report on Children*. 1971.

EXPERIMENTS, RACIAL HYGIENE, AND ETHICS

Adams, Carol A. *The Sexual Politics of Meat: A Feminist-Vegetarian Critical Theory*. New York: Continuum, 1990.

Ariditti, Rita, Renate Klein, and Shelley Minden, eds. *Test-Tube Women: What Future for Motherhood?*. London: Pandora Press, 1984.

Baruch, Elaine Hoffman, Amadeo F. D'Adamo Jr., and Joni Seager, eds. *Embryos, Ethics and Women's Rights: Exploring the New Reproductive Technologies*. New York and London: Harrington Park Press, 1988.

Collard, Andree, and Joyce Contrucci. *Rape of the Wild: Man's Violence Against Animals and the Earth*. Bloomington: Indiana University Press, 1989.

Corea, Gena. *The Mother Machine: Reproductive Technologies from Artificial Insemination to Artificial Wombs*. New York: Harper and Row, 1985.

Corea, G., et al. *Man-Made Women: How New Reproductive Technologies Affect Women*. Bloomington: Indiana University Press, 1987.

Diamond, Irene, and Gloria Orenstein, eds. *Reweaving the World: The Emergence of Ecofeminism*. San Francisco: Sierra Club Books, 1990.

Experimental Operations on Prisoners of Ravensbruck Concentration Camp. Warsaw: Wydawnictwo Zochodnie, 1960.

Fox, Michael Allen. *The Case for Animal Experimentation: An Evolutionary and Ethical Perspective*. Berkeley: University of California Press, 1986.

Freund, Paul A., ed. *Experimentation with Human Subjects*. New York: George Braziller, 1970.

*Gallagher, Hugh Gregory. *By Trust Betrayed: Patients, Physicians and the License to Kill in the Third Reich*. New York: Henry Holt and Co., 1990.

*Hunt, Linda. *Secret Agenda: The United States Government, Nazi Scientists and Project Paperclip, 1945–1990*. New York: St. Martin's Press, 1991.

Jones, James A. *Bad Blood: Tuskegee Syphilis Experiments*. New York: Free Press, 1981.

Katz, Jay. *Experimentation with Human Beings*. New York: Russell Sage Foundation, 1972.

Mason, Jim, and Peter Singer. *Animal Factories*. New York: Harmony Books, 1990.

*Merchant, Carolyn. *The Death of Nature: Women, Ecology and the Scientific Revolution*. New York: Harper Collins, 1980.

Mitscherlich, Dr. Alexander, and Fred Mielke. *Doctors of Infamy: The Story of the Nazi Medical Crimes*. Translated by Heinz Norden. New York: Henry Schuman, 1949.

Muller-Hill, Benno. *Murderous Science*. Translated by George R. Fraser. Oxford: Oxford University Press, 1988.

Nyiszli, Dr. Miklos. *Auschwitz: An Eyewitness Account of Mengele's Infamous Death Camp*. New York: Seaver Books, 1960.

Pappworth, M. H. *Human Guinea Pigs*. London: Routledge and Kegan Paul, 1967.

Phillips, Mary T., and J. A. Sechzer. *Animal Research and Ethical Conflict*. New York: Springer-Verlag, 1989.

*Proctor, Robert. *Racial Hygiene: Medicine under the Nazis*. Cambridge: Harvard University Press, 1988.

Regan, Tom, ed. *Animal Sacrifices: Religious Perspectives on the Use of Animals in Science*. Philadelphia: Temple University Press, 1986.

Schwarberg, Gunther. *The Murders at Bullenhauser Dam: The SS Doctors and the Children*. Bloomington: Indiana University Press, 1984.

Serpell, James. *In the Company of Animals: A Study of Human-Animal Relationships.* New York: Basil Blackwell, 1988.

*Singer, Peter. *Animal Liberation: A New Ethics for Our Treatment of Animals.* New York: Avon, 1975.

Sperling, Susan. *Animal Liberators: Research and Morality.* Berkeley: University of California Press, 1988.

Weinreich, M. *Hitler's Professors.* New York: YIVO, 1946.

GENERAL

Dawidowicz, Lucy. *The War Against the Jews 1933–1945.* New York: Bantam Books, 1986.

*Feig, Konnilyn G. *Hitler's Death Camps: The Sanity of Madness.* New York: Holmes and Meier, 1981.

Gilbert, Martin. *The Holocaust.* New York: Holt, Rinehart and Winston, 1985.

—. *The MacMillan Atlas of the Holocaust.* New York: MacMillan, 1982.

Hilberg, Raul. *The Destruction of the European Jews.* New York: Holmes and Meier, 1985.

Jewish Black Book Committee. *The Black Book: The Nazi Crime Against the Jewish People.* USA: The Jewish Black Book Committee, 1946.

Laqueur, Walter. *The Terrible Secret: Suppression of the Truth about Hitler's "Final Solution."* Boston: Little, Brown and Co., 1980.

Lanzmann, Claude. *Shoah: An Oral History of the Holocaust (The Complete Text of the Film).* New York: Pantheon Books, 1985.

Miller, Judith. *One by One by One: Facing the Holocaust.* New York: Simon and Schuster, 1990.

Polish Ministry of Information. *The Black Book of Poland.* New York: G.P. Putnam's Sons, 1942.

*Rosenberg, David, ed. *Testimony: Contemporary Writers Make the Holocaust Personal.* New York: Random House, 1989.

Rothschild, Sylvia. *Voices from the Holocaust.* New York: New American Library, 1981.

Schoenberner, Gerhard. *The Holocaust: The Nazi Destruction of Europe's Jews.* Originally published as *The Yellow Star.* Edmonton: Hurtig Publishers, 1985.

*Wiesel, Elie. *Against Silence: The Voice and Vision of Elie Wiesel.* Edited by Irving Abrahamson. New York: Holocaust Library, 1985.

GENOCIDE

Fein, Helen. *Accounting for Genocide: National Responses and Jewish Victimization during the Holocaust.* Chicago: The University of Chicago Press, 1984.

*Lifton, Robert J. *Nazi Doctors: Medical Killing and the Psychology of Genocide.* New York: Basic Books, 1986.

*Lifton, Robert J., and Eric Markusen. *The Genocidal Mentality: Nazi Holocaust and Nuclear Threat.* New York: Basic Books, 1990.

*Rubenstein, Richard L. *The Age of Triage: A Chilling History of Genocide from the Irish Famine to Vietnam's Boat People.* Boston: Beacon Press, 1983.

*Wallimann, Isidor, and Michael N. Dobkowski, eds. *Genocide and the Modern Age: Etiology and Case Studies of Mass Death.* New York: Greenwood Press, 1987.

HOMOSEXUALITY

Cooper, Emmanuel. *The Sexual Perspective: Homosexuality and Art in the Last 100 Years in the West.* New York and London: Routledge and Kegan Paul, 1986.

*Duberman, Martin Bauml, Martha Vicinus, and George Chauncey Jr., eds. *Hidden from History: Reclaiming the Gay and Lesbian Past.* New York: New American Library, 1989.

Faderman, Lillian. *Surpassing the Love of Men: Romantic Friendship and Love Between Women from the Renaissance to the Present.* New York: William Morrow, 1981.

*Faderman, Lillian, and Brigitte Ericksson, eds. *Lesbians in Germany: 1890s–1920s.* Tallahassee, Tenn. Naiad Press, 1990.

Heger, Heinz. *The Men With the Pink Triangles.* Boston: Alyson Publications, Inc., 1980.

Hirschfeld, Magnus. *Men and Women: The World Journey of a Sexologist.* New York: AMS Press, 1935.

*Plant, Richard. *The Pink Triangle: The Nazi War against Homosexuals.* New York: An Owl Book (Henry Holt and Co.), 1986.

*Rector, Frank. *The Nazi Extermination of Homosexuals.* New York: Stein and Day, 1981.

Steakley, James D. *The Homosexual Emancipation Movement in Germany.* New York: Arno Press, 1975.

ISRAEL AND ZIONISM

Avineri, Shlomo. *The Making of Modern Zionism: The Intellectual Origins of the Jewish State.* New York: Basic Books, 1981.

Freedman, Marcia. *Exile in the Promised Land.* New York: Firebrand Books, 1990.

*Grossman, David. *The Yellow Wind.* New York: Farrar, Straus and Giroux, 1988.

Hertzberg, Arthur. *The Zionist Idea.* New York: Atheneum, 1986.

Krausz, Ernest, ed. *The Sociology of the Kibbutz.* New Brunswick, N.J.: Transaction Books, 1983.

Lipman, Beata. *Israel: The Embattled Land.* London: Pandora, 1988.

Oz, Amos. *In the Land of Israel.* London: Fontana Paperbacks, 1983.

Sachar, Howard M. A History of Israel: *From the Rise of Zionism to Our Time.* New York: Alfred A. Knopf, 1986.

JEWISH HISTORY AND INFORMATION

Ausubel, Nathan. *Pictorial History of the Jewish People.* New York: Crown Publishers, 1989.

Ben-Sasson, H. H., ed. *A History of the Jewish People.* Cambridge: Harvard University Press, 1976.

*Eban, Abba. *Heritage: Civilization and the Jews.* New York: Summit Books, 1984.

Fast, Howard. *The Jews: Story of a People.* New York: A Laurel Book (Dell), 1968.

*Harris, Lis. *Holy Days: The World of a Hasidic Family.* New York: Summit Books, 1985.

Howe, Irving, and Eliezer Greenberg, eds. *Voices from the Yiddish.* New York: Schocken Books, 1975.

Klepfisz, Herzel. *Culture of Compassion: The Spirit of Polish Jewry from Hasidism to the Holocaust.* Translated by Curt Leviant. New York: KTAV, 1983.

Meyerhoff, Barbara. *Number Our Days.* New York: A Touchstone Book, published by Simon and Schuster, 1978.

Newman, Louis I., trans. *The Hasidic Anthology: Tales and Teachings of the Hasidim.* New York: Schocken Books, 1963.

Potok, Chaim. *Wanderings: Chaim Potok's History of the Jews.* New York: Fawcett Crest, 1984.

Rapoport, Nessa. *Preparing for Sabbath.* Sunnyside, N.Y.: Biblio Press, 1981.

Roskics, Diane K., and David G. Roskics. *The Shtetl Book.* New York: KTAV, 1979.

Waskow, Arthur I. *Seasons of Our Joy: A Handbook of Jewish Festivals.* New York: Summit Books, 1982.

Zborowski, Mark, and Elizabeth Herzog. *Life Is with People: The Culture of the Shtetl.* New York: Schocken Books, 1952.

LITERATURE

Bellow, Saul, ed. *Great Jewish Short Stories.* New York: Dell Co., 1963.

Chernin, Kim. *The Flamebearers.* New York: Random House, 1986.

*Duras, Marguerite. *War.* New York: Pantheon Books, 1986.

Eliach, Yaffa. *Hasidic Tales of the Holocaust.* New York: A Discus Book (Published by Avon), 1983.

*Friedlander, Albert, ed. *Out of the Whirlwind: A Reader of Holocaust Literature.* New York: Schocken Books, 1976.

Hersey, John. *The Wall.* New York: Alfred Knopf, 1950.

Howe, Irving, ed. *Jewish American Stories.* New York: New American Library, 1977.

*Kosinski, Jerzy. *The Painted Bird.* New York: Bantam Books, 1981.

Levy, Isaac Jack, trans. *And the World Stood Silent: Sephardic Poetry of the Holocaust.* Urbana: University of Illinois Press, 1989.

*Nomberg-Przytyk, Sara. *Auschwitz: True Tales from a Grotesque Land.* Chapel Hill: The University of North Carolina Press, 1985.

Piercy, Marge. *Gone to Soldiers.* New York: Fawcett Crest, 1987.

Potok, Chaim. *My Name Is Asher Lev.* New York, Ballantine, 1972.

*Sachs, Nelly. *O, the Chimneys: Selected Poems.* New York: Farrar, Straus and Giroux, 1967.

Singer, Isaac Bashevis. *An Isaac Bashevis Singer Reader.* New York: Farrar, Straus and Giroux, 1981.

*Wiesel, Elie. *Night.* New York: Bantam Books, 1960.

NUCLEAR POWER

Barker, Rodney. *The Hiroshima Maidens.* New York: Viking, 1985.

*Freeman, Leslie J. *Nuclear Witnesses: Insiders Speak Out.* New York: W. W. Norton and Co., 1982.

Gofman, John W. *"Irrevy": An Irreverent, Illustrated View of Nuclear Power.* San Francisco: Committee for Nuclear Responsibility, 1979.

Gofman, John W., and Arthur Tamplin. *Poisoned Power: The Case against Nuclear Power Plants before and after Three Mile Island.* Emmaus, Penn. Rodale Press, 1979.

Hersey, John. *Hiroshima.* New York: Alfred A. Knopf, 1946.

*Lifton, Robert J. *Death in Life.* New York: Random House, 1967.

Miller, Richard L. *Under the Cloud: The Decades of Nuclear Testing.* New York: Free Press, 1986.

Oe, Kenzaburo, ed. *The Crazy Iris and Other Stories of the Atomic Aftermath.* New York: Grove Press, 1985.

Osada, Dr. Arata. *Children of the A-Bomb.* Tokyo. Uchida Rokakuko Publishing, 1959.

Walker, Charles, Leroy C. Gould, and Edwarde J. Woodhowe, eds. *Too Hot to Handle? Social and Policy Issues in the Management of Radioactive Wastes.* New Haven: Yale University Press, 1983.

*Weart, Spencer R. *Nuclear Fear: A History of Images.* Cambridge: Harvard University Press, 1988.

PHILOSOPHY

*Frankl, Viktor. *Man's Search for Meaning.* New York: Pocket Books, 1963.

Friedlander, Saul. *Reflections of Nazism.* New York: Avon Books, 1982.

*Gottlieb, Roger S., ed. *Thinking the Unthinkable: Meanings of the Holocaust.* Mahwah, N.J.: Paulist Press, 1990.

Leul, Steven A., and Paul Marcus, eds. *Psychoanalytic Reflections on the Holocaust*. New York: KTAV, 1984.

*Roiphe, Anne. *A Season for Healing: Reflections on the Holocaust*. New York: Summit Books, 1988.

THE REICH AND THE SECOND WORLD WAR

*Arendt, Hannah. *Eichmann in Jerusalem: A Report on the Banality of Evil*. New York: Penguin, 1977.

*Engelmann, Bernt. *In Hitler's Germany: Everyday Life in the Third Reich*. New York: Pantheon, 1986.

Hitler, Adolf. *Mein Kampf*. Boston: Houghton, Mifflin Co., 1971.

*Shirer, William L. *The Nightmare Years, 1930–1940*. New York: Bantam Books, 1985.

—. *The Rise and Fall of the Third Reich: A History of Nazi Germany*. New York: Fawcett Crest, Ballantine Books, 1983.

Taylor, A. J. P. *The Origins of the Second World War*. England: Penguin Books, 1985.

RESISTANCE

Ainsztein, Reuben. *The Warsaw Ghetto Revolt*. New York: Holocaust Library, 1979.

Arad, Dr. Yitzhak. *Ghetto in Flames: The Struggle and Destruction of the Jews of Vilna in the Holocaust*. New York: Holocaust Library, 1982.

Arad, Dr. Yitzhak. *The Partisan: From the Valley of Death to Mount Zion*. New York: Holocaust Library, 1979.

*Laska, Vera. *Women in the Resistance and in the Holocaust: The Voices of Eyewitnesses*. Westport, Conn.: Greenwood Press, 1983.

*Novitch, Miriam. *Sobibor: Martyrdom and Revolt*. New York: Holocaust Library, 1980.

Rossiter, Margaret L. *Women in the Resistance*. New York: Praeger, 1986.

*Suhl, Yuri, ed. *They Fought Back: The Story of Jewish Resistance in Nazi Europe*. New York: Schocken Books, 1975.

Tec, Nechama. *When Light Pierced the Darkness: Christian Rescue of Jews in Nazi-Occupied Poland*. Oxford: Oxford University Press, 1986.

ROMANIES, ARMENIANS, AND OTHERS

*Bedoukian, Kerop. *Some of Us Survived: The Story of an Armenian Boy*. New York: Farrar, Straus, Giroux, 1978.

Clebert, Jean-Paul. *The Gypsies*. London: Penguin Books, 1969.

*Hancock, Ian. *The Pariah Syndrome: An Account of Gyspy Slavery and Persecution*. Ann Arbor, Mich.: Karoma Publishers, Inc., 1987.

Kherdian, David. *The Road from Home: The Story of an Armenian Girl*. New York: Greenwillow, 1979.

Ngor, Haing, and Roger Warner. *Haing Ngor: A Cambodian Odyssey*. New York: MacMillan, 1987.

*Ramati, Alexander. *And the Violins Stopped Playing: A Story of the Gypsy Holocaust*. New York: Franklin Watts, 1986.

Tomaseuic, Nebojsa Bato, and Rajko Djuric. Photographs by Dragoljub Zamurouic. *Gypsies of the World: A Journey into the Hidden World of GypsyLife and Culture*. New York: Henry Holt and Co., 1988.

Villa, Susie Hoogasian, and Mary Kilbourne Matossian. *Armenian Village Life before 1914*. Detroit, Mich.: Wayne State University Press, 1982.

SOVIET UNION

Ehrenburg, Ilya, and Vasily Grossman, eds. *The Black Book: Documenting the Nazis' Destruction of 1.5 Million Soviet Jews*. New York: Holocaust Library, 1980.

*Gilbert, Martin. *The Jews of Hope: The Plight of Soviet Jewry Today*. New York: Penguin Books, 1985.

Smith, Hedrick. *The Russians*. New York: Ballantine, 1976.

SURVIVORS

*Bergman, Martin S., and Milton E. Jucovy. *Generations of the Holocaust*. New York: Basic Books, Inc., 1982.

*Borowski, Tadeusz. *This Way for the Gas: Ladies and Gentlemen*. New York: Penguin Books, 1985.

*Des Pres, Terence, *The Survivor: An Anatomy of Life in the Death Camps*. New York: Oxford University Press, 1976.

*Donat, Alexander. *The Holocaust Kingdom: A Memoir*. New York: Holt, Rinehart and Winston, 1965.

Fenelon, Fania. *The Musicians of Auschwitz*. London: Michael Joseph, 1977.

*Hart, Kitty. *Return to Auschwitz*. New York: Atheneum, 1982.

*Hass, Aaron. *In the Shadow of the Holocaust*. Ithaca, N.Y.: Cornell University Press, 1990.

Hillesum, Etty. *An Interrupted Life: The Diaries of Etty Hillesum*. New York: Pantheon, 1983.

Kinsler, Florabel. *An Eriksonian and Evaluative Investigation of the Effects of Video Testimonies upon Jewish Survivors of the Holocaust*. A Dissertation Presented in Partial Fulfillment of the Requirements for the Degree Doctor of Philosophy. Los Angeles: International College, 1986.

Klein, Cecilie. *Sentenced to Live: A Survivor's Memoir*. New York: Holocaust Library, 1988.

Krystal, Dr. Henry, ed. *Massive Psychic Trauma*. New York: International University Press, Inc., 1968.

Langer, Lawrence L. *Holocaust Testimonies: The Ruins of Memory*. New Haven, Conn.: Yale University Press, 1991.

*Levi, Primo. *If Not Now, When?* Translated by William Weaver. New York: Penguin Books, 1986.

—. *Survival in Auschwitz*. New York: Summit Books, 1986.

—. *The Reawakening*. New York: Summit Books, 1986.

Lustig, Arnost. *Darkness Casts No Shadow*. Evanston, Ill.: Northwestern University Press, 1976.

—. *Night and Hope*. Washington, D.C.: Inscape,1976.

Marcus, Paul, and Alan Rosenberg, eds. *Healing Their Wounds: Psychotherapy with Holocaust Survivors and Their Families*. New York: Praeger, 1989.

*Moskovitz, Sarah. *Love Despite Hate: Child Survivors of the Holocaust and Their Adult Lives*. New York: Schocken Books, 1983.

Semprun, Jorge. *The Long Voyage*. New York: Grove Press, 1964.

Tec, Nechama. *Dry Tears: The Story of a Lost Childhood*. New York: Oxford University Press, 1984.

TORTURE, TERRORISM, AND VIOLENCE

*Amnesty International. *Torture in the Eighties*. London: Amnesty International, 1984.

Arendt, Hannah. *On Violence*. New York: Harvest/HBJ, 1970.

—. *The Origins of Totalitarianism*. New York: Harcourt, Brace, Jovanovich, 1973.

Bender, David, and Bruco Leone, eds. *Terrorism: Opposing Viewpoints*. St. Paul, Minn.: Greenhaven Press, 1986.

Bockle, Franz, and Jacques Pohier, eds. *The Death Penalty and Torture*. New York: A Crossroad Book/Seabury Press, 1979.

Bronowski, J. *The Face of Violence*. New York: George Braziller, 1955.

Cohen, Dr. Elie. *Human Behavior in the Concentration Camp*. New York: Universal Library (Gosset and Dunlap), 1953.

Ford, Franklin L. *Political Murder: From Tyrannicide to Terrorism*. Cambridge: Harvard University Press 1985.

Deeley, Peter. *Beyond Breaking Point*. London: Arthur Barker, Ltd., 1971.

May, Rollo. *Power and Violence*. New York: Norton, 1972.

Peters, Edward. *Torture*. New York: Basil Blackwell, 1985.

Stohl, Michael, and George A. Lopez. *The State as Terrorist: The Dynamics of Governmental Violence and Repression*. Westport, Conn.: Greenwood Press, 1984.

*Timerman, Jacobo. *Prisoner without a Name/Cell without a Number*. New York: Vintage Books (A Division of Random House), 1982.

Van Yelyr, R. G. *The Whip and the Rod*. London: Gerald G. Swan, 1941.

WOMEN

*Bridenthal, Renate, Alina Grossman, and Marion Kaplan, eds. *When Biology Became Destiny: Women in Weimar and Nazi Germany*. New York: Monthly Preview Press, 1984.

Cantor, Aviva, and Ora Hamelsdorf. *The Jewish Woman: 1900–1985. A Bibliography*. Fresh Meadows, N.Y.: Biblio Press, 1987.

*Delbo, Charlotte. *None of Us Will Return*. New York: Grove Press, 1968.

Evans, Richard J. *The Feminist Movement in Germany, 1894–1933*. London: Sage Publications, 1976.

Fenelon, Fania. *Playing for Time*. New York: Atheneum, 1977.

*French, Marilyn. *Beyond Power*. New York: Summit Books, 1985.

Gloseffi, Daniela, ed. *Women on War*. New York: A Touchstone Book (Simon and Schuster), 1988.

Greenberg, Blu. *On Women and Judaism: A View from Tradition*. Philadelphia: The Jewish Publication Society, 1981.

*Heinemann, Marlene E. *Gender and Destiny: Women Writers and the Holocaust*. Westport, Conn.: Greenwood Press, 1986.

Henry, Sondra, and Emily Taitz. *Written Out of History: Our Jewish Foremothers*. Fresh Meadows, N.Y.: Biblio Press, 1983.

Kaplan, Marion A. *The Jewish Feminist Movement in Germany*. Westport, Conn.: Greenwood Press, 1979.

*Katz, Esther, and Joan Ringelheim. *Proceedings of the Conference: Women Surviving the Holocaust*. New York: Institute for Research in History, 1983.

Kaye, Evelyn. *The Hole in the Sheet: A Modern Woman Looks at Orthodox and Hasidic Judaism*. Secaucus, N.J.: Lyle Stuart, 1987.

Kaye-Kantrowitz, Melanie, and Irena Klepfisz, eds. *The Tribe of Dina: A Jewish Women's Anthology*. Montpelier, Vt.: Sinister Wisdom Books, 1986.

*Koontz, Claudia. *Mothers in the Fatherland*. New York: St. Martin's Press, 1987.

*Lengyel, Olga. *Five Chimneys: The Story of Auschwitz*. Chicago: Ziff-Davis, 1947.

*Lerner, Gerda. *The Creation of Patriarchy*. New York: Oxford University Press, 1986.

*Plaskow, Judith. *Standing Again at Sinai: Judaism from a Feminist Perspective*. New York: Harper Collins, 1991.

Pogrebin, Letty Cottin. *Deborah, Golda and Me: Being Female and Jewish in America*. New York: Crown Publishers, 1991.

Schwertfeger, Ruth. *Women of Theresienstadt: Voices from a Concentration Camp*. Hamburg: Berg Publishers (Longwood), 1989.

WORK AND SLAVE LABOR

Anthony, P. D. *The Ideology of Work*. London: Tavistock Publications, 1984.

*Amott, Teresa L., and Julie A. Matthaei. *Race, Gender and Work: A Multi-Cultural Economic History of Women in the United States*. Boston: South End Press, 1991.

Baldwin, Roger N., ed. *A New Slavery: Forced Labor: The Communist Betrayal of Human Rights*. Dobbs Ferry, N.Y.: Oceana Publications, 1953.

Bradley, Harriet. *Men's Work, Women's Work*. Minneapolis: University of Minnesota Press, 1989.

Carlton, Richard K., ed. *Forced Labor in the "People's Democracies."* New York: Frederick A. Praeger, 1955.

*Coser, Lewis A. "Forced Labor in Concentration Camps." In *The Nature of Work*, edited by Kai Erikson and Steven Peter Vallas. New Haven: Yale University Press, 1990.

Davis, David Brian. *The Problem of Slavery in Western Culture*. Ithaca, N.Y.: Cornell University Press, 1966.

Elkins, Stanley M. *Slavery: A Problem in American Institutional and Intellectual Life*. Chicago: University of Chicago Press,1968.

*Ferencz, Benjamin B. *Less than Slaves: Jewish Forced Labor and the Quest for Compensation*. Cambridge: Harvard University Press, 1979.

Genovese, Eugene D. *The Slave Economies*. New York: John Wiley and Sons, Inc., 1973.

Hutchinson, Louise Daniel. *Out of Africa*. Washington, D.C.: Smithsonian Institution Press, 1979.

Killingray, David. *The Transatlantic Slave Trade*. London: B. T. Batsford Ltd., 1987.

*Klein, Gerda Weissmann. *All But My Life*. New York: Hill and Wang, 1957.

Koestler, Arthur. *Scum of the Earth*. New York: MacMillan and Co., 1941.

*Kogan, Eugen. *The Theory and Practice of Hell: The German Concentration Camps and the System Behind Them*. Translated by Heinz Norden. New York: Berkley Books, 1980.

Le Chene, Evelyn. *Mauthausen: The History of a Death Camp*. London: Methuen and Co., 1971.

Meltzer, Milton. *Slavery: From the Rise of Western Civilization to the Renaissance*. New York: Cowles Book Co., Inc., 1971.

Sandberg, Moshe. *My Longest Year*. Jerusalem: Yad Vashem, 1968.

*Solzhenitsyn, Alexander. *One Day in the Life of Ivan Denisovich*. New York: Signet, 1963.

Spiegel, Marjorie. *The Dreaded Comparison: Human and Animal Slavery*. Philadelphia: New Society Publishers, 1988.

Selected Filmography

Indicates films I found particularly illuminating.

Ambulance. Dir. Janusz Morganstern. Poland, 1962.

Art of the Third Reich. Dir. Hugh Martin. A&E-TV. United States, 1990.

Escape from Sobibor. Dir. Jack Gold. Zenith Productions (distributor). United States (filmed in Yugoslavia), 1987.

From the Bitter Earth: Artists of the Holocaust. Dir. Paul Morrison. BBC-TV, Great Britain. 1988.

Genbaku Shi: Killed by the Atomic Bomb. Dir. Gary W. DeWalt. Volta Pictures. New Mexico (filmed in Hiroshima), 1985.

Genocide. Dir. Arnold Schwartzman. Simon Wiesenthal Center (distributor). Los Angeles, 1981.

"Harvest of Despair." Dir. Slavko Nowytski. *Firing Line*. Dir. Warren Steibel. PBS-TV. United States, 1986.

Hotel Terminus: The Life and Times of Klaus Barbie. Dir. Marcel Ophuls. France, 1988.

Jud Suss. Nazi Propaganda Film. German Government. Dir. Veit Harlan. David Calvert Smith (distributor), 1940.

Judgment at Nuremburg. Dir. Stanley Kramer. United States, 1961.

Kitty: Return to Auschwitz. Dir. Peter Morley. Yorkshire TV. Great Britain, 1980.

Legacy of the Bomb. Dir. Noel Buckner and Rob Whittlesey. PBS-TV. United States, 1990.

Lodz Ghetto. Dir. Alan Adelson and Kathryn Taverna. United States (filmed in Poland), 1989.

"Men of Our Time: Hitler." Writer: Kingsley Martin. *Biography*. A&E-TV. United States, 1987.

"Monzano Mountains Nuclear Storage Facility." *KOAT News Report*. ABC-TV, Albuquerque. United States, 1992.

Murderers Among Us: The Simon Wiesenthal Story. Dir. Brian Gibson. HBO-TV. United States, 1990.

Never Forget. Dir. Joseph Sargent. TNT-TV. United States, 1991.

Night and Fog (Nuit et Brouillard). Dir. Alain Resnais. France, 1955.

The Night Porter (Il Portiere di Notte). Dir. Liliana Cavani. Italy, 1974.

"Operation Paperclip." *Primetime Live Report*. ABC-TV. United States, 1992.

Partisans of Vilna. Dir. Josh Waletzky. Ciesla Foundation Productions. United States, 1986.

Playing for Time. Dir. Daniel Mann. CBS-TV. United States, 1990. Based on Fania Fenelon's autobiographical account.

The Road to Total War 1, 2, 3. Dir. Barbara Sears. Canada, 1983.

Shoah. Dir. Claude Lanzmann. France, 1985.

The Sorrow and the Pity (Le Chagrin et la Pitie). Dir. Marcel Ophuls. Lausanne Television Rencontre (Switzerland). France, 1969.

Survivor Testimony. UCLA Holocaust Documentation Archives.

Survivor Testimony. Fortunoff Video Archive for Holocaust Testimony, Yale University.

A Time to Remember. Dir. C.J. Pressma. United States, 1984.

Triumph of the Spirit. Dir. Robert M. Young. Based on a story by Shimon Arama and Zion Haen.

Triumph of the Will (Triumph des Willens). Dir. Leni Riefenstahl. Germany, 1935.

"Tuskegee Experiments." *Primetime Live Report*. ABC-TV. United States, 1992.

Westinghouse Promo Video on WIPP. United States, 1990.

The WIPP Trail: Nuclear Waste Controversy. A Nation's Crisis Dumped on New Mexico. Dir. Penelope Place and Gay Dillingham. United States, 1989.

Witness to the Holocaust: The Trial of Adolf Eichmann. Dir. C. J. Pressma. United States, 1984.

The World at War: Genocide. Dir. Michael Darlow. BBC-TV. Great Britain, 1975.

Notes

Unless otherwise cited, all artwork is by Judy Chicago, all photography by Donald Woodman.

PART ONE

p 1 [I opened my door . . .] Amir Gilboa, "I Opened My Door," in *Tikkun* (A Bimonthly Jewish Critique of Politics, Culture & Society) May/June 1991

PART TWO

p 13 [The world is ruled . . .] Tadeusz Borowski, *This Way for the Gas, Ladies and Gentlemen* (New York: Penguin Books, 1985)

p 20 [top photo of Essen synagogue] Alte Synagogue, Essen, Germany

p 37 [photo of Nazi rally at Nuremberg] Heinrich Hoffman and Wilfred Bade, editors, *Deutschland Erwacht: Zigaretten-Bilderdienst* (Hamburg-Bahrenfeld: Werden, Kampf und Sieg, 1933) (Simon Wiesenthal Center Library and Archive, Los Angeles, Calif.)

p 40 [photo of Dachau at liberation] U.S. Army Signal Corps

p 42 [wartime photo of Ebensee work camp] Bundesministerium fur Inneres, Archiv des Offentlichen Denkmals und Museums Mauthausen

p 43 [prisoner drawing and wartime photo of armaments tunnels at Ebensee] Bundesministerium fur Inneres, Archiv des Offentlichen Denkmals und Museums Mauthausen

p 47 [wartime photo of prisoners at Mauthausen] Bundesministerium fur Inneres, Archiv des Offentlichen Denkmals und Museums Mauthausen

p 48 [Siminski's *In the Gas Chambers*] Janet Blatter and Sybil Milton, *Art of the Holocaust* (New York: Layla Productions, Inc. and The Rutledge Press, 1981)

p 49 [wartime photo of prisoners working at stone quarry] Bundesministerium fur Inneres, Archiv des Offentlichen Denkmals und Museums Mauthausen

p 49 [Siwek's *With the Spade*] Panstwowe Muzeum Oswiecim Brzezinka, Auschwitz, Poland

p 50 [Liebermann's *Die SS quält*] Panstwowe Muzeum Oswiecim Brzezinka, Auschwitz, Poland

p 50 [Latawiec's *Beati qui moritur*] Collection of Bronislaw Latawiec, Stalowa Wola, Poland

p 51 [Taussig's *The Shops in Terezin*] The State Jewish Museum, Prague, Czech Republic

p 52 [wartime photo of Jews in Theresienstadt] Archive of Photographs, The State Jewish Museum, Prague, Czech Republic

p 52 [Hoskova-Weissova's *Bialystok's Children Arriving in Terezin*] Collection of Helga Hoskova-Weissova, Prague, Czech Republic

p 55 [wartime photo of Jewish artifacts being sorted] Archive of Photographs, The State Jewish Museum, Prague, Czech Republic

p 58 [wartime photo of I. G. Farben Rubber Works] Panstwowe Muzeum Oswiecim Brzezinka, Auschwitz, Poland

p 59 [drawing of prisoners at Siemens plant] Leitung von G. Zorner, *Frauen-KZ Ravensbruck* (Berlin: VEB Deutscher Verlag der Wissenschaften, 1986)

p 60 [Koscielniak's *Panorama of Birkenau*] Collection of Mieczyslaw Koscielniak, Slupsk, Poland

p 61 [Tollik's *The Street in the Women's Camp*] Panstwowe Muzeum Oswiecim Brzezinka, Auschwitz, Poland

p 69 [wartime photo of Treblinka prisoners] YIVO Institute for Jewish Research

p 70 [Charyton drawing of prisoner transport] Jewish Historical Institute, Warsaw, Poland

p 76 [wartime photo of death march] KZ-Gedenkstatte Dachau Museum Archiv und Bibliothek, Dachau, Germany

PART THREE

p 85 [Study of the Holocaust . . .] Yehuda Bauer, "Whose Holocaust?" in *Mainstream* vol. 26, no. 9 (Nov. 1980)

p 92 [medieval anti-Semitic engraving] Joshua Trachtenberg, *The Devil and the Jews: The Medieval Conception of the Jew and Its Relation to Modern Anti-Semitism* (Philadelphia: The Jewish Publication Society of America, 1983)

p 97 [thirteenth-century colophon] Bibliotheque Nationale, Paris, France

p 105 [Aloebert drawings of homosexuals in camps] Bundesministerium fur Inneres, Archiv des Offentlichen Denkmals und Museums Mauthausen

p 105 [It is often assumed by casual students . . .] Erwin J. Haeberle, "Swastika, Pink Triangle and Yellow Star: The Destruction of Sexology and the Persecution of Homosexuals in Nazi Germany," in *Hidden from History: Reclaiming the Gay and Lesbian Past*, edited by Martin B. Duberman et al. (New York: NAL-Dutton, 1989)

p 106 [wartime photo of torture at Buchenwald] Archives F.N.D.I.R.P. (Federation Nationale des Deportes et Internes Resistants et Patriotes), Paris, France

p 110 [historic photo of gay bar] Dr. Ilse Kokula

p 114 [The majority of TRU waste . . .] from a promotional pamphlet on WIPP published by the Department of Energy

p 114 [Entering the world of defense intellectuals . . .] Carol Cohn, "Sex and Death in the Rational World of Defense Intellectuals," in *Signs* Summer 1987

p 114 [Nazi and nuclear ideologies . . .] Robert J. Lifton and Eric Markusen, *The Genocidal Mentality: Nazi Holocaust and Nuclear Threat* (New York: Basic Books, 1990)

p 114 [I'm sitting in my tractor . . .] Tom Bailie, "Growing Up as a Nuclear Guinea Pig," in *The New York Times* July 22, 1990, copyright © 1990 by

The New York Times Company, reprinted by permission

p 115 [I am the daughter of a U.S. Air Force Colonel . . .] Sandra Marlow, in a National Association of Atomic Veterans newsletter

p 115 [I was a uranium miner . . .] from testimony given at the National Citizens' Hearings for Radiation Victims held in Washington, D.C. in 1980 and quoted in Leslie J. Freeman, *Nuclear Witnesses: Insiders Speak Out* (New York: W. W. Norton and Co., 1982)

p 115 [They all had skin blackened by burns . . .] Hiro-shima survivor quoted in Robert Lifton, *Death in Life* (New York: Random House, 1967)

p 115 [There are only 90,000 people . . .] Henry Kissinger, as quoted in Robert C. Kiste, *The Bikinians: A Study in Forced Migration* (Menlo Park, Calif.: Cummings, 1974)

p 119 [Accusations have been leveled . . .] Walter Laqueur, *The Terrible Secret: Suppression of the Truth about Hitler's "Final Solution"* (Boston: Little, Brown and Co., 1980)

p 120 [I saw the trainloads of Jews arrive . . .] Jorge Semprun, *The Long Voyage* (New York: Grove Press, 1964)

p 123 [When I speak of the banality of evil . . .] Hannah Arendt, *Eichmann in Jerusalem* (New York: Penguin, 1977)

p 128 [Armed resistance was the last ring . . .] from proceedings of the Conference on Women Surviving the Holocaust

p 130 [photo of women sewing Nazi flags] Landesbildstelle Berlin, Germany

p 131 [Kowner drawing of women sewing] Jewish Historical Institute, Warsaw, Poland (this art is also used as a screen on page 125)

p 131 [Whose memory will be respected . . .] Dr. Joan Ringelheim, "Thoughts about Women and the Holocaust," in *Thinking the Unthinkable: Meanings of the Holocaust*, edited by Roger S. Gottlieb (Mahwah, NJ: Paulist Press, 1990)

p 134 [Nowakowski's *Nazi and Child*] from the estate of Waldemar Nowakowski

p 134 [Many SS men committed suicide . . .] *Newsletter of Jerome Riker International Study of Organized Persecution of Children* vol. 6, no. 1 (Spring 1989)

p 134 [At times, my life seemed not to be my own . . .] Helen Epstein, *Children of the Holocaust* (New York: Bantam Books, 1980)

p 134 [The men and women who carried out the Final Solution . . .] Alice Miller, *For Your Own Good: Hidden Cruelty in Childrearing and the Roots of Violence* (New York: Farrar, Straus, Giroux, 1983)

p 135 [Our sensitization to the cruelty . . .] Alice Miller, *For Your Own Good* (ibid.)

p 136 [Two-thirds of the world's peoples . . .] the statistics are drawn from the United Nations, *Report on Children*, 1971

p 140 [Jew badge] W. S. Konecky Associates

p 147 [wartime photo of Dachau experiment] KZ-Gedenkstatte Dachau Museum Archiv und Bibliothek, Dachau, Germany

p 147 [photo of animal experiment] People for the Ethical Treatment of Animals (PETA)

p 147 [Nazi racial science . . .] Robert Proctor, *Racial Hygiene: Medicine under the Nazis* (Cambridge: Harvard University Press, 1988)

p 149 [Documents provided by the Department of Energy . . .] "American Nuclear Guinea Pigs: Three Decades of Radiation Experiments on U.S. Citizens," a report prepared by a House Subcommittee on Energy and Commerce, Nov. 1986

p 149 [It has been nearly sixty years . . .] Isabel Wilkerson, "Blacks Assail Ethics in Medical Testing," in *The New York Times* June 3, 1991

p 150 [wartime photo of V-2 rocket] U.S. Army Signal Corps

p 150 [photo of moon walk] NASA

p 150 [There is a reluctance to accept the facts of history . . .] from a report prepared by Dr. Mitscherlich on the Nuremberg trials published in 1949 and quoted in Hugh Gregory Gallagher, *By Trust Betrayed: Patients, Physicians and the License to Kill in the Third Reich* (New York: Henry Holt and Co., 1990)

p 151 [photo of Hartheim hospital] Edition Hentrich, Berlin, Germany

p 151 [The Nazis did not direct their physicians to kill . . .] and [When Hitler gave the German doctors license . . .] Hugh Gregory Gallagher, *By Trust Betrayed: Patients, Physicians and the License to Kill in the Third Reich* (New York: Henry Holt and Co., 1990)

p 152 [The Reproduction Revolution . . .] Gena Corea, "What the King Cannot See," from *Embryos, Ethics and Women's Rights: Exploring the New Reproductive Technologies*, edited by Elaine Hoffman Baruch et al., copyright 1987 Gena Corea, and from *The Mother Machine*, by Gena Corea, copyright © 1985 by Gena Corea, by permission of HarperCollins Publishers

p 155 [The American plantation . . .] Stanley Elkin, *Slavery: A Problem in American Institutional and Intellectual Life*

p 156 [photo of slave collar] David Killingray, *The Transatlantic Slave Trade* (London: B. T. Bratsford, Ltd., 1987)

p 156 [The institution of slavery was universal throughout much of history . . .] Milton Meltzer, *Slavery: From the Rise of Western Civilization to the Renaissance* (New York: Cowles Book Co., Inc., 1971)

p 157 [It was forced labor that marked the day . . .] Eugene Kogan, *The Theory and Practice of Hell: The German Concentration Camps and the System Behind Them*, translated by Heinz Norden (New York: Berkley Books, 1980)

p 157 [Koscieniak drawing of prisoner being beaten] Panstwowe Muzeum Oswiecim Brzezinka, Auschwitz, Poland

p 158 [No one is innocent of the Holocaust . . .] Richard Smith, "Murderous Objectivity: Reflections on Marxism and the Holocaust," in *Thinking the Unthinkable: Meanings of the Holocaust*, edited by Roger S. Gottlieb (Mahwah, NJ: Paulist Press, 1990)

p 158 [photo of Nazi rally] Heinrich Hoffman and Wilfred Bade, editors, *Deutschland Erwacht: Zigaretten-Bilderdienst* (Hamburg-Bahrenfeld: Werden, Kampf und Sieg, 1933) (Simon Wiesenthal Center Library and Archive, Los Angeles, CA)

p 158 [photo of Klan rally] The Bettmann Archive

p 162 [We are told that when we become the majority . . .] Judah Magnes, "Like All the Nations?" in *The Zionist Idea*, edited by Arthur Hertzberg (New York: Atheneum, 1986)

p 163 [It is often difficult to listen . . .] Florabel Kinsler, *An Eriksonian and Evaluative Investigation of the Effects of Video Testimonies upon Jewish Survivors of the Holocaust.* A Dissertation Presented in Partial Fulfillment of the Requirements for the Degree Doctor of Philosophy (Los Angeles: International College, 1986)

p 163 [I have exposed myself to you . . .] Cecilie Klein, *Sentenced to Live: A Survivor's Memoir* (New York: Holocaust Library, 1988)

p 164 [One man who had spent five years . . .] Martin S. Bergman and Milton E. Jucovy, *Generations of the Holocaust* (New York: Basic Books, 1982)

p 164 [Confronting radical evil . . .] Terence Des Pres, *The Survivor: An Anatomy of Life in the Death Camps* (New York: Oxford University Press, 1976)

PART FOUR: Photo Sites and Attributions for Color Plates

Bones of Treblinka [plate 3]: Treblinka memorial site, Poland

Banality of Evil / Struthof [plate 4]: Inn, with bathhouse converted to gas chamber, Struthof, France

Wall of Indifference [plates 5 and 6]: Train in woods, Frankfurt, Germany

Treblinka / Genocide [plate 9]: Treblinka memorial site, Poland

Pink Triangle / Torture [plate 11]: Pansy bed courtesy of Santa Fe Greenhouses, Inc., Santa Fe, NM

Lesbian Triangle [plates 13 and 14]: (left) Guard tower at Majdanek Concentration Camp, Lublin, Poland (right) Interior of barracks at Birkenau, Auschwitz, Poland

Banality of Evil / Then and Now [plate 15]: (left) Celle, Germany (right) Albuquerque, NM

Im/Balance of Power [plates 16 and 17]: (center) Historic photo of Warsaw Ghetto: Yad Vashem photo, Jerusalem, Israel (top left) Israeli refugee camp, 1948: Cornell Capa and Richard Whelan, editors, *Robert Capa Photographs* (New York: Alfred A. Knopf, 1985), Robert Capa photo (top right) Abused child: Eli H. Newberger, editor, *Child Abuse* (Boston: Little, Brown and Co., 1982) (bottom right) Vietnam napalm victim: Peter Krebs, *Die Kinder Von Vietnam*, Nick Up photo (bottom left) Starving children: Donald McCullin, *The Destruction Business* (London: Open Gate Books, 1971), Donald McCullin photo

Arbeit Macht Frei / Work Makes Who Free? [plates 18–20]: (center panel 1 left) Klan rally in Birmingham, AL, 1960s: David M. Cholmers, *Hooded Americanism: The First Century of the Ku Klux Klan, 1865–1965* (New York: Doubleday and Company, Inc., 1965) (center panel 1 right) Laborers returning after picking cotton on Alexander Knox's Mt. Pleasant plantation, ca. 1870: Edward Campbell Jr. and Kym Rice, editors, *Before Freedom Came: African-American Life in the Antebellum South* (Charlottesville: University Press of Virginia, 1991), George N. Barnard photo (center panel 2 left) Historic photo of the Mauthausen quarry: Andre Leroy, *La Déportation* (Paris: Federation Nationale des Deportes et Internes Resistants et Patriotes, 1967) (center panel 2 right) Historic photo of Nazi rally at Nuremberg: Heinrich Hoffman and Wilfred Bade, editors, *Deutschland Erwacht: Zigaretten-Bilderdienst* (Hamburg-Bahrenfeld: Werden, Kampf und Sieg, 1933) (Simon Wiesenthal Center Library and Archive, Los Angeles, CA)

See No Evil / Hear No Evil [plate 21]: (1) U.S. atmospheric nuclear test: Los Alamos National Laboratory (LANL) photo (2) Crematoria at Dachau, Germany (3) Train in woods in Frankfurt, Germany (4) Truck transporting nuclear waste on New Mexico highway

Four Questions [plates 22–24]: (panel 1 left) Nazi high-altitude experiment at Dachau: KZ-Gedenkstatte Dachau Museum Archiv und Bibliothek photo, Dachau, Germany (panel 1 right) Monkey experiment at Silver Spring, MD: People for the Ethical Treatment of Animals (PETA) photo (panel 2 left, photo collage) Interior of tunnel at Ebensee labor camp, Historic photo of mountainside from the tunnel at Dora labor camp: U. S. Army Signal Corps, Historic photo of V-2 rocket: U. S. Army Signal Corps (panel 3 left) Hartheim Hospital: Edition Hentrich photo, Berlin, Germany

Legacy [plates 25 and 26]: Remains of crematoria at Birkenau, Auschwitz, Poland

ABOUT THE AUTHOR

Judy Chicago is an artist, writer, teacher, and thinker whose work and philosophy have had an international impact on art and culture. She is best known for *The Dinner Party*, a collaborative, multimedia installation that presents a symbolic history of women in Western civilization through a series of thirty-nine place settings, set on a triangular banquet table forty-eight feet per side. *The Dinner Party* has traveled extensively throughout the United States and to five other countries, where it has been seen by approximately one million viewers during its fourteen showings; its continuing influence will be examined in an upcoming commemorative exhibition.

In the 1980s Chicago worked on the *Birth Project*, another collaborative effort. This series of needleworked images celebrating birth and creation in Western art was exhibited in a hundred venues around the United States. She then created *Powerplay*, a series of drawings, paintings, weaving, cast paper pieces, and bronzes that explore how male definitions of power affect the world in general and men in particular. The thought processes and research that went into *Powerplay* were combined with a growing interest in her own Jewish heritage that led directly to her investigation of the Holocaust.

Other books by Chicago include *Through the Flower, The Dinner Party, Embroidering Our Heritage*, and *Birth Project*. There have been four films made about the artist's work, and she has lectured widely to diverse audiences all over the world. She lives in New Mexico with her husband, photographer Donald Woodman.

ABOUT THE PHOTOGRAPHER

Donald Woodman holds an MFA in photography from the University of Houston. He worked as an architectural photographer with Ezra Stoller in New York and was Minor White's assistant at the Massachusetts Institute of Technology. Mr. Woodman's work can be found in numerous museum collections, including the Victoria and Albert Museum in London and the Museum of Art and History in Fribourg, Switzerland, as well as in various private collections. His work has appeared in such magazines and newspapers as *Vanity Fair, Art in America* and *New York Newsday*.